Minorities in Entrepreneurship

This book is dedicated to

My mother, Rosetta Ann, for her precious gifts
(2/11/1916–17/11/2011)
(GW)

My entrepreneurial children, Fern and Lloyd
(MD)

My wonderful godparents, Renee and Peter
(SF)

Minorities in Entrepreneurship

An International Review

Glenice J. Wood

Senior Research Fellow, University of Ballarat, Australia and Co-Director, Davidson and Wood

Marilyn J. Davidson

Professor Emerita in Work Psychology, Manchester Business School, University of Manchester, UK and Co-Director, Davidson and Wood

Sandra L. Fielden

Senior Lecturer in Organisational Psychology, Manchester Business School, University of Manchester, UK

Edward Elgar

Cheltenham, UK • Northampton, MA, USA

Published by
Edward Elgar Publishing Limited
The Lypiatts
15 Lansdown Road
Cheltenham
Glos GL50 2JA
UK

Edward Elgar Publishing, Inc.
William Pratt House
9 Dewey Court
Northampton
Massachusetts 01060
USA

A catalogue record for this book is available from the British Library

Library of Congress Control Number: 2011936345

ISBN 978 1 84980 242 0

Typeset by Columns Design XML Ltd, Reading
Printed and bound by MPG Books Group, UK

Contents

Author biographies

Marilyn J. Davidson is Professor Emerita, Manchester Business School, University of Manchester, UK and Co-Director of Davidson and Wood Equality and Diversity Consultants, based in the UK and Australia. She has published over 150 academic papers and 22 books in the area of equality and diversity in the workplace. Her most recent books include the *International Research Handbook on Successful Women Entrepreneurs* (2010, with S.L. Fielden) and *Women in Management Worldwide* (2011, with R.J. Burke). In 2009 she was recipient of the British Psychology Society Award for Promoting Equality. Her current research interests include entrepreneurs, women in management, lesbian, gay and bisexuals in the workplace, gender pay gaps, occupational stress and gender differences.

Sandra L. Fielden is a Senior Lecturer in Organisational Psychology in the Manchester Business School at the University of Manchester. She is well known globally for her work as Editor of the Emerald journal *Gender in Management: An International Journal* over the last ten years, and has been awarded Editor of the Year 2002, 2005 and for Outstanding Service in 2010. She has published two books and numerous chapters in the area of women's entrepreneurship and her current research interests include gender and ethnic entrepreneurship, gender in management, coaching and mentoring, sexual harassment and evaluation studies.

Glenice J. Wood is currently a Senior Research Fellow with the School of Business in the University of Ballarat, Australia, where she was formerly an Associate Professor in Management. She is also a Co-Director of Davidson and Wood, Equality and Diversity Consultants, based in the UK and in Australia. She has published widely in the areas of gender in management, women in management and women entrepreneurs, and has contributed numerous chapters to international publications in the above areas, as well as to textbooks for management students. She has also published a book entitled *Sixteen Australian Managers Ten Years On: Rhetoric and Realities* (2007), which followed-up Australian male and female managers who had aspired to achieve senior management promotions. Her current research interests include women in the workplace, gender differences in promotional outcomes, mentoring and entrepreneurs.

1. Introduction: minorities in entrepreneurship – an international review

Entrepreneurship is the engine fuelling innovation, employment generation and economic growth. Only by creating an environment where entrepreneurship can prosper and where entrepreneurs can try new ideas and empower others can we ensure that many of the world's issues will not go unaddressed.

(Klaus Schwab, Founder and Executive Chairman,
World Economic Forum, 2009, p. 6)

INTRODUCTION

It is widely acknowledged that national economies as well as local communities benefit enormously from the introduction of new business ventures (De Clercq and Arenius, 2006; Anderson et al., 2009). Entrepreneurial activities provide more than economic advantages; they are also capable of providing significant social changes (Bosma et al., 2008). Because of the recognition of the importance of entrepreneurial activities, particularly in the industrialized economies of Western societies (Peredo et al., 2004), the field of entrepreneurial research has enjoyed prominence over the previous two decades. This literature has furnished researchers with an awareness of the general characteristics, strategies and motivations of those who take up a business venture, as well as underscoring the importance of the entrepreneur's contribution to the economic development of the country.

From this knowledge base, we have been able to draw together a clear picture of the entrepreneur. According to Frederick et al. (2007), an entrepreneur is 'a person who habitually creates and innovates to build something of recognized value around perceived opportunities' (p. 76). A typical entrepreneur is considered to be male, native born, usually between 35 and 55 years old who operates a business venture in Western developed countries such as Europe, the US, UK and Australia. The set of characteristics that are generally attributed to the 'entrepreneur' include: total commitment, determination and perseverance; calculated risk-taking and risk-seeking; drive to achieve and grow; opportunity orientation and goal orientation and persistent problem-solving (Frederick et al., 2007). These characteristics describe an individual who is capable of working long hours, with high levels of commitment and an ability to persevere against all odds. Furthermore, this group have the confidence in themselves to make the differences they want to achieve in their lives and in their communities (ibid.).

There has long been an awareness that entrepreneurial activity is influenced by culture and customs, which, amongst other things, will impact on the proportions of people who feel it is acceptable to start up a business venture of their own (e.g., Rafiq, 1992). The Global Entrepreneurship Monitor (GEM) recognizes the impact of cultural attitudes toward entrepreneurial activity on the way various populations will view the suitability of taking up business ventures or entering into self-employment. Such attitudes can be entrenched and difficult to change: 'National attitudes towards entrepreneurship in general are unlikely to change dramatically. Such attitudes include the degree to which people view entrepreneurship as a good career choice, and the degree to which the media pays attention to entrepreneurship' (Bosma et al., 2008, p. 29).

Despite the awareness of cross-cultural variations in entrepreneurial activity, to date, the vast majority of entrepreneurial literature has focused on the typical or 'mainstream' entrepreneur. It is clear, however, that some segments of the population do not participate in new business ventures to the same extent as the mainstream population, with many minority groups facing particular obstacles and difficulties. For example, female entrepreneurs do not participate in creating or owning new businesses as frequently as men in the vast majority of 41 GEM countries (Allen et al., 2007) or in the UK (Fielden and Davidson, 2005, 2010), the US (Bosma et al., 2008) or Australia (Wood, 2010), suggesting some additional barriers to women taking up an entrepreneurial business venture.

Other minority groups, such as Indigenous people, may also have unique barriers that prevent them participating in entrepreneurial activities to the same extent as mainstream entrepreneurs (Anderson, 2004; Anderson et al., 2006; Peredo and Anderson, 2006). For example, they may experience discrimination, prejudice and stereotypical views held by the wider community, as well as the negative views of their own communities (e.g., Foley, 2006; Foley and Pio, 2009). Possibly a greater obstacle for some Indigenous minorities is that entrepreneurial attitudes may no longer be prevalent in their culture, making the perception of an entrepreneurial venture even more remote (see Frederick et al., 2007). In Australia, Indigenous people have been described as 'a dispossessed and disadvantaged minority living under a hegemony, which has much dissimilarity to their own social, economic and cultural traditions' (Hindle and Moroz, 2009, p. 7). Obviously, such a reality is not seen as conducive to participating in entrepreneurial ventures (Frederick and Foley, 2006).

While we are aware that Indigenous individuals have different experiences in entrepreneurship compared to mainstream entrepreneurs, there has been a relatively small amount of research that has considered the applicability of established knowledge to a wider range of minority groups taking up entrepreneurial ventures. For example, we do not know definitively whether the motivators and barriers that are now recognized for the mainstream entrepreneur are experienced similarly by different minority groups who set up their own businesses. Indeed, indications are that generalizations drawn from mainstream research may not be applicable to all minority groups; according to Peredo et al. (2004) this is very much the case for Indigenous entrepreneurs.

Certainly, evidence suggests that in the new millennium minority entrepreneurship is an important phenomenon as the number of minorities entering small business ownership, for example, women, black, black Asian minority ethnic, disabled people, third age/retired people, gay people, migrants and Indigenous populations, has increased significantly across the world (Dana, 2007). These groups make a crucial contribution to the economic growth and development of local, national and global economies. Yet, despite their increasing numbers, they have received little attention from the academic community, and to date, there have been limited research publications on the experiences of business ventures operated by minority groups drawn from a wide range of demographic, cultural, social, economic and educational backgrounds.

It is our view that widening the field of our knowledge into the drivers of entrepreneurial activity amongst minority groups can be very beneficial. Studies into entrepreneurial minority groups will provide 'a richer understanding of individual segments [and this] can lead to development of sound theory regarding the larger population' (Schindehutte et al., 2005, pp. 27–8). Apart from the capacity to build on theoretical frameworks, expanding our knowledge on the characteristics, motivations and obstacles faced by entrepreneurs who operate on the fringes of mainstream society may facilitate government strategies to address the barriers the minority entrepreneurs may uniquely face. Such a focus would provide the necessary structures and processes to assist minority groups who engage in entrepreneurial ventures to reach their full potential.

The aim of this book, therefore, is to present a comparative, up-to-date, international review of eight minority groups of entrepreneurs within one book. The focus is on drawing together the available literature on the characteristics, aspirations and motivations of each minority group of entrepreneurs reviewed. The Global Entrepreneurship Monitor (Bosma et al., 2008), reports that when there is 'opportunity recognition', people may be 'pulled' into a business venture as their main motivator. However, others who feel that they may be unemployed in the near future, or who believe that they are unable to earn a living in any other way, may be 'pushed' into taking up an entrepreneurial venture. This group of entrepreneurs can be described as 'necessity-motivated' (ibid.), and the book aims to investigate the degrees of 'push' versus 'pull' motivational factors in developing business enterprises in these different minority groups. Furthermore, we have aimed to pull together the available literature on what specific challenges and barriers may have been experienced in either the early stage of the business venture set-up or at a later stage of business development. In addition, we have showcased stories of success in each specific minority group and finally focused on future projections and developments (including research initiatives) for each of the entrepreneurial groups.

While it is recognized that the selection of minority groups included in this book is not comprehensive, it is a selection that has been possible to review because of the available accessible research and literature. We are aware of other minority groups who are becoming engaged in entrepreneurial activities, such as war veterans and ex-offenders. However, the lack of available literature in these areas has meant that to date there is only very limited published material and much of it concentrates on small business training and initiatives for veterans and ex-offenders, rather than on in-depth research of the experiences, barriers and profiles of these entrepreneurs (US Census Bureau Online, 2007; Smith, 2009).

The literature that is available on veterans' and ex-offenders' entrepreneurial activities suggests these would certainly be fruitful areas of research in the future. In 2007 in the US for example, veteran-owned firms accounted for 9 per cent of all non-family businesses, with California having the most veteran-owned businesses (9.8 per cent of all such firms) (US Census Bureau Online, 2007). In fact, we include as one of our case studies in Chapter 8 on 'Disabled Entrepreneurs', a highly successful UK veteran business owner who suffered war injuries in Iraq. Furthermore, in relation to ex-offender entrepreneurs, studies in the UK carried out by Rieple and her associates in the late 1990s, for example, revealed that prisoners appeared to be more entrepreneurial than other occupational groups, that many had worked in their own businesses in the past and that an even higher proportion intended to do so in the future (Rieple et al., 1996; Rieple, 1998). These authors advocated the development of taught business skills in the prison population and Rieple (1998, p. 254) concluded:

Although individual prisons or probation areas may have a relatively small number of individuals within their remit, in total there are possibly some six or seven thousand current offenders (that is, those who are serving community orders or who are on post-sentence licences) who are running their own businesses in the UK alone. This figure could be multiplied several times if those indicated by our survey who intend to start their own businesses in the future actually do so. There is therefore a potentially large population of offenders who might benefit from training in small business skills, and who if sufficiently encouraged may become the successful entrepreneurs of the future.

With the prison population in England and Wales having doubled since the mid-1990s to record numbers of over 85 000 in 2010 (Verkaik, 2010), Rieple's comments above regarding this group of minority entrepreneurs would seem even more relevant today. Therefore, this group of entrepreneurs may well form an important minority group worthy of further study.

STRUCTURE OF THE BOOK

The layout of this book has been informed by the degree of marginalization and discrimination that may be experienced by various groups of people who fall outside mainstream entrepreneurial activity. In terms of the sequence of the chapters, we have subjectively placed the groups we consider to be the least disadvantaged first – through either marginalization or discrimination and prejudice – through to those groups who may experience more severe barriers to them taking up entrepreneurial activities. It is recognized that there will be significant variability within each of these minority entrepreneurial groups, both within and between countries throughout the world.

Chapter 2 on 'Younger Entrepreneurs' and Chapter 3 on 'Older Entrepreneurs' will explore the factors that motivate these 'minority' entrepreneurs to take up business ventures in various countries, as well as examine the particular barriers and obstacles that hinder their potential success. In particular cultures, age exerts an impact on people's attitudes about whether it is acceptable, appropriate, or perhaps possible to take up entrepreneurial ventures. This is evident in the data on early-stage entrepreneurial activity from all three economy classifications of the GEM, that is, factor-driven, efficiency-driven and innovative-driven economies (Bosma et al., 2008). In some cultures, age can also exert an influence on the proportion of individuals who take up training prior to starting a business, as this activity appears to decrease with age (ibid.). For example, in India and Germany, training was most frequently taken up by the 25–34-year-old age group, while in Turkey, only 10 per cent of this age group took up training, while the proportion was 60 per cent in Chile and Finland (ibid.). For older entrepreneurs aged between 55 and 64 years of age, 33 per cent of nascent entrepreneurs took up training in Finland, compared to only 4 per cent in Egypt (ibid.). These chapters examine the influences of age on those who operate as entrepreneurs at either end of the age spectrum.

Chapter 4 reviews the situation of 'Women Entrepreneurs' who appear to face particular obstacles. The barriers female entrepreneurs face are embedded in the culture and social mores that exist in any given country. Obviously, such differences in the experiences of men and women in these various countries will reflect differing educational levels, workforce participation, economic development of the country, and attitudes toward entrepreneurship from both the culture of the country, and the individual (ibid.). This chapter also explores the motivators for women wanting to pursue an entrepreneurial career, while examining the particular barriers they may face. These factors, in particular, are of great importance, as there is clearly an economic case for encouraging more women to start their own business. In the US, there has been recognition for more than three decades of the importance of this segment of the population in taking up entrepreneurial ventures (Prowess, 2011). However, in the UK, a similar level of government support has not been achieved. In fact, it has been estimated that Britain would add 750 000 more businesses if female entrepreneurship was at the same level as has been achieved in the US (ibid.).

In Chapter 5, we turn our attention to 'Ethnic Minority Entrepreneurs'. In this book, we have defined ethnic minority entrepreneurs as being those who retain a strong association and personal involvement with their country and culture of origin, but who were born in the country of their current residence (Chaganti and Greene, 2002). The distinction between ethnic minority entrepreneurs and immigrant entrepreneurs is based on the country of birth. For example, Rath (2010) has concluded that ethnic entrepreneurship occurs when first-generation immigrants set up businesses to meet the needs of their own ethnic communities, and in so doing, create ethnic markets. However, in the literature reviewed, it is acknowledged that there are examples of a considerable overlap in some studies where participants may have been termed 'ethnic', 'immigrant' (e.g., Peredo et al., 2004), and on some occasions 'Indigenous' populations have been likened to 'ethnic outsiders to the dominant culture' (Foley, 2003, p. 135). There is clearly a need for a commonly agreed definition within these areas of potential overlap.

In Chapter 6, we focus on 'Immigrant Entrepreneurs', which we define as individuals who have entered the host country to pursue work opportunities but who were born outside that country. This group often become involved in business ventures shortly after their arrival in the host country, and their businesses may fall outside the areas that have been traditionally seen as 'ethnic minority businesses'. That is, this group of entrepreneurs may be involved in the development of innovative areas of business, and be delivering their product or ideas across a wide range of sectors in the community at large (e.g., Desiderio and Salt, 2010). This minority group of entrepreneurs is of particular interest, as currently they become involved in entrepreneurial activities at a slightly higher rate than do native-born citizens in most OECD countries (12.7 per cent compared to 12 per cent respectively), however, it does appear that survival rates may be lower than those experienced by native entrepreneurs (ibid.). Nevertheless, immigrant entrepreneurs are contributing significantly to the employment creation of many countries. Therefore, this chapter endeavours to draw a picture of some of the characteristics of immigrant entrepreneurs in various countries, and to deepen understanding of what may facilitate or hinder their entry into business ventures.

Chapter 7 looks at 'Lesbian, Gay and Bisexual (LGB) Entrepreneurs' from a global and international perspective. This is the only group of entrepreneurs featured in the book who in many countries throughout the world could face criminal proceedings, imprisonment or even the death penalty (in at least seven countries), if they were 'open' about their sexual orientation (IDAHO-UK, 2009). This degree of persecution is not restricted to developing or Muslim countries, but is still found in developed Western countries such as the US where in more than half the states LGBs still have no legal protection against homophobic discrimination (Herek et al., 2009). It is therefore not surprising that research in this area has only really emerged in the past decade or so (Davies, 2010). Indeed, LGB business owners have often remained hidden, as unlike ethnicity, gender, some disabilities and age, sexual orientation is easier to conceal. Nevertheless, as with the other featured minority entrepreneurs, this chapter highlights the potential economic importance of LGB business owners as well as evidence of their outstanding entrepreneurial successes in countries in which they feel safe from legal persecution (Galloway, 2007). Even so, the chapter clearly emphasizes that throughout the world, LGB business owners continue to face varying degrees of homophobic discrimination and prejudice (Davidson, 2011). Furthermore, in parallel to their other minority entrepreneurial counterparts, LGBs are made up of different individuals in relation to factors such as age, gender, ethnicity, nationality, personalities and disabilities and can face potentially different oppressive layers of discrimination (Iwasaki and Ristock, 2007).

Chapter 8 focuses on 'Disabled Entrepreneurs' and it has been estimated that between 10 per cent and 20 per cent of the world's population has some kind of disability (De Klerk, 2008; Disabled World, 2010). This chapter explores the plight of entrepreneurs with disabilities ranging from cognitive, physical, sensory and intellectual impairments to those with various types of chronic disease and mental illness. What is evident is that similar to other minority entrepreneurs, the available research literature on this group of individuals is very sparse and tends to constitute predominantly US and European (including UK) studies (e.g., Holub, 2001; Jones and Latrielle, 2006; Larsson, 2006). Like all other disabled and non-disabled entrepreneurs, females in this group are in a minority compared to their disabled male counterparts (Larsson, 2006). However, unlike other entrepreneurial minorities, both male and female disabled business owners are much more likely to work part-time (due to health issues etc.). In addition, their self-employment rates decrease with age and often in parallel with the severity of their disabilities (Boylan and Burchardt, 2002).

In Chapter 9, 'Indigenous Entrepreneurship' is considered. Along with the conventions adopted in the Global Entrepreneurship Monitor (Hindle and Rushworth, 2002), in this book Indigenous (with a capital 'I') will be the convention adopted as a mark of respect for Indigenous peoples of all nations. Indigenous peoples, in contrast to immigrant populations, 'almost always involve individuals that have a close attachment to ancestral territories and the natural resources in them' (Peredo et al., 2004, p. 14). There is a growing awareness of the significant role Indigenous entrepreneurship can take in the areas of economic and social development (Hindle and Rushworth, 2002). This area of entrepreneurial activity is increasingly being seen as the way forward for Indigenous people to achieve more equity in the development of their countries of birth. For example:

> Stimulation of Indigenous entrepreneurship has the potential to repair much of the damage through creation of an enterprise culture, which fully respects Indigenous traditions but empowers Indigenous people as economic agents in a globally competitive modern world. There is growing world-wide awareness that policies directed to developing Indigenous entrepreneurship have the 'win-win' potential of enhancing Indigenous self-determination, while reducing welfare costs. (Hindle and Rushworth, 2002, p. 41)

In Australia, while there has been a recognition of the potential that may exist in Indigenous entrepreneurship (Wood and Davidson, 2011), efforts to facilitate the development of entrepreneurial business ventures amongst the Indigenous population have not enjoyed universal success (Hindle and Rushworth, 2002). In contrast, there are increasing levels of Indigenous entrepreneurship in other countries, such as the US and Canada. In Canada, the numbers of Indigenous people involved in their own businesses has grown at twice the national average – for men and women alike (ibid.).

However, many Indigenous groups worldwide continue to suffer severe social disadvantage, including very poor health, inadequate education and poverty (Peredo et al., 2004). Although a focus on Indigenous entrepreneurship has begun to generate a body of literature (Peredo and Anderson, 2006), further research in this area is required (Frederick and Foley, 2006). Possibly, entrepreneurial enterprises will provide a mechanism for Indigenous people to become economically independent and improve their living conditions. This chapter will analyse what we know of the facilitators for small business operation in the Indigenous communities, with a particular focus on the barriers that may impede their success.

Finally, Chapter 10 concludes the book, by pulling together the themes that have emerged in the various chapters. It starts off by comparing the similarities and differences that may exist in the mainstream entrepreneurial populations across the various countries compared to the different minority group business owners reviewed throughout the book. It then compares and contrasts the push and pull factors that motivate entrepreneurs from the various minority groups, as well as the barriers and challenges that face those who set up business ventures outside the acceptable boundaries of mainstream entrepreneurship. Finally, constructive recommendations for ways forward in terms of future research and business support and development are offered. Given the potential of successful entrepreneurial ventures to positively influence the quality, and in fact quantity, of life for many of the minority groups reviewed in the forthcoming chapters, we believe this book makes an important contribution to the extant knowledge of non-mainstream entrepreneurs.

REFERENCES

Allen, I.E., A. Elam, N. Langowitz and M. Dean (2007), *Global Entrepreneurship Monitor 2007, Report on Women and Entrepreneurship*, available at: http://www.gemconsortium.org; accessed 8 August 2011.

Anderson, R. (2004), 'Indigenous entrepreneurship: is it, and if so what is it?' (panel symposium proposal), Annual Meeting of the Academy of Management, New Orleans, LA, USA.

Anderson, R., B. Honig and A.M. Peredo (2006), 'Communities in the new economy: where social entrepreneurship and Indigenous entrepreneurship meet', in C. Steyaert and D. Hjorth (eds), *Entrepreneurship as Social Change*, Cheltenham, UK and Northampton, MA, USA: Edward Elgar, pp. 56–78.

Anderson, R., D. De Clercq, B. Honig and F. Schlosser (2009), 'Workshop on fostering entrepreneurship among people with special needs through entrepreneurial mentoring programs', Anaheim: USASBE Proceedings.

Bosma, N., Z. Acs, E. Autio, A. Coduras and J. Levie (2008), *Global Entrepreneurship Monitor, 2008 Executive Report*, Universidad del Desarrollo, Santiago, Chile, Babson College, MA, USA and London Business School, UK.

Boylan, A. and T. Burchardt (2002), *Barriers to Self-employment for Disabled People*, London: Report for the Small Business Service, October.

Chaganti, R. and P.G. Greene (2002), 'Who are ethnic entrepreneurs? A study of entrepreneursapos: ethnic involvement and business characteristics', *Journal of Small Business Management*, **40** (2), 126–43.

Dana, L.-P. (2007) (ed.), *Handbook on Ethnic Minority Entrepreneurship*, Cheltenham, UK and Northampton, MA, USA: Edward Elgar.

Davidson, M.J. (2011), 'The dark side of the rainbow: a research model of occupational stress and lesbian, gay and bisexuals (LGBs) in the workplace', in S. Grosch (ed.), *Diversity in the Workplace*, London: Gower.

Davies, G.S. (2010), 'A diversity integrative model of the factors affecting lesbian, gay and bisexual career choice intentions', MSc dissertation, University of Manchester, Faculties of Humanities, Manchester, UK.

De Clercq, D. and P. Arenius (2006), 'The role of knowledge in business start-up activity', *International Small Business Journal*, **24** (4), 339–58.

De Klerk, T. (2008), 'Funding for self-employment of people with disabilities. Grants, loans, revolving funds or linkage with microfinance programmes', *Lepra Review*, **79** (1), 92–109.

Desiderio, M.V. and J. Salt (2010), 'Main findings of the conference on entrepreneurship and employment creation of immigrants in OECD countries', 9–10 June, Conference Paper, Paris.

Disabled World (2010), available at: http://www.disabled-world.com; accessed 20 November 2010.

Fielden, S.L. and M.J. Davidson (eds) (2005), *International Handbook of Women and Small Business Entrepreneurship*, Cheltenham, UK and Northampton, MA, USA: Edward Elgar.

Fielden, S.L. and M.J. Davidson (eds) (2010), *International Research Handbook on Successful Women Entrepreneurs*, Cheltenham, UK and Northampton, MA, USA: Edward Elgar.

Foley, D. (2003), 'An examination of Indigenous Australian entrepreneurs', *Journal of Developmental Entrepreneurship*, **8** (2), 133–51.

Foley, D. (2006), 'Indigenous Australian entrepreneurs: not all community organisations, not all in the outback', Discussion Paper No. 279/2006, Centre for Aboriginal Economic Policy Research.

Foley, D. and E. Pio (2009), 'Inextricable identity and ideology: Indigenous women entrepreneurs in Australia and Hawaii', 6th Annual Australian Graduate School of Entrepreneurs (AGSE) Conference, Adelaide, South Australia.

Frederick, H.H. and D. Foley (2006), 'Indigenous populations as disadvantaged entrepreneurs in Australia and New Zealand', *The International Indigenous Journal of Entrepreneurship, Advancement, Strategy and Education*, **11** (2), available at: http://www.Indigenousjournal.com/IIJEASVolIIIss2Frederick.pdf; accessed 3 August 2010.

Frederick, H.H., D.F. Kuratko and R.M. Hodgetts (2007), *Entrepreneurship: Theory, Process and Practice*, South Melbourne, Victoria: Nelson Australia.

Galloway, L. (2007), 'Entrepreneurship and the gay minority. Why the silence?', *Entrepreneurship and Innovation*, **8** (4), 271–80.

Herek, G.M., J.R. Gills and J.C. Coogan (2009), 'Internalized stigma among sexual minority adults: insights from a social psychological perspective', *Journal of Counseling Psychology*, **56** (1), 32–43.

Hindle, K. and P. Moroz (2009), 'Indigenous entrepreneurship as a research field: developing a definitional framework from the emerging canon', *International Entrepreneurial Management Journal*, available at: http://kevinhindle.com/system/resources/BAhbBlsHOgZmSSJDMjAxMC8xMC8yMi9JbmRpZ2Vub3VzX2VudHJlcHJlbmV1cnNoaXBfYXNfYV9yZXNlYXJjaYXJja F9maWVsZC5wZ GYGOgZFVA/Indigenous_entrepreneurship_as_a_research_field.pdf; accessed 4 August 2011.

Hindle, K. and S. Rushworth (2002), *Global Entrepreneurship Monitor, Australia, 2002*, Melbourne, Australia: Swinburne University of Technology.

Holub, T. (2001), 'Entrepreneurs among people with disabilities', Los Angeles ERIC Clearinghouse on Entrepreneurship Education, available at: http://www.celcee.edu/products/digest/Diig01-05; accessed 20 November 2010.

IDAHO-UK (2009), 'International day against homophobia and transphobia', available at: http://www.idaho.org.uk/; accessed 18 August 2011.

Iwasaki, Y. and J.L. Ristock (2007), 'The nature of stress experienced by lesbians and gay men', *Anxiety, Stress and Coping*, **20** (3), 299–319.

Jones, M.J. and P.L. Latrielle (2006), 'Disability and self-employment: evidence from the UK', WELMERC School of Business and Economics, University of Wales, Swansea, Wales, Working Paper, June.

Larsson, S. (2006), 'Disability management and entrepreneurship: results from a nationwide study in Sweden', *The International Journal of Disability Management Research*, **1** (1), 159–68.

Peredo, A.M. and R.B. Anderson (2006), 'Indigenous entrepreneurship research: themes and variations', in C.S. Galbraith and C.H. Stiles (eds), *Developmental Entrepreneurship: Adversity, Risk, and Isolation*, Oxford: Elsevier, pp. 253–73.

Peredo, A.M., R.B. Anderson, C.S. Galbraith, B. Honig and L.-P. Dana (2004), 'Towards a theory of Indigenous entrepreneurship', *International Journal of Entrepreneurship and Small Business*, **1** (1/2), 1–20.

Prowess (2011), 'Promoting women's enterprise support', available at http://www.prowess.org.uk/facts.htm; accessed 26 March 2011.

Rafiq, M. (1992), 'Ethnicity and enterprise: a comparison of Muslim and non-Muslim-owned Asian businesses in Britain', *New Community*, **19** (1), 43–60.

Rath, J. (2010), 'Ethnic entrepreneurship: concept paper', European Foundation for the Improvement of Living and Working Conditions, Institute for Migration and Ethnic Studies (IMES) at the University of Amsterdam.

Rieple, A. (1998), 'Offenders and entrepreneurship', *European Journal on Criminal Policy and Research*, **6** (2), 235–56.

Rieple, A., M. Harper and A. Bailey (1996), 'Ex-offenders and enterprise', *The Howard Journal of Criminal Justice*, **35** (2), 131–47.

Schindehutte, M., M. Morris and J. Allen (2005), 'Homosexuality and entrepreneurship: implications of gay identity for the venture-creation experience', *The International Journal of Entrepreneurship and Innovation*, **6** (1), 27–40.

Smith, R. (2009), 'Entrepreneurship: a divergent pathway out of crime', in K. Jaishankar (ed.), *International Perspectives on Crime*, Newcastle-upon-Tyne: Cambridge Scholars Publishing.

US Census Bureau Online (2007), 'Survey of business owners – veteran-owned firms', available at: http://www.census.gov/econ/sbo/get07sof.html?10; accessed 29 March 2011.

Verkaik, R. (2010), 'Rising number of prisoners is "out of control"', *The Independent*, 24 April.

Wood, G.J. (2010), 'Australia', in S.L. Fielden and M.J. Davidson (eds), *International Handbook of Women and Small Business Entrepreneurship*, Cheltenham, UK and Northampton, MA, USA: Edward Elgar, pp. 10–25.

Wood, G.J. and M.J. Davidson (2011), 'A review of male and female Australian Indigenous entrepreneurs: disadvantaged past – promising future?', *Gender in Management*, **26** (4), 311–26.

World Economic Forum (2009), *Educating the Next Wave of Entrepreneurs – Unlocking Entrepreneurial Capabilities to Meet Global Challenges of the 21st Century*, Report of the Global Educational Initiative, Switzerland: World Economic Forum.

2. Younger entrepreneurs

> Despite the fact that most young people do not see themselves as entrepreneurs, we do not believe there is a shortage of ambition. Instead, the ambitions and skills of young people simply need to be tapped and focused towards entrepreneurial aims. The results show that 51% of young people would like to be their own boss and only one in 10 want to work for a big company.
>
> (Tenner Tycoon, 2011, p. 16)

INTRODUCTION

Most previous entrepreneurial literature has utilized adult participants (Turker and Selcuk, 2009), however, making a decision to move into an entrepreneurial venture can occur at various key points throughout an individual's life. Such decision points may occur on leaving school, enrolling on a course in entrepreneurship, being dissatisfied in current employment that may lack the opportunity for autonomy, or leaving full-time employment at the point of retirement (Singh and DeNoble, 2003). All of the factors that are brought to bear at these various stages will impact on decisions that may result in self-employment (Singh and Verma, 2001).

This chapter will explore the group of entrepreneurs who primarily fall below 30 years of age. This group is a minority; for example, the Australian Bureau of Statistics reported that only 3 per cent of entrepreneurs in Australia (ABS, 2008) were 24 years of age and under. While this is a small proportion of the overall entrepreneurial activity, it would nevertheless be of interest to have an understanding of the barriers and facilitators that may be experienced by these younger entrepreneurs in their efforts to set up their own business ventures.

According to the Global Entrepreneurship Monitor (GEM) *Executive Report*, the greatest proportions of entrepreneurs occur between the ages of 25 and 34 in high- and middle-income countries (Minniti et al., 2005). In these countries, younger entrepreneurs (18–24 years of age) were more likely to become involved in an entrepreneurial venture than were people over 55 years of age (ibid.). However, as seen in Table 2.1, in Australia, older entrepreneurs (55+) are more likely to be involved in small business operations, according to the Australian Bureau of Statistics (ABS, 2008). (This latter group will be discussed in more detail in the following chapter.)

Table 2.1 General demographics of small business operators by age, 2007 (n = 1.9 million)

Business operators	Total (%)	15–24 years (%)	25–54 years (%)	55+ (%)
Male	68	3.7	67.8	28.4
Female	32	1.4	72.5	26.0
Total business operators	100	3.0	69.3	27.7

Source: Australian Bureau of Statistics (2008).

As outlined in Table 2.1, the proportions of Australian business operators who fell at either end of the age spectrum were markedly different, with only 3 per cent being between 15 and 24 years of age, and a greater proportion of operators (28 per cent) being 55 or over (ABS, 2008). Over two-thirds of entrepreneurs in Australia were between 25 and 54 years of age and there has been an increase in the proportion of male business operators under 30 years of age; in 2003, 65 per cent of operators were in this category whereas in 2004, the figure was 73 per cent. In contrast, female operators in the same age group decreased by 1.7 per cent at that time (ABS, 2004).

There is a further interesting gender difference in some of the age groups of young entrepreneurs in Australia. For example, 3.4 per cent of male business operators were between 20 and 24 years of age, compared to only 0.9 per cent of females in the same age group (ABS, 2008). However, in the 35–44 age bracket, female business operators began to outnumber their male counterparts (30 per cent female compared to 25.3 per cent male), and at 45–54, slightly more females were business operators (29 per cent) than their male counterparts (27.8 per cent) (ibid.). There are many reasons why these disparities may be occurring, and one obvious possibility is that a proportion of women leave the workforce temporarily when they have their children, and take on the primary responsibility of care until their children begin school. After this period, many women return to paid employment, or as these statistics suggest, some start a business venture (Fielden and Davidson, 2010).

In the UK, in 2001 the proportion of young people (16–24 years of age) who considered starting up a business was 17 per cent; by 2003 this had fallen to 14 per cent (*Enterprise*, 2005). However, in 2007, an estimated 550 businesses were started weekly by young entrepreneurs under 25 years of age; this represented 7 per cent of all start-up business ventures in England and Wales. Almost two-thirds of young people surveyed in the South West and London stated they wished to be self-employed (65 per cent and 64 per cent respectively); in the North East and East Midlands the numbers were lower, although they come close to half of the sample (42 per cent and 48 per cent respectively) (UK Women's Enterprise Task Force, 2007). Young men showed a greater propensity to want to set themselves up in business than young women (64 per cent compared with 50 per cent respectively) (ibid.). However, in 2006, these aspirations were not directly translating into action; at that time, the proportion of young entrepreneurs between the ages of 18 and 24 in the UK was predominantly made up of young males (6.8 per cent compared to females at 1.9 per cent) (Kwong, 2006). Three years later, a more positive picture was emerging, with levels of female entrepreneurship in the UK reported to be at 47 per cent of the male entrepreneurial activity (Levie and Hart, 2009).

Nevertheless, there is a growing proportion of young female students in the UK (51 per cent in the 14–19 age group) who now state that they want to become entrepreneurs, which is slightly less (4 per cent) than the figure cited by young male students. This figure is markedly greater than that reported in 2004 (35 per cent female compared to 55 per cent male) (UK Women's Enterprise Task Force, 2007). This positive shift in attitude may reflect a general belief in this age cohort that entrepreneurial ventures constitute a career choice that is positively viewed in the UK (*Enterprise*, 2005). In some other countries, increasing rates of new venture desirability by female students have also been reported. For example, Veciana et al. (2005) reported very similar aspirations by male and female students in Puerto Rico (50.4 per cent and 49.6 per cent respectively) who expressed a desire to become an entrepreneur. However, the Catalan (Spanish) students in their sample followed the more traditional pattern of 61.3 per cent of male students, compared to 38.7 per cent females expressing the view that a new business venture was desirable.

The recent publication of the GEM *Executive Report* (Bosma et al., 2008) provides some useful statistics on age and early-stage entrepreneurial activity in other countries, reported in three economic categories: factor-, efficiency-, or innovation-driven economies. Countries classified as 'innovation-driven economies' include Norway, Finland, Denmark, Iceland, Netherlands, France, Germany, Greece, Italy, Israel, Japan, Slovenia, Republic of Korea, United Kingdom, Ireland and United States. In these countries, the bulk of early-stage entrepreneurial activity was carried out by 25–34-year-olds (10 per cent), with 8 per cent being conducted by

35–44-year-olds, and 6 per cent by 45–54-year-olds. In contrast, 18–24-year-olds in the GEM data account for only 5 per cent of the early-stage entrepreneurial activity, with a smaller proportion again (3 per cent) being carried out by 55–64-year-old operators (ibid.).

As a comparison, in countries classified as having factor-driven econo-mies (e.g., Bolivia, Bosnia and Egypt), 24 per cent of early-stage entrepre-neurial activity was carried out by 25–34-year-olds. In efficiency-driven economies (e.g., Argentina, Brazil, Hungary and Turkey) there was 14 per cent in the similar age group, compared to only 10 per cent in innovation-driven economies (e.g., Belgium, Denmark, United Kingdom and the United States) (ibid.). The disparity in the figures may well reflect different proportions of 'necessity' entrepreneurs, who take up self-employment because of the lack of other employment options available to them.

Despite the lower proportion of young people involved in early-stage entrepreneurial activity in the innovation-driven economies represented in the above data, it has been long recognized that this is a cohort of significant importance. For example, in an early publication, Lorrain and Raymond (1991) reported that in the US, more than one-third of the 230 000 new businesses started in 1987 were set up by young people, and 250 000 college students at around that time had started their own busi-nesses (ibid.). In addition, these authors reported that in Canada, 4 per cent of independent entrepreneurs were under 25 years of age, and almost a quarter were under 30 years of age. In Quebec alone, almost 14 per cent of business owners were young entrepreneurs, which equated to 16 000 indi-viduals who were less than 30 years of age (ibid.). More recently in the US, the numbers of young entrepreneurs is approaching one-third (31.5 per cent) of the total entrepreneurs. In a sample of 584 385 business operators, 184 338 were operated by 20–34-year-old entrepreneurs (Fairlie, 2009).

Overall these figures represent a significant proportion of young people worldwide entering into a business venture, but despite this, we know very little about what influences the young entrepreneur. It is important to gain knowledge in this area, as the way in which we work in the future will be influenced by the innovative nascent business ventures currently under development by the young entrepreneur (Henderson and Robertson, 2000). In particular, it is important to widen understanding of the motivating factors of people younger than 25 years of age, in order to examine 'which factors affect their intentions to start-up a business in the future' (Turker and Selcuk, 2009, p. 143). The youth of today will provide us with the next batch of up and coming entrepreneurs, and hence it is essential that we focus on entrepreneurial intention, and how this can be fostered (Turker and Selcuk, 2009). This knowledge will ensure adequate and appropriate policy mechanisms are designed and implemented, after providing the necessary appropriate educational opportunities.

YOUNGER ENTREPRENEURS: GENERAL CHARACTERISTICS

In the past, there have been strongly held beliefs about the suitability of young people to enter into business dealings, as young business operators have been seen as 'at risk'. For example, early research concluded that people under 30 were less capable of succeeding in setting up business ventures because of their lack of work experience, management skills, knowledge base or general maturity (Lorrain and Raymond, 1991).

However, consideration of some cross-cultural research begins to paint a different picture of the young entrepreneur. For example, research by Kazmi (1999) has provided a snapshot of the young second-generation Indian entrepreneur. In this study, all but one of the 36 participants were male, and the average age was 25 years, with the range being between 23 and 29 years of age. On average these entrepreneurs entered into their businesses when they were 21; almost a quarter (24) of the group were married, and were supported by their spouses – directly or indirectly. The majority of the group held postgraduate degrees, with two-thirds being in the area of engineering, accountancy or management; 28 of the 36 had previous business experience before starting their own ventures, or joining the established family business (ibid.). The entrepreneurial competencies of this group were assessed, and the following picture emerged. The entire sample was judged to be highly achievement oriented, and a significant majority were considered to display effective leadership qualities, as well as managerial skills. These included superior human relations skills, such as an aptitude to maintain a successful interpersonal relationship with their community, suppliers, creditors and their employees (ibid.). They were further distinguished by their 'emotional stability' (ibid., p. 72). Most displayed high levels of motivation, as well as effective administrative skills. Not surprisingly, the majority of the group were considered to be both creative and innovative in their ideas and to have high levels of risk-taking ability. They were also judged to be visionary in their ability to look ahead and plan for the future.

In contrast, a study by Roberts and Tholen (1998) reported on young people aged below 30 in seven former communist countries, and focused on the experiences of a self-employed group in a relatively new way of working (i.e., new businesses set up to secure self-employment were seen as a novelty in 1996–97), as well as on their attitudes toward their futures. A total of 550 self-employed young business operators participated in the study, and the authors noted that representation of female entrepreneurs was very low (ibid.). This research identified some important characteristics believed to be shared by young entrepreneurs in the post-communist environment, who were frequently described as 'overwhelmingly radical and internationalist' (ibid., p. 60). The businesses the young entrepreneurs were involved in were micro in size. Most were sole operators in their business ventures and they did not employ others. This group of young entrepreneurs tended to lack trust in official programmes set up to support new business ventures. All participants were characterized by working long hours, and showed a total dedication to the success of their new business venture. Illustrations of this were seen in the lack of holidays taken by the group in the study; these occurred rarely. Their lives were described in quite austere terms, for example, 37 per cent of the sample stated that they had not been to a bar or restaurant over the previous four weeks. More typically, their working week tended to exceed 60 hours per week. Overall, there was a view expressed that in order to be successful, they had to 'dedicate their lives to building up their businesses' (ibid.).

A further study (Ang and Hong, 2000) provided information regarding the characteristics of the young entrepreneur by investigating university students in two Asian locations: Hong Kong and Singapore. Ang and Hong looked at the role of personality and motivational factors in entrepreneurial interest, and reported that risk-taking, persistence and an internal locus of control were important personality characteristics of their sample of university students. They concluded that these characteristics were not normally found in the East Asian culture from which the sample was drawn. In addition, the authors reported that the predictors of entrepreneurial spirit were different for their Hong Kong sample, compared to the Singaporean sample. In particular, the quality of persistence was only found to be important in the Hong Kong sample, while internal locus of control and a consuming interest in money were rated highly by the Singaporean sample. In contrast, risk-taking was a common personality characteristic for both groups (ibid.).

In an attempt to characterize the young entrepreneur, attitudes toward success could add a useful dimension. It would appear that business operators in this age group may have a different perspective of what constitutes 'success' than do an older generation of self-employed business people. In the past, recognition, a sense of achievement and financial success were deemed to be the important underpinnings of being successful (Cull, 2006). For younger entrepreneurs, their views of success may be focused on the sense of freedom and independence they can achieve. In a study in Canada, Cull reported that young participants stated that freedom to be in charge of their lives was an important element in success as was the opportunity to enjoy the business operation through a positive attitude to the entrepreneurial venture. In addition, recognition was important and the ability to be independent (ibid.).

Other researchers, such as Alstete (2002), studied college students in New York, and reported that the ability to make money was seen as a potential benefit of being involved in entrepreneurial activity by only 17 per cent of the sample ($n = 54$). Having greater control (47 per cent) and greater satisfaction (28 per cent) in their work were more important (ibid.). Therefore, although it would appear that success for the young entrepreneur may include the desire for financial gains (ibid.), other aspects of 'success' may be seen as more important. These attitudes reflect the more commonly held views on the benefits of entrepreneurship, which encompass the ability to reach an individual's optimal potential while making a difference – in their own lives, or the lives of others, achieving personal control, making a meaningful contribution to society, enjoying the work being done and gaining financial benefits (Scarborough and Zimmerer, 2000). Achieving these goals could be viewed as 'success' by the young entrepreneur in their business venture.

YOUNGER ENTREPRENEURS: ASPIRATIONS AND MOTIVATIONS

It is evident that some young people start considering entrepreneurship before they have completed their formal education. The extant literature has examined factors that are influential in young people considering a career in an entrepreneurial activity. Numerous studies have been conducted in diverse countries, and there appears to be a huge interest shown by students considering a career in a sole-operated business.

Studies focusing on career aspirations have been particularly illuminating. In the early 1980s, 40.7 per cent of students in the UK, and more than a third of Irish students (34.3 per cent) were reported to have an interest in starting their own business (Scott and Twomey, 1988). Recent figures suggest that this trend continues, with more than half of 16–21-year-olds in the UK aspiring to become self-employed at some later stage (UK Women's Enterprise Task Force, 2007).

Similar trends have been noted in the US, where there has been a considerable shift in the proportions of students who aspire to being self-employed. In the early 1980s, Scott and Twomey (1988) reported that a quarter of students in their study had aspirations to become self-employed, whereas ten years later, a national survey of high school students in the US indicated that two-thirds (66.9 per cent) aspired to start their own business (Kourilsky and Walstad, 1998). Recent research suggests that this trend is continuing strongly. Blanchflower and Oswald (2007) reported that 49 per cent of young people under 25 in the UK aspired to be self-employed, with 59 per cent feeling similarly in the US. Of interest in this study is the strong preference for self-employment by young people of a similar age reported in other European countries, for example, Cyprus and Hungary (68 per cent), Estonia (71 per cent), Italy (74 per cent) and Portugal (78 per cent). In Canada, similar upward trends have been noted, with 8.9 per cent of students aspiring to self-employment in 1987, and 10.9 per cent a decade later. In the Netherlands, similar increases were noted, with 9.9 per cent of students aspiring to self-employment in 1987, and an increase to 11.3 per cent in 1996 (Wang and Wong, 2004).

It is interesting to note the variability amongst different countries. This suggests that in some cultures, acceptance of an entrepreneurial role may be higher. Alternatively, it may be that certain cultures foster a predisposition toward entrepreneurial activity. This possibility is borne out in early research by Parnell et al. (1995) when they examined degrees of propensity toward entrepreneurial activities by students from diverse cultures; they found that US students had a stronger entrepreneurial predisposition compared to Egyptian students. Certainly, there is a recognition of cultural forces that need to be considered in a given cultural context. Lee et al. (2005) explored cultural influences on young people's attitudes toward starting a business venture in the US and Korea, and revealed that there was a belief that entrepreneurship education should be customized to meet the needs of each cultural context, suggesting that unique factors were at play in each country. In other words, no one 'programme' would be adequate to ideally meet the needs of each country.

Previous work experience may also be a significant factor in influencing the ambition of university students to consider an entrepreneurial career (Scott and Twomey, 1988). Another factor may be the role of socio-cultural factors. Begley et al. (1997) reported that social status alone could be considered to be a factor in influencing young people to take up a business venture. The public perception of entrepreneurs, along with the amount of encouragement afforded young university students, were also found to be factors in aspirations to become entrepreneurs (Veciana et al., 2005). However, this study highlighted that young people can aspire toward an entrepreneurial career, but their aspirations may be hindered by an expectation that such a reality may not be forthcoming. If expectations are low, this would be expected to reduce the actual intention of a young person to enter into a business venture.

A recent study by Turker and Selcuk (2009) reported only two predictors for entrepreneurial intention in their sample of 300 university students in Turkey. These were the support of the education setting in which they operated, and the structural support of the external environment. The latter support was considered to be more significant than the former. Therefore, there appear to be numerous factors that influence young students (18+ years of age) to consider enterprise as a career. These factors include 'individual or psychological components, social and economic features' (Henderson and Robertson, 2000, p. 282). Effective training and business education are also recognized to be important.

Alstete (2002) reported that students in the US had a strong desire to maintain a lifestyle that was flexible, allowing them high degrees of personal freedom. They also viewed making money as a significant factor and this was linked to the ability to make profits in a successful entrepreneurial business that would bring about security in an early retirement. In addition, young employees may also be attracted to the idea of going into business by lower levels of organizational commitment they may have to their current places of employment. All of the above factors were found to influence the aspirations of young people in their considerations of an entrepreneurial career (ibid.).

The ability to ensure some degree of financial security was also influential in the aspirations of young students in Scotland and England. Henderson and Robertson (2000) concluded that of the two-thirds of their sample who stated they would venture into their own business, making money and having the opportunity to be their own boss were seen as the key drivers. Similarly, Ang and Hong (2000) concluded that their sample of East Asian Chinese students residing in Hong Kong and Singapore expressed a desire for money and security as their primary motivators in considering an entrepreneurial venture. In Singapore, Wang and Wong (2004) reported that 'gender, family, business experience and educational level' (p. 170) were significant factors in explaining entrepreneurial interest. However, in their large sample of 5326 undergraduate students in engineering, computing and science, they concluded that while their participants reported high levels of desire to run their own businesses, there appeared to be inadequate preparation to make this a reality. Knowledge of running a business was lacking, and there was a propensity to be risk-averse to making their goals a reality. These authors concluded that aspirations to start a new business venture did not necessarily translate into actual self-employment in a number of industrialized countries.

However, there are various factors that do motivate and sustain young entrepreneurs once they start their business ventures. These include having greater satisfaction in the work being done, and having the capacity to provide for the family, as well as having something to leave the children. Another motivator for younger entrepreneurs is the existence of other family members who are already in business (Lorrain and Raymond, 1991), and this appears to have a particular influence on decisions of young people to take up a similar path (Scott and Twomey, 1988). Shaver and Scott (1991) have also suggested that young entrepreneurs who have an entrepreneurial family background may choose to move into some form of self-employment as soon as their formal schooling is completed.

Attitudes are also key as an influencing factor for young people. Primarily, attitudes are powerful in terms of the self-image a person has of themselves, and their abilities. Perceptions are also important in relation to views about what running a small business involves. These factors play a part in making decisions about possible careers, and these will be linked to the individual's personal ambitions (Henderson and Robertson, 2000). These authors are of the view that: 'if a young person's social environment is conducive to entrepreneurship and the individual has positive personal experience of a business venture, he or she may well be drawn towards entrepreneurship' (p. 283). In support of this view, they found that students whose backgrounds were affluent were more likely to see entrepreneurship as a positive possibility. In addition, their study reported that the main influences on career choices for undergraduate students were their own personal experiences, followed by family or friends. Interestingly, teachers or careers guidance counsellors were seen as a very small influence, because of a perception that they 'do not always demonstrate sufficient knowledge of, and enthusiasm for, entrepreneurship as a career choice' (p. 286).

YOUNGER ENTREPRENEURS: CHALLENGES AND BARRIERS

In addition to an understanding of what aspirations and motivators influence and sustain the young entrepreneur, it is important to explore what challenges and barriers are faced by this cohort. One barrier experienced by entrepreneurs of all age groups appears to be the difficulties they face in obtaining financial credit. It is possible that this impediment would create more difficulties for the young entrepreneur.

As expected, early researchers have reported that young entrepreneurs find barriers in the lack of credibility afforded them by bankers, suppliers, customers and so on because of the perceived risk involved relating to young entrepreneurs (Stevenson, 1987; Lorrain and Raymond, 1991). Apparently, young entrepreneurs lack credibility in the eyes of the business community in which they operate, and this is perceived as a major problem for young entrepreneurs. Such a perspective is likely to have a negative impact on accessing credit through normal channels.

In relation to accessing finance, research by Roberts and Tholen (1998) in East-Central Europe and three states of the former Soviet Union reported that very few young entrepreneurs in these countries drew on the services of banks, accountants or solicitors. Cash economies were the norm. In this study, the source of income assistance for young entrepreneurs was families and personal friends, as in most of these countries, credit facilities were not available. Of interest was the finding that this 'limitation' did not appear to overly concern the young small business operators who stated that 'they would have been crippled by the interest charges' (ibid., p. 60). Therefore, the bulk of start-up capital was generated through personal savings, or from family members. Government programmes were available to assist people starting up their own businesses in all of the countries included in the research. However, these did not appear to be reaching the majority of the young people considering new business ventures. Rather, friends, or families, were seen as the safest source of advice regarding appropriate business practices (Roberts and Tholen, 1998).

This issue of difficulty in accessing mainstream sources of finance has also been found in a study by Turner and Nguyen (2005). This research focused on young entrepreneurs in Vietnam who were increasingly becoming involved in establishing entrepreneurial ventures such as export/import businesses, or managing in the service sector. The sample for the study was 75 young male and female business operators of a slightly older age group (between 25 and 35 years of age), located in Hanoi. One of the key findings of the study was the realization that access to formal credit and loans through banks and other financial institutions was extremely complex. For many young entrepreneurs, gaining a bank loan was thought to be 'nothing more than a dream' (Nguyen et al., 2001, p. 16). According to Ronnas (2001), 95 per cent of entrepreneurs in Vietnam used their own capital as well as relying on interest-free loans from friends and relatives. A miniscule portion of the sample in this study (less than 1 per cent) took out a bank loan. Therefore, family and friends appeared to be the key providers of finance and support for young entrepreneurs in Vietnam, and issues of trust and distrust were paramount. In terms of setting up new business ventures, it appeared that in Vietnam, trust only occurred in a very narrow circle of family, with perhaps a few close friends; there was a strong distrust of people outside this circle (Turner and Nguyen, 2005).

YOUNGER ENTREPRENEURS: STORIES OF SUCCESS

Despite the difficulties that may be experienced by the young entrepreneur, the following stories of success provide ample evidence of entrepreneurial spirit in the young. The first case study describes the classic 'rags to riches' story of the Australian, Reginald Murray Williams, who began his working life at 16 years of age. He turned his hand to numerous entrepreneurial ventures throughout his life, experiencing the cycles of debt, expansion and success. The second case study describes the young entrepreneur Poppy King, who in the mid-1990s set up a company at the age of 18 and became a household name in Australia. She experienced great success after only a few years, followed by a series of significant setbacks that led to a restructure of her company, and a new direction for her energies and entrepreneurial ventures.

BOX 2.1   REGINALD MURRAY (R.M.) WILLIAMS – CAMEL BOY, DROVER, WELL DIGGER, MINER, HISTORIAN, AUTHOR, LEATHERWORKER, BOOTMAKER AND BUSINESSMAN

Reginald Murray Williams (R.M.) was born in 1908, seven years after Federation, on a farm in Mid North, South Australia, and worked since the age of 16 as a camel 'boy', drover, well digger, miner, historian, author, leatherworker, bootmaker and businessman. From an early age, R.M. 'went bush' – stone building and lime burning in Victoria and on the Western Australian goldfields. He joined the missionary explorer William Wade in the late 1920s as a camel boy, and trekked across Australia's central western deserts, learning valuable bush lore and survival skills from the Aboriginal peoples of the area. During this period, he honed his stock handling and bushcraft skills from the stockmen of the desert fringe cattle stations.

At the onset of the Great Depression (1932) R.M. and his young family were living 'rough' in the Gammon Ranges of South Australia, barely making a living by digging wells. During this time he met an itinerant saddler named 'Dollar Mick', a self-taught genius in leatherworking, and his exceptional skills were passed on to the 24-year-old R.M. who made and sold his first pair of riding boots for 20 shillings. R.M. was well equipped to know what was required in the way of riding boots, as he had worked on some of the great pastoral runs of the interior as a stockman and drover.

His products began to be sought after, with patronage by the cattle king, Sir Sidney Kidman, and he set up the beginnings of his first factory in 1932 in an iron woodshed behind his father's house in a suburb in Adelaide, South Australia. At this time, there was no available capital and little help, however, he built up a team of dedicated craftsmen and took out advertisements in the rural press that asked customers for cash with their orders. R.M. developed his business over the next few decades, diversifying into bush saddlery, equipment and the company's trademark moleskins, jeans and bush shirts. However, this early success brought with it some significant challenges. R.M. had to borrow money in order to expand his business and to keep up with the orders that were flowing in, and this led to debt.

However, the entrepreneurial spirit was alive and well in R.M., and when he was approached by an elderly women who owned a gold mine in Tennant Creek in the Northern Territory, he could not resist the opportunity, seeing it as a way to get out of debt. He raised the capital through family and friends, and the mine was purchased. Eventually, the mine struck gold, and 'Nobles Nob' became one of the richest small gold mines in Australia. Despite the fact that 'many millions' were made through the gold mine, and R.M. was living the life of a successful businessman, he was not happy, and he chose to go back to a simple life in the bush, where he felt he belonged.

R.M. Williams passed away on 4 November 2003 aged 95, after living the life of an Australian icon. He had married twice, and had nine children. He was a unique Australian identity, contributing to his community in numerous ways. For example, he was the founder of the Australian Roughriders Association, and helped to form the Equestrian Federation of Australia in 1951. He also established the Stockman's Hall of Fame in Longreach in 1988, and was the editor of *Hoofs and Horns* magazine in the early 1950s. In addition, he published five books of Australian poetry. Today, the R.M. Williams family own many properties, with the bushwear business, established by R.M. as a young entrepreneur, continuing to enjoy the success of being recognized as an Australian trademark throughout the world.[1]

BOX 2.2 POPPY KING – FOUNDER OF POPPY INDUSTRIES

Poppy King was 18 when she started her business in 1992, with capital of just $40 000. Her first foray into the commercial world was with a range of lipsticks called 'Seven Virtues'. She produced 100 samples of seven colours and, in less than three years, built her cosmetic business into an empire with an $8 million annual turnover. At its height, Poppy King was named by *Time* magazine as a Global Leader of the New Millennium. Her company was featured in *Vogue*, *Elle* and *Harpers* fashion magazines. It appeared that Poppy King could do no wrong, and she became a household name in Australia during this period. In 1995, her entrepreneurial skills were recognized when she was named 'Young Australian of the Year'. In 1996, she held the position of Managing Director of Poppy Industries, and was also a member of the federal government's Small Business Council.

However, in 1997, turnover fell from $6 million to $4 million and pre-tax losses neared $1 million. This dramatic change was put down to the appearance of copycat brands of lipstick on the market. Additional capital was brought in by a couple who acquired a half share in the business and injected $3.5 million into the company, but the business continued to decline, with the partners unable to agree on the direction they should take to break into the US market.

By the following year, the dispute between the partners was beyond resolution. In August 1998, an audit found that the business was 'on its last legs'. The co-owners resigned as directors and Poppy continued to run the business on her own, while launching new products in Melbourne. However, in September 1998, the business was placed in the hands of the receiver. Adam Trescowthick subsequently acquired it in 1998 for $1.3 million, and Poppy King was reinstated as CEO of the company.

In 2002, Poppy King started working with Estee Lauder, and she moved to New York, where she took up the role of Vice President of Prescriptives in charge of creative marketing. She left this role in 2005 and tried her hand at writing her first book, *Lessons of a Lipstick Queen: Finding and Developing the Great Idea That Can Change Your Life*. While working on the book, Poppy launched 'Lipstick Queen' in 2006, and introduced another range of lipsticks that featured opaque and sheer options for each colour.

In the last few years, Poppy has continued to work on various projects in New York: TV, public speaking and new product launches. She has retained hands-on involvement with Poppy Industries, and markets and promotes herself with the same enthusiasm she had when she started out in business almost 20 years ago. King says that she has learnt to say no to some opportunities, and to work out what the important fundamentals of the business are and prioritize accordingly. This time around, she wants to focus on making sure her timing is right and doing one thing at a time, properly, and making decisions with her head, rather than her heart.

This philosophy is obviously working to her advantage, and the entrepreneurial spirit is still driving her business ventures. In 2011, Poppy King has produced a range of glosses and lipsticks for Boots No. 7 in the UK. Poppy focused on what she believes motivates women to wear lip colour, and she set about designing a colour to 'match' each reason. The end result is a range of seven lipsticks, each with complementing lip glosses. It appears that another cycle in Poppy King's entrepreneurial ventures is about to begin.[2]

YOUNGER ENTREPRENEURS: SUMMARY

In summary, even though young entrepreneurs make up a small proportion of the total entrepreneurial activity in the majority of countries, their involvement is considered to be essential for the ongoing national growth of a country (Henderson and Robertson, 2000). Although there is growing interest in the field of entrepreneurship in general, we need to know more about young nascent entrepreneurs who are considering setting up a business venture or who may have recently begun some entrepreneurial activity. The current lack of knowledge is somewhat surprising given that the Generation Y (i.e., those born between 1977 and 1995) burgeoning population, who may not be driven by the same goals or values as the Baby Boomer generation (born between 1946 and 1964), will possibly be looking for other ways of working – ways that increase their independence while providing them with adequate levels of income. Entrepreneurial ventures may increasingly offer an appropriate vehicle for these goals, and this cohort.

There are some cross-cultural similarities emerging in the available literature on the young entrepreneur. In terms of characteristics, the young entrepreneur appears to be highly achievement oriented; many of them display leadership qualities and managerial skills. Interpersonal relationships are important to them, and they are prepared to work extraordinarily hard to achieve their goals. An ability to take risks, to persevere in the face of adversity and to operate from an internal locus of control were also considered to be characteristics of this group in the selection of literature reviewed. The young entrepreneurs also appeared to have a strong desire to have an element of freedom in their working lives; to be independent and in charge of their own destiny. Overall, they displayed a strongly positive attitude to their entrepreneurial venture.

Aspirations of younger people to become entrepreneurs appear to be growing, particularly in the UK with dramatic changes being noted in the numbers of young women who now report they wish to start up a business venture (UK Women's Enterprise Task Force, 2007). In terms of motivations, in addition to expressing a desire for security and a desire for financial gain, young entrepreneurs stated that they were motivated by being their own boss, trying to reach their optimal potential and by making a difference both in their lives, and in the lives of others. Being able to provide for their families, and leave something to their children, were also seen as highly motivating. Many expressed the desire to make a meaningful contribution to society.

One common denominator appears to be that young entrepreneurs have an added difficulty of accessing financial backing for the entrepreneurial venture, and young business operators appear to face this obstacle regardless of their country of origin. Understanding what inspires, drives and maintains the young entrepreneur is essential for governments and policymakers in both the public and private sectors. Knowledge of the barriers and constraints faced by the young entrepreneur will also assist in enhancing participation levels.

Even though the proportion of entrepreneurs who fall into the 'young' category may be considered to be small in relation to the total cohort of entrepreneurs in a given country, their contribution to a dynamic economy is significant, and the successes enjoyed by many of this group are worthy of serious study and reflection. For example, in the United States, a list of the 50 richest young entrepreneurs under 30 years of age with online businesses is published annually. This list includes the highest earner, Mark Zuckerberg, 23 years of age, the founder of 'Facebook', with a reported net worth of $US700 million. The youngest entrepreneur in this list is Ashley Qualls, who at 17 is reported to have a net worth of $US4 million in her web company 'WhateverLife' (Top Young Entrepreneurs, 2010).

YOUNGER ENTREPRENEURS: THE FUTURE

Certainly, different age cohorts are recognized as having different sets of skills. According to Yeaton (2008), Generation Y individuals are believed to have highly developed technological skills and the ability to multitask and this group of people are now at an age where they have finished their studies and are entering the workforce, or establishing themselves in a career. With the Western phenomenon of the ageing population, Generation Y represents a large proportion of the population, making up approximately a quarter of it in some Western countries, for example, in Australia (28 per cent) and in the US (26 per cent) (Rugimbana, 2000). Furthermore, the predictions are that Generation Y members will make up more than one-third of the US population by 2015 (Pelton and True, 2004). This group of people may well have a different way of looking at things, as well as a different set of needs. It has been suggested that Generation Y individuals may be characterized by an ability to cope with risk, and being more amenable to change in general. In addition, it is anticipated that this group will widely adopt technology to enable them to develop networks to turn their ideas into ways of enlarging their customer base (Hunt and Virasa, 2009).

It seems clear that 'the future working environment will depend heavily on the creativity and individuality of the young' (Henderson and Robertson, 2000, p. 279). In this context, entrepreneurship can be viewed 'as a set of qualities influencing behaviour and enabling individuals to be flexible and creative in the face of change' (ibid.). Such qualities may be particularly suited to the young entrepreneur.

Without doubt, we are seeing a radical change in our workplaces. We no longer see employees who dedicate their entire working lives to one organization, and in return for this loyalty, they are looked after until their retirement. Financial security was won in this exchange. More typically, we are now seeing employees changing their place of work frequently, negotiating the type of work they want to be involved in – in particular as it relates to the length of hours they are prepared to give in an effort to retain some kind of work–life balance in their lives and those of their families. Increasingly also, there are radical changes in work roles (Pocock, 2003; McCrindle Research, 2007; McPherson, 2007).

Henderson and Robertson (2000) suggested that a new way of working in the future could be termed a 'portfolio career', which is characterized by workers having periods of self-employment, salaried work, and on occasion, unemployment. If such a way of working is to become a reality in the new millennium, entrepreneurial skills will become a key focus for those who wish to continue working, but traditional avenues of work have been closed to them. It is not uncommon now for increasing numbers of males in some Western countries to stay at home and fulfil the role of full-time carer for small children while their wives and partners continue on in paid employment. In addition, there is likely to be much more uncertainty about the way in which we work in the future, and individuals will need to be able to take on the responsibility of continually re-inventing themselves for different avenues of work, and of course for their financial security (Henderson and Robertson, 2000; ABS, 2007). Such an environment is likely to be conducive to an increase in entrepreneurial activity; possibly young entrepreneurs may be best suited to adapt to the radical changes that are taking place in the workplace.

We need to look to our young entrepreneurs, as they *are* our future. In recognizing this, secondary schools, universities and training institutions should consider the curriculum design of the programmes they offer. From the extant literature, we have learned that students feel that they learn very little about entrepreneurship from formal classes in university. To accommodate the projected growth in entrepreneurship (especially in the young) Henderson and Robertson (2000) counsel that educational institutions need to consider the way they deliver programmes in entrepreneurship; the focus of such programmes, the time at which they are offered, the degree of practical applied activities in the course and so on. 'Flexibility and creativity will be necessary survival skills in the workplace' (ibid., p. 286) and such an environment will stimulate and foster entrepreneurial activity in the future. We may be a long way from achieving that ideal. In a British study, when young people were asked what they learnt most during their education, they responded that they learnt least about starting an enterprise (less than 10 per cent) compared to maths and English (65 per cent). Even more damning was the finding that more than two-thirds of the students in this study felt they lacked the necessary skills to start a business (*Enterprise*, 2005). The recent Tenner Tycoon study (2011) confirmed these perceptions; it found that 41 per cent of students surveyed (1034 students between the ages of 14 and 19) believed that schools did not do enough to prepare young people to start up a business venture, with only 2 per cent of the sample believing that schools adequately prepared them for entrepreneurial activities.

The benefits of having young entrepreneurs in a society are manifold. Young entrepreneurs who are successful will generate business for the country in which they live. They will employ others. They will become mentors and role models, which may motivate other young people to follow in their path. They will not be forced to rely on governments for pension support in their old age. The successes of young entrepreneurs over the past

20 years have seriously challenged the view that young people entering into a business venture constitute a risk because of their lack of perceived skills in management, limited work experience and immaturity.

NOTES

1. Sources: adapted from the following: http://www.rmwilliams.com.au/home.asp? pageid=B1B2147C197AA576; http://en.wikipedia.org/wiki/R._M._Williams; http:// www.rmwilliams.com.au/home; all accessed 13 December 2010.
2. Sources: adapted from the following: http://en.wikipedia.org/wiki/Poppy_King; http:// www.australianoftheyear.org.au/recipients/?m=poppy-king-1995l; 'Lawyers suggest mediation for Poppy King dispute', 13 August 1998: http://www.liv.asn.au/about-liv/media-centre/Media-Releases/Lawyers-Suggest-Mediation-For-Poppy-King-Dispute. aspx?rep=1&glist=0&sdiag=0; 'News and views with Sting', Fiona Byrne, *The Sunday Herald Sun*, 10 February 2002; 'Poppy grows back', Laura Kendall, *The Advertiser*, 4 July 2007; 'Lippy king', Jenny Wills, *The Sunday Telegraph*, 14 April 2002; 'Poppy's new life', Christine Caulfield, *Sunday Herald Sun*, 10 December 2006; http://www.boots.com/en/ No-7/No7-Poppy-King/Interview-with-Poppy-King/; all accessed 9 May, 2011.

REFERENCES

Alstete, J.W. (2002), 'On becoming an entrepreneur: an evolving typology', *International Journal of Entrepreneurial Behaviour and Research*, **8** (4), 222–34.

Ang, S.H. and D.G.P. Hong (2000), 'Entrepreneurial spirit among East Asian Chinese', *Thunderbird International Business Review*, **42** (3), 285–309.

Australian Bureau of Statistics (ABS) (2004), 'Characteristics of small business', Catalogue No. 8127.0, Canberra: Australian Government Publishing Service.

Australian Bureau of Statistics (ABS) (2007), 'Mature age workers. Australian social trends', Catalogue No. 4102.0, Canberra: Australian Government Publishing Service.

Australian Bureau of Statistics (ABS) (2008), 'Counts of Australian business operators, 2006 to 2007', Catalogue No. 8175.0, Canberra: Australian Government Publishing Service.

Begley, T.M., W.L. Tan, A.B. Larasati, A. Rab and E. Zamora (1997), 'The relationship between socio-cultural dimensions and interest in starting a business: a multi-country study', *Frontiers of Entrepreneurship Research*, Babson Conference Proceedings, available at: www.babson.edu/entrep/fer/papers97/ beg.htm; accessed 5 August 2011.

Blanchflower, D.G. and A.J. Oswald (2007), 'What makes a young entrepreneur?', IZA Discussion Paper No. 3139, November, 2007.

Bosma, N., Z. Acs, E. Autio, A. Coduras and J. Levie (2008), *Global Entrepreneurship Monitor, 2008 Executive Report*, Universidad del Desarrollo, Santiago, Chile, Babson College, MA, USA and London Business School.

Cull, J. (2006), 'Mentoring young entrepreneurs: what leads to success?', *International Journal of Evidence-based Coaching and Mentoring*, **4** (2), Autumn, 8–18.

Enterprise (2005), 'Building an enterprise culture: enabling the enterprise revolution', November, Issue 3, Confederation of British Industry (CBI), UK.

Fairlie, R.W. (2009), *Kauffman Index of Entrepreneurial Activity, 1996–2008*, Kauffman, The Foundation of Entrepreneurship.

Fielden, S.L. and M.J. Davidson (eds) (2010), *International Research Handbook on Successful Women Entrepreneurs*, Cheltenham, UK and Northampton, MA, USA: Edward Elgar.

Henderson, R. and M. Robertson (2000), 'Who wants to be an entrepreneur? Young adult attitudes to entrepreneurship as a career', *Career Development International*, **5** (6), 279–87.

Hunt, B. and T. Virasa (2009), 'Generation Y: an emerging entrepreneurial phenomenon', Conference Proceedings, Applied Geoinformatics for Society and Environment, Stuttgart, Germany, 2009.

Kazmi, A. (1999), 'What young entrepreneurs think and do: a study of second-generation business entrepreneurs', *Journal of Entrepreneurship*, **8** (1), 67–77.

Kourilsky, M.L. and W.B. Walstad (1998), 'Entrepreneurship and female youth: knowledge, attitudes, gender differences and educational practices', *Journal of Business Venturing*, **13** (1), 77–88.

Kwong, C.C.Y. (2006), 'Female entrepreneurship: an exploration of activity and attitudes across the UK', Institute for Small Business and Entrepreneurship, 29th National Conference, October–November, 2006.

Lee, S.M., D. Chang and S.-B. Lim (2005), 'Impact of entrepreneurship education: a comparative study of the U.S. and Korea', *International Entrepreneurship and Management Journal*, **1** (1), 27–43.

Levie, J. and M. Hart (2009), *Global Entrepreneurship Monitor: United Kingdom Monitoring Report*, University of Strathclyde Business School.

Lorrain, J. and L. Raymond (1991), 'Young and older entrepreneurs: an empirical study of difference', *Journal of Small Business*, **8** (4), 51–61.

McCrindle Research (2007*)*, *Striking a Work–Life Balance: Understanding Attraction & Retention in Today's Workforce*, available at: http://www.converge international.com.au/docs/WorkLifeBalanceWhitePaper-Smallfilesize.pdf; accessed 17 March 2011.

McPherson, M. (2007), *Work–Life Balance, Employee Engagement and Discretionary Effort*, Auckland: Equal Employment Opportunities Trust, available at: http://www.eeotrust.org.nz/content/docs/reports/Employee%20Engagement%202007%20Report%20-%20Review.doc; accessed 8 August 2011.

Minniti, M., W.D. Bygrave and E. Autio (2005), *Global Entrepreneurship Monitor, 2005, Executive Report*, Babson College and London Business School.

Nguyen, P.Q.T., T.A. Bui and M.T. Han (2001), 'Doing business under the new enterprise law: a survey of newly registered companies', Private Sector Discussion Paper No. 12, Hanoi: Mekong Project Development Facility.

Parnell, J.A., W.R. Crandall and M. Menefee (1995), 'Examining the impact of culture on entrepreneurial propensity: an empirical study of prospective American and Egyptian entrepreneurs', *Academy of Entrepreneurship Journal*, **2** (1), 39–52.

Pelton, L.E. and S.L. True (2004), 'Teaching business ethics: why Gen Y?', *Marketing Education Review*, **14** (3), 63–70.

Pocock, B. (2003), *The Work Life Collision*, Sydney: The Federation Press.

Roberts, K. and J. Tholen (1998), 'Young entrepreneurs in East-Central Europe and the former Soviet Union', *IDS Bulletin*, **29** (3), 59–64.

Ronnas, P. (2001), 'Introduction', in P. Ronnas and B. Ramamurthy (eds), *Entrepreneurship in Vietnam: Transformations and Dynamics*, Copenhagen: Nordic Institute of Asian Studies and Singapore: Institute of South-East Asian Studies, pp. 1–28.

Rugimbana, R. (2006), 'Generation Y: how cultural values can be used to predict their choice of electronic financial services', *Journal of Financial Service Marketing*, **11** (4), 301–14.

Scarborough, N.M. and T.W. Zimmerer (2000), *Effective Small Business Management: An Entrepreneurial Approach*, Upper Saddle River, NJ: Prentice-Hall.

Scott, M. and D. Twomey (1988), 'Long-term supply of entrepreneurs: student career aspirations in relation to entrepreneurship', *Journal of Small Business Management*, **26** (4), 5–13.

Shaver, K. and L. Scott (1991), 'Person, process, choice: the psychology of new venture creation', *Entrepreneurship Theory and Practice*, **16** (2), 23–45.

Singh, G. and A. DeNoble (2003), 'Early retirees as the next generation of entrepreneurs', *Entrepreneurship Theory and Practice*, **27** (3), 207–26.

Singh, G. and A. Verma (2001), 'Patterns of employment and working time among early retirees of a telecommunications firm', in S. Houseman and A. Nakamura (eds), *Working Time in Comparative Perspective, Volume II: Studies of Working Time over the Life Cycle and Nonstandard work*, Kalamazoo: Upjohn Institute for Employment Research.

Stevenson, L. (1987), 'Towards understanding young founders', in N.C. Churchill, J.A. Hornaday, B.A. Kirchhoff, O.J. Krasner and K.H. Vesper (eds), *Frontiers of Entrepreneurship Research*, Wellesley, MA: Babson College.

Tenner Tycoon (2011), *Make Money, Make a Difference: Backing Britain's Future*, report available at: http://www.tenner-tycoon.org/sites/default/files/make money makeadifferencereport_2011_0.pdf; accessed 22 June 2011.

Top Young Entrepreneurs (2010), 'The rich list', available at www.retireat21.com/top-young-entrepreneurs; accessed 20 July 2010.

Turker, D. and S.S. Selcuk (2009), 'Which factors affect entrepreneurial intention of university students?', *Journal of European Industrial Training*, **33** (2), 142–59.

Turner, S. and P.A. Nguyen (2005), 'Young entrepreneurs, social capital and doi moi in Hanoi, Vietnam', *Urban Studies*, **42** (10), 1693–710.

UK Women's Enterprise Task Force (2007), 'Increasing the quantity and quality of women's enterprise', Statistics and Trends, SBS Analytical Unit, UK.

Veciana, J.M., M. Aponte and D. Urbano (2005), 'University attitudes to entrepreneurship: a two countries comparison', *International Journal of Entrepreneurship and Management*, **1** (2), 165–82.

Wang, C.K. and P.-K. Wong (2004), 'Entrepreneurial interest of university students in Singapore', *Technovation*, **24** (2), 163–72.

Yeaton, K. (2008), 'Recruiting and managing the "why?" generation', *The CPA Journal*, **78** (4), 68–72.

3.   Older entrepreneurs

> The New Retirement Survey conducted for Merrill Lynch ... builds upon conventional wisdom that boomers are not interested in pursuing a traditional retirement of leisure. The majority of boomers relate they plan to keep working and earning in retirement, but will do so by cycling between periods of work and leisure, thus creating a new model of retirement.
>
> (Harris Interactive, 2005)

INTRODUCTION

Many Western and developing countries face the issue of an ageing and growing population. This will have significant implications on the economy of a country, the finances of governments and living standards in general (Swan, 2010). In addition, strategic planning has to go into the development of adequate infrastructure to enable the health care system to be capable of supporting the needs of the ageing population. In particular, when the population ages, this reduces the number of people in the workforce, and hence there are less funds available to support those who do not work, typically after 60 or 65 years of age (ibid.). In Australia, the ageing population will bring about a reduction in the proportion of working age people, with only an estimated 2.7 people of working age to support each Australian aged 65 years and over by 2050. This number will be reduced dramatically from what was available in 1970 (7.5 people), and this continues to decline; in 2010, there were five people of working age supporting those over 65 years of age (ibid.). In countries where low population growth is anticipated, greater challenges will be faced with the ageing of the population. For example, Japan has a low population growth and its old age dependency ratio is projected to be only 1.4 people of working age to support every person aged 65 years or older (ibid.).

An ageing population exerts a significant impact on the slowing of economic growth. Traditionally, the view has been that as the proportion of the working age population falls, the rate of labour force participation across the whole population will also fall. In Australia, this participation rate for people aged 15 years and over is projected to fall to less than 61 per cent by 2049–50, compared with 65 per cent in 2010. Therefore, the ageing population will necessitate governments of whatever persuasion over the next four decades, continuing 'to pursue productivity enhancing and nation building reforms through prudent investment in social and economic infrastructure, and policies to support skills and human capital development' (ibid., p. xii). To achieve this goal of economic growth, productivity growth will be essential. However, productivity growth is more difficult to sustain with an ageing population, particularly if that population continues to follow the traditional trend of leaving paid employment, ceasing work of any kind and entering into a phase of leisure. This places fiscal pressure on governments to continue to maintain – and extend – the services expected of them.

One of the areas that may contribute significantly to the desired productivity growth is through a growing proportion of newly retired men and women taking up an entrepreneurial venture at the end of their formal 'working lives', that is, typically at ages 55 onward. The reality of this possibility has been made clear in a large-scale online and telephone survey, conducted to understand the aspirations of a large proportion of employees who were approaching retirement in the US – named the 'baby boomers'. Merrill Lynch, a leading financial management and advisory company with offices in 36 countries around the world, commissioned the 'New Retirement Survey' in 2004, and the sample was a cross-section of 2348 US adults (1061 men, 1287 women) between the ages of 40 and 58 (Harris Interactive, 2005). The results highlighted the strong aspirations of this sample to continue to work and earn a living: just over three-quarters (76 per cent) of baby boomers surveyed expressed an intention to continue working and earning into their retirement years. While the sample felt they would 'retire' at around 64 years of age, a high proportion saw this as the beginning of 'an entirely new job or career' (ibid., p. 22).

The results of this survey highlight the potential of older workers to take up entrepreneurial ventures after they have finished their 'formal' working lives. In the past, it was taken for granted that when an employee reached the accepted retirement age, they would enter into a period in their lives dominated by leisure. From the results of the Merrill Lynch Retirement Survey, it is obvious that a new model of retirement is required for many retirees. For many, continuing to work will be seen not only as a possibility, but a viable option.

In the US, early research estimated that a third of retirees would return to some form of work after initial retirement (Beck, 1986). This proportion jumped dramatically in one decade. In 1999, the American Association of Retired Persons (AARP) found that 80 per cent of survey respondents planned to work past their retirement, with 17 per cent stating they wished to start their own business ventures (Roper Starch Worldwide, 1999). In recent US figures, this growth appears to have eventuated. Fairlie (2009) reported that the 55–64 age group had the highest level of business creation between 2007 and 2008, with this group making up 20.3 per cent of the overall entrepreneurial activity in a sample of 584 385 US entrepreneurs. This age group experienced the largest increase in start-up ventures of all the age groups in the database (i.e., 20–34, 35–44 and 45–54) (ibid.), and hence was the cohort with the highest entrepreneurial activity rate at that time.

Self-employment continues to be an important source of jobs in the United States. In 2009, 15.3 million individuals were self-employed (Hipple, 2010); of this group, 21.4 per cent of men and 14 per cent of women were classified as 'unincorporated self-employed' in the 65+ age group; this age group continues to have a higher self-employment rate than that of younger workers in the US (ibid.). Clearly, the proportion of older entrepreneurs is growing, and according to Wassel (2010) the 55–64-year-old cohort has the highest rate of business venture participation, at almost one-third higher than the rate of entrepreneurial activity of younger individuals.

Some interesting data on older entrepreneurs is available from the Global Entrepreneurship Monitor (GEM), which reports on entrepreneurial attitudes and perceptions in 43 participating countries (Bosma et al., 2008). The GEM *Executive Report* highlights that in countries classified as 'innovation-driven economies' (e.g., Belgium, Germany, United Kingdom, Norway and the United States), the proportion of entrepreneurs aged between 55 and 64 years of age involved in early-stage entrepreneurial activity is lower (4 per cent) than that of countries classified as 'factor-driven economies' (e.g., Iran, Egypt, India, Ecuador and Bolivia) (11 per cent) or as 'efficiency-driven economies' (e.g., Romania, Turkey, Russia, Hungary, South Africa and Mexico) (6 per cent) (ibid.).

Despite these small proportions of entrepreneurial activity in the 55+ age group, the older cohort of entrepreneurs continues to receive a significant (and increasingly urgent) focus from governments worldwide (Kautonen et al., 2008), in part because of a growing awareness that the extended life expectancy of Western world populations will place an untenable burden on current retirement and pension practices. With the challenge of an ageing and growing population for many Western and developing countries, creative strategic planning will be required from governments in order to address these demands. For example, over the next several decades, areas relating to the ageing population will impact on labour force participation in general, the demand for skilled labour, and health and housing. These will each have significant policy implications in Australia (ABS, 2010).

Undoubtedly, people in many Western countries are living longer and the percentage of individuals aged over 55 is steadily increasing. In Australia for example, 12 per cent of the current Australian population are aged between 65 and 84 years of age, and in 2050, this is estimated to grow to 17 per cent of the overall population (Swan, 2010). Some population forecasts have set this even higher (e.g., ABS, 2008 predicted that one-quarter of the population would be aged 65 and over by 2056). According to Langan-Fox et al. (2010) this will set up a 'growing dependency ratio', which will create significant problems (ibid., p. 248): 'In many nations such as Australia, USA, Germany, France, and the UK and many of the Scandinavian countries, there are as many citizens over 65 as there are under 15, dependent on the working population' (World Bank, 2003, cited in Langan-Fox et al., 2010).

A growing number of entrepreneurs will emerge from this cohort of older recent retirees, and they have the capacity to make a significant contribution to the economy, as well as enhancing their own quality of life, and increasing their economic and social worth well into their older age. Therefore, the issue of retaining the skills and expertise of older workers is one of great importance, and has far-reaching implications. It is on the one hand a significant social objective; on the other, it has very serious economic ramifications when the talents and experiences of older workers are lost at the point of retirement, as there is a huge drain of human capital. To illustrate, in the UK in 2003, it was estimated that there were 2.4 million people in England between the ages of 50 and 64 who were categorical about not wanting to work (PRIME Initiative, 2004). In addition, 1.4 million people over 50 received an incapacity benefit. A further sobering statistic was that an estimated 3 per cent of this age group had a pension that was considered sufficient to be able to support them comfortably (Kautonen et al., 2008). This represents a huge number of people who could potentially become involved in entrepreneurial ventures, and who therefore remain an untapped resource.

OLDER ENTREPRENEURS: GENERAL CHARACTERISTICS

In general, limited information is available to the researcher when considering the characteristics of entrepreneurs who take up business ventures over the age of 50. However, there are some notable exceptions. Kautonen (2008) has provided a clear picture of entrepreneurial activity in Finland of 'third age' (50 years and over) business operators. He reported that 16 per cent of small firms were established by individuals in this age group, and hence considered that the cohort was one that is worthy of further research, even though their start-up rate was less than half of the start-up of entrepreneurs in the 'prime age' group (between 20 and 49 years of age) in the Finnish sample.

One of the areas that has been explored in previous literature focuses on the competencies of older people. Researchers such as Singh and DeNoble (2003) and Weber and Schaper (2004) have reported that older entrepreneurs have some attributes that make them more able to start and run a business. These include their accumulated human and social capital, as well as the financial assets they may have accrued throughout their lifetimes. According to Rostad (2010), older entrepreneurs are more likely to have higher levels of capital to finance the initial start-up of the business.

Older entrepreneurs are characterized by their previous experiences in the workplace; these are believed to enhance the likelihood of new business start-ups (Rotefoss and Kolvereid, 2005). Such previous experiences can be influential in the success of an entrepreneurial venture, depending on whether it is 'novice' (a business set up without prior experience in an entrepreneurial activity), or 'serial' (where several businesses have been set up previously). It has been suggested that the latter type of entrepreneurial venture has a greater chance of success (Kautonen, 2008).

Such attributes and skills equip the older entrepreneur well. Researchers claim that the survival rates of business ventures set up by older entrepreneurs is higher than those of their younger counterparts. For example, Rostad (2010) referred to a recent study carried out by the US Duke University on 550 new-technology small business entrepreneurs. The researchers found that the older 55–64-year-old age group had twice as much success when starting a new business venture compared to the 20–34-year-old age group (ibid.).

Vaughn (2011) concurs with these results and refers to a recent US study published by the Kauffman Foundation. In this study, US entrepreneurs over 55 years of age were almost twice as likely to enjoy successful start-ups compared to their younger counterparts. The higher levels of success were attributed to better education and business experience of the older entrepreneurs. To illustrate, the report outlines that older entrepreneurs who had achieved 'Ivy League' degrees had higher employment levels and average sales (55 employees and \$6.7 million) than founders of technological companies with high school education (18 employees and \$2.2 million) (ibid.). Higher education therefore appears to be equated with greater success in business ventures for older entrepreneurs (ibid.).

However, previous research has reported that older entrepreneurs, in general, have lower levels of education, with the majority not having post-secondary qualifications (Weber and Schaper, 2004). According to

Parker (2004), this group only appear to seek higher qualifications if they consider that enhanced relevant skills are the likely outcomes. More research is obviously required into the educational characteristics of older people taking up entrepreneurial ventures, as we have insufficient information on this area from previous studies (Kautonen, 2008).

It is clear that not all people in this age cohort are attracted to setting up a business venture. It has been suggested that older people may not have the same desire to set up an entrepreneurial activity (Curran and Blackburn, 2001), and that motivation may be lower for potential older entrepreneurs, although ability is not considered to be an issue (Kautonen, 2008). In fact, competencies may increase with age, while *intentions* to take on entrepreneurial ventures appear to decrease (Rotefoss and Kolvereid, 2005).

The issue of gender distribution is of interest when considering older entrepreneurs. Some researchers, such as Weber and Schaper (2004) proposed that it was males who made up the majority of this cohort. This finding was supported by a study in the UK that found that almost two-thirds of contacts made to an enterprise support organization focusing on older entrepreneurs were made by males (PRIME Initiative, 2006). Kwong (2006) concurs with this finding, and reports that in the 55–64 age group in the UK, 4.1 per cent of males were involved in early-stage entrepreneurial ventures, compared to only 1.8 per cent of females. Although it is recognized that younger women may experience conflict because of their family commitments to partners and/or children, as well as with elder care responsibilities, such issues should not impact to the same extent on older females wishing to start up new business ventures (McKay, 2001).

OLDER ENTREPRENEURS: ASPIRATIONS AND MOTIVATIONS

In terms of aspirations when setting up a new business venture, both 'pull' and 'push' factors have been considered in relation to the older entrepreneur. It has been suggested that a small-scale business venture may be perceived as a way of keeping active, enhancing social inclusion and 'giving back' to society; in other words, 'pulling' individuals back into business activities (Kautonen et al., 2008). 'Push' factors capable of exerting an influence on older workers include lack of retirement funds or pension entitlements (Weber and Schaper, 2004), as well as dissatisfaction with current work roles, insufficient training opportunities or general age discrimination (Webster and Walker, 2005). In addition, a limited pool of paid employment may also force individuals into considering entrepreneurial ventures (Singh and DeNoble, 2003). The recognition that a growing number of people approaching retirement are now looking for some balance in their lives that may include work and leisure will necessitate a new way of approaching the question of future financial security (Harris Interactive, 2005).

A useful tool for analysing the motivation of older entrepreneurs has been offered by a model that adds considerably to our understanding of the 'pull' and 'push' factors that may be in operation for this cohort of entrepreneurs. Singh and DeNoble (2003) proposed that there were three sub-groups: 'constrained entrepreneurs', 'rational entrepreneurs' and 'reluctant entrepreneurs'. Constrained entrepreneurs are believed to be drawn to entrepreneurial possibilities, but previous work responsibilities may have made it impossible for them to pursue other options. Rational entrepreneurs weigh up what might be their best option; continuing as an employee, or taking the chance of setting up their own business venture. Reluctant entrepreneurs may become self-employed because of limited employment opportunities and insufficient resources to contemplate a comfortable retirement. The first two sub-groups are motivated to consider entrepreneurial ventures through 'pull' factors, whereas the latter group operates on the basis of 'push' factors (Kautonen, 2008).

Few research projects have been carried out on early retirees who move into entrepreneurial ventures (Singh and DeNoble, 2003). Some of this group become self-employed 'reluctantly' (Galbraith and Latham, 1996). Other early retirees see self-employment as an employment option that provides a bridge between full employment and full retirement; the onus here being on the individual (e.g., Baucus and Human, 1994; Galbraith and Latham, 1996; Singh, 1998). It was believed that almost a third of early retirees who returned to paid employment after they had retired, would have aspirations to take up an entrepreneurial self-employment option (Singh, 1998). It is interesting to compare these estimates with more recent data. As noted previously, three-quarters of respondents to a Retirement Survey in the US expressed the desire to work after they had formally retired, possibly in a new job or career (Harris Interactive, 2005).

It would seem that more knowledge is required through research about the ageing population in all Western nations in particular, and the propensity of a proportion of retirees to become self-employed after taking retirement at the 'traditional' time. This appears to represent a rich source of future research projects (Singh and DeNoble, 2003) to enhance knowledge of the aspirations and motivators of older entrepreneurs, and holds the promise of a beneficial outcome, both socially and economically, for communities at large.

OLDER ENTREPRENEURS: CHALLENGES AND BARRIERS

Despite the advantages that the older entrepreneur may have accrued, there are also particular problems for this cohort when considering new business ventures. According to Brown (2000), there are commonly held perceptions about the inappropriateness of older people taking up certain positions and age discrimination is therefore a particularly significant challenge. In some cultures, age is valued and revered. In others, such as Western cultures, older people are often seen as dependent individuals who have little to contribute to society at large (Kautonen et al., 2008). Such attitudes are highly likely to play a key role in possible negative attitudes of banks, lending agencies, financial advisers, as well as a biased view by customers as to the ability of the older entrepreneur to successfully run and sustain their business. In addition, limited opportunities for training also create barriers for the older entrepreneur (Brown, 2000).

Fear of the lack of available finance may also become a disincentive for older people to consider a business venture of their own (Singh and DeNoble, 2003). While older workers may have available funds at retirement to set up a business, they will also be relying on those funds to sustain them in retirement, and hence there will be conflicting demands on their financial resources.

Health concerns are another barrier facing the older entrepreneur, according to Curran and Blackburn (2001). In addition, a propensity to consider themselves as 'definitely retired' in a study of 463 people in the UK, aged 50–75, also created a mindset that was not conducive to starting up a business venture. This study reported a very small proportion of participants (4 per cent) who actually expressed an interest in becoming self-employed. It is also possible that a desire for instant returns, as opposed to future possibilities, may be underlying decisions of many older people at the point of retirement (Kautonen et al., 2008).

OLDER ENTREPRENEURS: STORIES OF SUCCESS

The following case studies highlight the success of four senior entrepreneurs; three are based in Australia, and one in the US. The first entrepreneur, Pat La Manna, was an immigrant to Australia who overcame many obstacles to eventually become highly successful, and was widely honoured for his contributions to the community. The second entrepreneur has undertaken numerous business ventures over a 50-year period, and she has recently entered into another entrepreneurial phase by setting up the hugely popular Stephanie Alexander Kitchen Garden Foundation in 2004. The third case outlines the success of Wally Blume who became an entrepreneur at 61 years of age, and who is now enjoying great success in his own business, Denali Flavors. Finally, the last case outlines the entrepreneurial activities of Eve Mahlab, businesswoman, lawyer and women's rights activist extraordinaire over more than 50 years.

BOX 3.1 PAT LA MANNA, SENIOR AUSTRALIAN OF THE YEAR, ENTREPRENEUR AND PHILANTHROPIST

Pat was born in Italy, and emigrated to Australia in 1948 when he was 16 years of age. His childhood in post-war Italy was poverty-stricken, and one of Pat's early memories was of his mother struggling to keep the family together 'scratching around in the field for weeds that she would bring back and cook up for us'. Pat's father travelled to Australia to earn money for his family; however, it took 12 years before Pat could join his father in Australia. At this time, he possessed only the clothes he wore, knew no English language and had had very little education. From humble beginnings of picking potatoes in the country in Victoria, Pat worked very hard, saving as much money as he could along the way. With the assistance of his father, Pat took on a job in a fruit shop so that he could learn the language, writing down unfamiliar words each day to assist in his learning. Although he earned less than he did by picking potatoes, he saw it as a way to improve his level of English, which he believed would open up new opportunities.

Pat had to deal with racism and many barriers during these early years in Australia, which were difficult for everyone. To many Australians, having immigrants coming into the country was a bitter reminder of the war that had taken the lives of many Australian servicemen. Pat persevered to overcome these challenges and barriers, and started his first business, a fruit shop, in 1953. His father was so proud of his work ethic and tenacity that he assisted him financially to enable him to start up in his own business.

Pat built this business into a real success, doubling the intake within three months through sheer hard work and being honest with his customers and suppliers. This became the hallmark of his dealings with others. His reputation was based on this, and his business grew and expanded. Eventually, his fruit and vegetable shops were set up in all major shopping centres throughout Victoria. He introduced self-service, and implemented home deliveries. After almost 20 years, Pat ventured into a highly successful banana wholesale business in 1972.

But it is the success of his entrepreneurial ventures in later life, and his philanthropical attitudes to life and others' misfortunes, that really define his life. Pat is a person who 'gives back' to his community in spades. He has been an active member of the Lions Club for over 40 years, having founded the Lions Club of the Melbourne Markets in 1972, which enjoys the accolade of being the highest fundraising Lions Club in Australia. He has supported numerous charities in Australia and overseas, including starting the Hand-to-Hand Appeal for the Bionic Hands Department at the Melbourne Royal Children's Hospital, raising almost $200 000 in this area.

Pat suffered a stroke in his late 60s and after he recovered, he set up the 'Pat La Manna Cancer and Research Stroke Foundation', which has raised over $1.5 million for scientific research. In 2009, at the age of 76, Pat La Manna was awarded the Senior Australian of the Year Award to recognize the phenomenal contribution he has made to his community and his adopted country.[1]

BOX 3.2 STEPHANIE ALEXANDER – SERIAL ENTREPRENEUR

Although the name Stephanie Alexander in Australia has been synonymous with fine food, excellent restaurants and wonderful books on cooking and travels for over four decades, it is her later entrepreneurial venture that is perhaps the most impressive. Initially, Stephanie trained to become a librarian and left Australia when she was 21 to travel in France. After returning to Australia, and with a passionate interest in food and cooking, she opened her first restaurant, Jamaica House, in 1964. Although this was successful, it did take a personal toll on her private life. Refreshed, in 1976, she opened the iconic Stephanie's Restaurant in Melbourne, which was a landmark institution in that city for over 21 years.

In 1985, Stephanie turned her hand to writing, enjoying growing success in this area. Her fifth book, *The Cook's Companion* in 1996, sold over 400 000 copies, and she believed this was because the book was meeting a need in younger people who had little understanding of how to cook, or the importance of using fresh food in their daily lives. Her success as an author continues, and she has recently published her tenth book, *Cooking and Travelling in South-West France.*

Another business venture began in 1997, when she opened the Richmond Hill Café & Larder with three partners, one of whom was her daughter. This was an informal café, which featured a marvellous cheese room and produce room, providing a sense of neighbourhood and community; this venture was extremely successful, passing into new ownership in 2005. It seems that Stephanie was highly skilled at 'reading the moment' to introduce new ventures in the world of fine food.

During these early years in the Richmond Hill Café & Larder, Stephanie became preoccupied with the way children relate to food; she had a strong belief that the more children were able to enjoy food as a positive experience, the easier it would be for them to appreciate fine food throughout their life. This philosophy led her to develop a gardening and cooking programme at Collingwood College in 2001, one of Melbourne's inner city schools, and this experience led her to establish the not-for-profit 'Stephanie Alexander Kitchen Garden Foundation' in 2004. The knowledge gained from setting up this venture culminated in a new book, *Kitchen Garden Cooking with Kids*, which traced the development of the Collingwood project, as well as providing information that would offer a blueprint for other primary schools to set up their own programmes.

The foundation provided the funding to expand the gardening cooking programme into other primary schools. Stephanie has enjoyed the support of philanthropic foundations, individuals who shared her vision, and governments, and in 2006, the Stephanie Alexander Kitchen Garden Foundation received grants of $2.4 million from the Victorian State government to support 40 new kitchen garden programmes in Victorian primary schools following the successful model at Collingwood College. In 2007, the Australian government announced that it had agreed to roll out the programme to support 190 additional projects around Australia by 2012.[2]

BOX 3.3 WALLY BLUME, FOUNDER OF DENALI FLAVORS

Wally Blume went into business for himself when he was 61 years of age, after working in the dairy business for over 20 years. He started out his working life with Kroger, a large grocery chain in the US, and later took the role of sales and marketing director for a major dairy company in Michigan, and it was here that he first gained experience in marketing new ice cream flavours. However, when another company took over the business, he decided that it was time to think about going out on his own. He felt that the innovative practices that had characterized the original company had changed. This decision was expedited when the new company decided to market a tomato ice cream. Blume summed up his thoughts in this way: 'It doesn't take a Rhodes Scholar to understand that chocolate fudge and peanut butter cups are going to outsell tomato ice cream every day of the year'.

In 1995, along with some colleagues, Blume decided to start up a business that would develop and market their own flavour combinations. One of their early creations was the 'Moose Track', a chocolate and peanut butter combination that found its niche in the market, and was a huge success. Despite this success, in 2000, Blume pooled together all of his resources, mortgaging his house and every other asset he could, pulling together sufficient capital to buy out his partners and start out on his own: 'I hocked everything. I mean, it was house, cars'. Although Wally Blume put everything on the line, he strongly believed that he knew the business so well that he would be able to make it even more successful. He hired three salespeople immediately, and paid them large salaries as a motivator. This business decision paid off within one month, as one of the salespeople signed up two huge accounts on his first sales trip to the East Coast and this deal covered his annual salary within four weeks of him joining the company. Right from the start, Blume put the focus on getting the right people onto the team.

Blume believes that he made the correct decision to set up his own national ice cream enterprise, as he was convinced that he could run the company better on his own. Because of this view, he felt that 'there was just no downside to the risk'. Therefore, in the same year, he set up Denali Flavors, a marketing and licensing company to create new ice cream and dessert concepts for independent regional dairies. This allowed the smaller dairies to compete with the larger national dairy brands.

Wally Blume does concede that starting out on his own in his 60s may have been seen by others as a risky proposition, however he believes his work experience and his age gave him a real advantage. He admits that if he had not understood the business as well as he did, then such a branching out on his own would have been very risky. He was aware that there were potential risks, but he focused on pursuing his belief that: 'If we just keep right on going, this is just an absolutely dynamite investment and I'll get a fairly quick payback'. Knowing the business as well as he did, he saw the potential that was still untapped. He had a very strong idea of the right way to proceed; this led him to pay off his loans in two years.

Today, Denali Flavors has grown at an average of 10 per cent per year for over a decade. The company earns about $80 million annually and has licensing agreements with a large number of manufacturers. Denali has 40 different flavours under its banner, and none of these is based on a vegetable! Denali Flavors sells its products in all 50 states as well as Canada, and its flavours are available in every major US market. Although Wally Blume is now 70, his entrepreneurial spirit does not appear to have waned in any way. He has now launched two additional ventures: a sauna business and a boat pontoon outfit, and it would appear that he is just getting started! His business acumen has ensured his financial security, and he is known as a very generous donor to various international charities.[3]

BOX 3.4 EVE MAHLAB, BUSINESSWOMAN, LAWYER AND WOMEN'S RIGHTS ACTIVIST

Eve Mahlab was born in Vienna in 1937, migrating to Australia with her family at the age of two. She graduated in law, and practised as a solicitor, but found it difficult to balance her legal career with her family. This led her to establish a home-based employment agency in 1964, and this business eventually became a national small business specializing in human resources and publishing.

She became a member of the Coordinating Committee of the Women's Electoral Lobby in Victoria from 1972 to 1976, because she believed that 'women get the crumbs from the government and philanthropic funding tables'. According to Eve Mahlab, at that time, women rarely got a mention. In her view, there is still considerable room for improvement. She believes that the United Nations, as well as national and state governments, do not allocate budgets appropriately with due consideration for women.

From 1980, she was a member of the Victorian government Committee of Inquiry into the Status of Women. She is an active member of the Liberal Party, having stood for pre-selection on a number of occasions. In 1982, her business skills were recognized when she was named the Qantas-Bulletin Australian Business Woman of the Year.

However, another phase to her various successful careers opened up when she retired from active business management in 1987, at the age of 50. At this time, she began to take up board appointments and became involved in film and other projects. She is also actively engaged in making significant contributions of her time and expertise to her community, including the Coordinating Committee of the Women's Electoral Lobby, the Advisory Board of the Centre for Philosophy and Public Issues at Melbourne University, the Monash University Council, Westpac Banking Corporation, Film Australia, and the Walter and Eliza Hall Institute of Medical Research.

At this time, she also founded some other entrepreneurial ventures, such as the 'Know Biz (Business Education) Association', providing links between business and schools, and also co-founded the 'Australian Chapter of Femmes Chefs d'Enterprises' (the international association of Women Business Owners).

In 1988, she received the Order of Australia for her services to business and the community, government and women's issues. In 1997, Eve Mahlab received an honorary Doctorate of Law from Monash University. She has been the subject of numerous television documentaries and books, including *Tall Poppies* and the *Fabulous Fifties*. In 2001, she was awarded a Centenary Medal 'for service to the community through business and commerce'.

More recently, in 2007, Eve co-founded and convened the 'Australian Women Donors Network', which has as its primary focus the development of women and girls. The network actively promotes investment in women and girls through enhancing understanding and support within their own network, as well as the community at large, as to the importance of this goal. The aim is to bring about positive social change that the network believes will be of benefit to all of society; this is achieved through encouraging the funding of projects that invest in women and girls specifically, and by heightening awareness about gender in mainstream society. The network brings together women who give 'money, time, voice or skills' to advance the status of women, and in this area, Eve Mahlab is recognized as a lifelong advocate. She firmly believes that the time is right for change: 'Indeed, I believe that we are witnessing the third wave of the Women's Movement, the first got us the vote, the second liberated us from our virtual confinement to unpaid house and caring work, and the third, in the wake of women gaining education, influence and wealth will see the financial empowerment of women and the resulting benefit to families, the community and the country'.

Her entrepreneurial flair is now firmly focused on improving the lot of women and girls in society, and it looks like she will continue to work tirelessly to bring about the positive social change that she believes is possible.[4]

OLDER ENTREPRENEURS: SUMMARY

There have been dramatic increases in the proportions of early retirees who are taking up an entrepreneurial self-employment option. Over a decade ago, Singh (1998) estimated that almost a third of early retirees would return to paid employment, possibly through an entrepreneurial venture. More recent research highlights the rapid increase in this phenomenon. The Merrill Lynch Retirement Survey (Harris Interactive, 2005) reported that three-quarters of its large sample planned to continue earning a living throughout their retirement, possibly in a new career.

Older entrepreneurs may be characterized by particular competencies and attributes that make starting and running a business relatively easy. For example, their accumulated human and social capital, as well as secure financial backing, places them in a privileged position to strike out into an entrepreneurial venture. Researchers such as Singh and DeNoble (2003) and Weber and Schaper (2004) have reported that compared to many other entrepreneurial groups, older entrepreneurs have some attributes that make them more able to start and run a business.

However, while competencies may increase with age, it has been recognized that the desire to enter into a business venture may decline (Rotefoss and Kolvereid, 2005). Education levels have been reported to be lower in cohorts of older entrepreneurs, who tend to only seek higher qualifications if they believe they will acquire enhanced relevant skills (Parker, 2004), although recent reports refute this, indicating that higher levels of education are tied to greater success in the business venture (Vaughn, 2011). The majority of older entrepreneurs are male, and the proportions are similar to those found in the general entrepreneurial population (i.e., approximately two-thirds male, and one-third female) (Wood, 2011).

The older entrepreneur can encounter particular challenges, including age discrimination and the lack of training opportunities available to the younger workers (Brown, 2000). In addition, fear of lack of available finance may become a disincentive for older people to consider a business venture of their own, according to Singh and DeNoble (2003). Available financial resources may be required to self-fund the retirement, creating conflicting demands on what would otherwise be a 'guaranteed' source of income. In addition, older entrepreneurs may face particular barriers when they approach banks or lending agencies for money to start up a new business venture. There may be subtle societal attitudes and stereotypes that perpetuate the myth that older people have lived their life and have nothing further to offer (Kautonen et al., 2008). Finally, older entrepreneurs may also have concerns about ongoing health issues (Curran and Blackburn, 2001), and this can create a mindset that is aversive to the risk-taking that may be required in setting up a business venture.

OLDER ENTREPRENEURS: THE FUTURE

Much more research is needed in the area of the older entrepreneur. Webster and Walker (2005) have formulated a theoretical framework based on research knowledge at that time, highlighting the employment options available to the older worker; returning to some form of employment, remaining unemployed, or considering self-employment through small business ventures. The model incorporated the prerequisite prior experiences, skills and attitudes considered important in order to participate in training and skills development, which in turn was hypothesized to result in growth of the business venture. What is evident from this theoretical model is that it illustrates how older entrepreneurs are often quite unique in that they may choose entrepreneurship instead of early retirement after acquiring relevant life and work experiences that have the capacity to set them up well for taking up business ventures (Langan-Fox et al., 2010).

Up until quite recently, 'retirement' was seen as a phase a person moved into when they had reached the end of their formal working life, that is, at age 55 or 60, they then retired and sat back and relaxed. However, times are certainly changing. This may be driven to a large extent by the huge proportion of 'baby boomers' who are hitting retirement age at this time. It may also have a lot to do with a slowly increasing life expectancy. In the past, most people felt particularly privileged to live to 'three score years and ten'. However, in 2011, the average world life expectancy was 67.07 years for both sexes (CIA, *The World Fact Book*, 2011). In the more developed countries, life expectancy is substantially higher, for example in Monaco, the figure is 89.73, in Japan, the average life expectancy is 82.25, in Australia, the figure is 81.81 and in the UK, 80.95 (ibid.). This means that for the majority of people in the more developed and wealthier countries, they are more likely to enjoy good health, and can look forward to between 20–25 years of life after retirement.

Merrill Lynch's Retirement Survey has alerted us to the emergence of a new model of retirement that will now be required for the burgeoning numbers of older retirees who may potentially become entrepreneurs. This survey has provided researchers with 'a complex and illuminating review of the kind of lifestyles, work-styles and recreation activities that boomers envision for their future' (Harris Interactive, 2005, p. 22). Survey respondents spoke of a desire to 'cycle between periods of work and leisure' (ibid.), as they continued to work well past what was once believed to be a finishing point for employees. Some of the highlights of the survey offer some illuminating insights into the hopes, aspirations and desires of those approaching retirement, and hence may provide a useful base for research projects into this important area in the future. The key features of the Merrill Lynch Retirement Survey included the following:

- The vast majority of those surveyed wanted to start another job or career after the age of 64. While two-thirds of those surveyed agreed that they would stop working formally 'at some point', they saw this as commencing in their late 60s, rather than at the traditional age of 60 or 65.
- Respondents did not want a life of full-time leisure *or* work. Rather, they opted for a choice that would allow 'cycling' between work and leisure (42 per cent), part-time work (16 per cent), starting up an entrepreneurial venture of their own (13 per cent) or returning to some other form of full-time work (6 per cent). Only a very small proportion (17 per cent) hoped they would not have to work again for their income.
- While finances were a major reason for 37 per cent of the sample stating they wanted to continue to earn an income, two-thirds of the sample believed that 'continued mental stimulation and challenge is what will motivate them to stay in the game' (ibid.)

- The new retiree was motivated by accumulating the necessary resources for a comfortable retirement (81 per cent) rather than reaching a certain age (56 per cent).
- All of these factors will have a significant bearing on the time that retirement savings will be drawn upon, as this may no longer be the primary source of income – at least initially, for the newly retired.
- An interesting gender difference was noted in the data: male retirees aspire to work less, spending more time relaxing. For female retirees however, they aspire to explore 'new opportunities for career development, community involvement and continued personal growth' (Harris Interactive, 2005, p. 23).

According to the data provided by this large-scale US survey, there is a huge potential for a large proportion of people in their 60s to start up a business venture once they have 'officially retired'. The enthusiasm is there, and along with the wealth of skills and experience accumulated through a lifetime of working as an employee, older entrepreneurs may be an increasingly important segment of the working population into the future.

NOTES

1. Sources: adapted from the following: http://www.australianoftheyear.org.au/; http://www.health.gov.au/internet/main/publishing.nsf/Content/ageing-acat-acatchat-2009-summer.htm and http://www.thesenior.com.au/news.asp?publication=andarticletype=General%20NewsandArticleID=1079; all accessed 8 August 2011.
2. Sources: adapted from the following: http://en.wikipedia.org/wiki/Stephanie_Alexander; http://www.stephaniealexander.com.au/mylife.htm; and http://www.australianofthe year.org.au/; all accessed 8 August 2011.
3. Sources: adapted from the following: 'Late bloomers: these entrepreneurs are tapping a lifetime of experiences in their business', http://www.entrepreneur.com/slideshow/200236; S. Perman (2009), 'Senior entrepreneurs: their time has come', *Businessweek*, 8 June 2009, http://www.businessweek.com/smallbiz/content/jun2009/sb2009068_927403.htm; all accessed 8 August 2011.
4. Sources: adapted from the following: http://www.womenaustralia.info/biogs/AWE 4421b.htm; http://www.vwt.org.au/store/files/1265087969.pdf; http://www.curriculum.edu.au/cce/mahlab,9153.html; http://www.womendonors.org.au/index.php?option=com _contentandview=articleandid=38andItemid=95; and www.womendonors.org.au; all accessed 8 August 2011.

REFERENCES

Australian Bureau of Statistics (ABS) (2008), 'Population projections Australia, 2006–2101', media release dated 4 September 2008, Catalogue No. 3222.0, available at: http://www.abs.gov.au/Ausstats/abs@.nsf/Latestproducts/3222.0 Media%20Release12006%20to%202101?opendocument&tabname=Summary&

prodno=3222.0&issue=2006%20to%202101&num=&view=; accessed 17 August 2011.

Australian Bureau of Statistics (ABS) (2010), 'Population by age and sex, Australian states and territories', Catalogue No. 3201.0, June.

Baucus, D. and S. Human (1994), 'Second-career entrepreneurs: a multiple case study analysis of entrepreneurial processes and antecedent variables', *Entrepreneurship Theory and Practice*, **19** (2), 41–60.

Beck, S. (1986), 'Mobility from preretirement to postretirement job', *The Sociological Quarterly*, **27** (4), 515–31.

Bosma, N., Z. Acs, E. Autio, A. Coduras and J. Levie (2008), *Global Entrepreneurship Monitor, 2008 Executive Report*, Universidad del Desarrollo, Santiago, Chile, Babson College, MA, USA and London Business School, UK.

Brown, R. (2000), 'Getting old and grey? The implications of demographic change and population ageing for the Scottish labour market', Glasgow: Scottish Enterprise.

Central Intelligence Agency (CIA) (2011), 'Country comparison: life expectancy at birth', *The World Fact Book*, available at: https://www.cia.gov/library/publications/the-world-factbook/rankorder/2102rank.html#top; accessed 8 August 2011.

Curran, J. and R. Blackburn (2001), 'Older people and the enterprise society: age and self-employment propensities', *Work, Employment and Society*, **15** (4), 889–902.

Fairlie, R.W. (2009), 'Kauffman index of entrepreneurial activity, 1996–2008', available at: http://ssrn.com/abstract=1395945; accessed 10 May 2011.

Galbraith, C. and D. Latham (1996), 'Reluctant entrepreneurs', *Frontiers of Entrepreneurial Research* conference papers, Babson Park: Center for Entrepreneurial Studies.

Harris Interactive (2005), *The New Retirement Survey*, Merrill Lynch, available at: http://www.retirement-jobs-online.com/retirement-survey.html; accessed 10 May 2010.

Hipple, S.F. (2010), 'Self-employment in the United States', *Monthly Labor Review*, September, 17–32.

Kautonen, T. (2008), 'Understanding the older entrepreneur: comparing third age and prime age entrepreneurs in Finland', *International Journal of Business Science and Applied Management*, **3** (3), 3–13.

Kautonen, T., S. Down and L. South (2008), 'Enterprise support for older entrepreneurs: the case of PRIME in the UK', *International Journal of Entrepreneurial Behaviour and Research*, **14** (2), 85–101.

Kwong, C.C.Y. (2006), 'Female entrepreneurship: an exploration of activity and attitudes across the UK', Institute for Small Business and Entrepreneurship, 29th National Conference, October–November, 2006.

Langan-Fox, J., E. Karami and J.M. Canty (2010), 'Not over-the-hill ... yet! The older entrepreneur', paper presented at the 7th AGSE International Entrepreneurship Research Exchange, 2–5 February, University of the Sunshine Coast, Qld. Melbourne: SUT (February).

McKay, R. (2001), 'Women entrepreneurs: moving beyond family and flexibility', *International Journal of Entrepreneurial Behaviour and Research*, **7** (4), 148–65.

Parker, S.C. (2004), *The Economics of Self-employment and Entrepreneurship*, Cambridge: Cambridge University Press.

PRIME Initiative (2004), *Towards a 50+ Enterprise Culture: A PRIME Report*, January, available at: http://prime.org.uk/2004/01/towards-a-50-plus-enterprise-culture-a-prime-report/; accessed 9 August 2010.

PRIME Initiative (2006), *Olderpreneur Outcomes – A Follow-up Study of What Happened to People Aged Over 50 Who Contacted PRIME about Starting in Business*, available at: http://prime.org.uk/wp-content/uploads/2009/03/prime_report_on_olderpreneur_outcomes_2006.pdf; accessed 8 August 2011.

Roper Starch Worldwide (1999), *Baby Boomers Envision their Retirement: An AARP Segmentation Analysis: Key Findings*, Roper Starch Worldwide Inc. and AARP, available at: http://boomersint.org/aarp.htm; accessed 8 August 2011.

Rostad, E. (2010), 'Are older entrepreneurs more successful?', The Entrepreneur School Blog. How to start a business, available at: http://blog.theentrepreneurschool.com/are-older-entrepreneurs-more-successful-1992; accessed 8 August 2011.

Rotefoss, B. and L. Kolvereid (2005), 'Aspiring, nascent and fledgling entrepreneurs: an investigation of the business start-up process', *Entrepreneurship and Regional Development*, **17** (2), 109–27.

Singh, G. (1998), 'Work after early retirement', unpublished PhD dissertation, School of Graduate Studies, University of Toronto.

Singh, G. and A. DeNoble (2003), 'Early retirees as the next generation of entrepreneurs', *Entrepreneurship Theory and Practice*, **27** (3), 207–26.

Swan, W. (MP) (2010), *Intergenerational Report 2010. Australia to 2050: Future Challenges*, available at http://www.treasury.gov.au/igr/igr2010/report/pdf/IGR_2010.pdf; accessed 11 May 2011.

Vaughn, C. (2011), 'The Zuckerberg fallacy: older entrepreneurs as the drivers of innovation', Founder's Toolbox Blog, available at: http://www.goodwinfoundersworkbench.com/posts/zuckerberg-fallacy-older-entrepreneurs-drivers-innovation/; accessed 8 August 2011.

Wassel, J. (2010), 'Older entrepreneurs as the new economic frontier', *The Gerontologist*, **50** (6), 863–5.

Weber, P. and M. Schaper (2004), 'Understanding the grey entrepreneur', *Journal of Enterprising Culture*, **12** (2), 147–64.

Webster, B. and B. Walker (2005), 'Smart training for the older entrepreneur', paper presented at the International Council of Small Business World Conference, Melbourne, June.

Wood, G.J. (2011), 'Women in management in Australia', in M.J. Davidson and R.J. Burke (eds), *Women in Management Worldwide – Progress and Prospects*, Aldershot: Gower Publishing.

4.   Women entrepreneurs

[T]here is no one set of factors that influence women's entrepreneurial activity, rather it is a combination of different factors dependent on the individual. Age, domestic circumstances, education, socio-economic group, employment history, previous personal income, culture and geographic location, all influence the weight of each factor.

(Fielden and Davidson, 2005, p. 265)

INTRODUCTION

The number of women entering small business ownership has increased significantly across the world and these women make a crucial contribution to the economic growth and development of local, national and global economies, especially in emerging economies (Allen et al., 2008). Furthermore, countries that have exhibited the highest rates of entrepreneurial activity are typically characterized by a more widespread involvement of women (Fielden and Davidson, 2010). Although the increase in women's entrepreneurship has reduced the gap between men and women's entrepreneurship in many countries, men are still about twice to two-thirds more likely to be involved with entrepreneurial activity (Allen et al., 2008).

As can be seen in Table 4.1, this difference in activity rate is also stage dependent, with comparably more women in the early stages than in the established stage of entrepreneurship. This does of course vary between countries, with the greatest disparity between developed economies (i.e., those thought to be the most developed and therefore less risky in terms of investment) and emerging economies (i.e., business and market activity in industrializing or emerging regions of the world). There often appears greater parity in the entrepreneurial activity levels of women and men in emerging economies, which may be attributed to economic, political and legislative similarities (Delmar, 2003). However, previous research on the global situation of women entrepreneurs clearly shows that it is the socio-cultural traditions and values that have the greatest impact on women's involvement in entrepreneurial activity, regardless of legislation that supports women's progression (Fielden and Davidson, 2010). Traditional gender roles inherent in patriarchal societies generally lead to restricted access to labour markets, feminized occupations, glass ceilings, discrimination and stereotypes (e.g., Syed, 2010).

Table 4.1 illustrates that in the factor-driven economies (i.e., the lowest stage of development), the lowest levels of women's entrepreneurial activity are seen in the Middle Eastern countries, with women accounting for less than a third of all entrepreneurs (Kelley et al., 2010), whereas in Sub-Saharan African countries there is more or less equal participation between men and women. In the efficiency-driven economies (i.e., middle-stage development) Eastern European countries account for the lowest levels of women's entrepreneurial activity, with Turkey exhibiting the lowest level. In contrast, Latin American countries have higher levels of participation, with Costa Rica and Mexico reporting almost equal participation by gender. Innovation-driven sectors, for example, Australia, the US, Malaysia, Belgium and Switzerland, have the highest levels of women's entrepreneurial activity, whereas Taiwan, the Republic of Korea and Japan have comparatively low participation rates (ibid.) (see Table 4.1).

Despite the increasing numbers of women business owners around the globe, as an international community they have received little attention from the academic community and research into the experiences of women entrepreneurs is confined to a relatively small number of established markets (Fielden and Davidson, 2010). This is partly because women are more likely to locate their ventures in lower-order services, that is, those that only service a limited geographical area, with their businesses remaining small in terms of employment, sales, profitability and market share (Carter and Marlow, 2007). Consequently, women's enterprises have tended to be seen as poor or under-performers (Ahl, 2006).

However, the importance of women's entrepreneurship is not only in relation to the global economy; women also make a valuable contribution to the diversity of entrepreneurial activity in local economies, that is, exploiting new business opportunities (Verheul et al., 2004), which is essential if countries are to maintain strong levels of entrepreneurship during fluctuating global economies. Also a large proportion of previous research has tended to treat entrepreneurship as gender-neutral (Lewis, 2006), with an inherent assumption that women's entrepreneurial activity will simply mirror that of men. Interestingly, even when there is evidence to show that gender is a key factor in determining the entrepreneurial experience, there is a growing perception that gender is no a longer relevant issue (Fielden and Davidson, 2010). However, as can be seen in the following sections, the reality does not always match the rhetoric.

Table 4.1 Rates of entrepreneurial activity across countries by gender 2007

	Early stage (%)		Established (%)		Overall business (%)	
	Men	Women	Men	Women	Men	Women
Argentina	17.52	11.34	15.78	4.16	33.30	15.50
Austria	3.06	1.84	7.25	4.78	10.31	6.61
Belgium	4.30	1.98	1.86	0.93	6.16	2.91
Brazil	12.73	12.71	12.70	7.24	25.43	19.95
Chile	16.45	10.43	11.89	5.59	28.33	16.02
China	19.27	13.43	9.66	7.04	28.93	20.47
Colombia	26.91	18.77	15.49	7.84	42.41	26.60
Croatia	9.44	5.13	5.79	2.67	15.23	7.80
Denmark	6.21	4.56	8.54	3.43	14.75	8.00
Finland	8.96	4.81	10.31	4.80	19.27	9.60
France	4.14	2.21	2.52	0.95	6.66	3.16
Greece	7.96	3.46	14.59	12.04	22.56	15.51
Hong Kong	14.33	5.82	7.51	3.75	21.84	9.56
Hungary	9.29	4.52	5.88	3.81	15.17	8.33
Iceland	17.40	7.44	13.43	3.98	30.83	11.42
India	9.51	7.49	8.69	2.18	18.21	9.66
Ireland	10.57	5.87	12.66	5.38	23.22	11.25
Israel	7.12	3.75	3.61	1.10	10.72	4.84
Italy	6.69	3.30	8.87	2.17	15.56	5.48
Japan	3.47	5.22	8.72	8.57	12.20	13.79
Kazakhstan	11.17	7.64	6.80	4.80	17.97	12.44
Latvia	7.70	1.41	4.90	2.02	12.60	3.43
Netherlands	6.64	3.70	8.59	4.07	15.24	7.77
Norway	8.59	4.28	8.20	3.50	16.79	7.78
Peru	25.74	26.06	18.07	12.40	43.80	38.46
Portugal	11.70	5.92	9.79	4.44	21.49	10.36
Puerto Rico	3.16	2.97	4.05	0.89	7.21	3.87
Romania	4.95	3.09	3.34	1.70	8.30	4.79
Russia	3.79	1.64	1.63	1.73	5.41	3.37
Serbia	12.11	5.06	7.74	2.83	19.85	7.88
Slovenia	6.84	2.68	6.84	2.31	13.69	4.99
Spain	9.75	5.48	8.17	4.57	17.92	10.06

Table 4.1 (continued)

	Early stage (%)		Established (%)		Overall business (%)	
	Men	Women	Men	Women	Men	Women
Sweden	5.78	2.47	6.87	2.48	12.65	4.95
Switzerland	7.59	4.92	8.56	4.60	16.15	9.52
Thailand	27.78	25.95	23.22	19.47	51.00	45.42
Turkey	8.65	2.41	9.47	1.32	18.12	3.73
UK	7.41	3.60	7.59	2.55	15.00	6.15
United States	11.98	7.25	6.47	3.48	18.45	10.73
Uruguay	17.33	7.19	8.63	4.54	25.96	11.73
Venezuela	23.50	16.81	5.87	4.90	29.37	21.71

Source: Adapted from Allen et al. (2008).

WOMEN ENTREPRENEURS: GENERAL CHARACTERISTICS

There are a number of demographic factors that can have an impact on a woman's decision to embark on an entrepreneurial career, such as age, marital status and educational background. However, factors such as human and social capital, career orientation and experience also have a significant influence on the experiences and success of women entrepreneurs (Fielden and Davidson, 2010).

Almost three decades ago, an early study by Watkins and Watkins (1984) found that women entrepreneurs in the US tended to have a median age of 32 years, while a more recent study reported that female entrepreneurs tended to be much older, with the ages ranging from 40 to 50 years (Mattis, 2004). Furthermore, in 2001 a report by the UK Cabinet Office stated that entrepreneurship was a mid-life choice, with the majority of women setting up their own business after the age of 35. However, three years later the greatest increases in women's entrepreneurship were seen in the 25–34-year-old age group (Harding, 2004).

Although the majority of studies around the world have found that a high proportion of women entrepreneurs are in their 30s and 40s (Taylor and Newcomer, 2005), this is not the full story as it tends to incorporate women in all stages of entrepreneurship. If the figures are broken down between early stage and established women entrepreneurs, a different picture emerges. In emergent and developed economies women in early-stage entrepreneurship are predominantly between the ages of 25 to 34, whereas established women entrepreneurs are spread across a wider range from 45 to 54 (Allen et al., 2008). This is an important distinction as age is also related to women's entrepreneurial motivation, with younger women influenced more by wealth creation and the opportunity to take a leadership role, and older women influenced more by the barriers they encounter in the workplace (van der Boon, 2005). It is predicted that this younger age group will become increasingly prominent as serial entrepreneurs, continually creating or seeking an environment that affords them the challenges they need (Martin and Tulgan, 2001).

Studies have frequently found that women entrepreneurs are less likely to be married than their male counterparts. For example, in the UK, a study by Carter et al. (2001) revealed that while the majority of entrepreneurs were likely to be married (80 per cent men, 67 per cent women), women were more than twice as likely to be divorced, and four times more likely to be widowed. Very early research indicated that widowed women exhibit higher entrepreneurial rates than any other category, while single women account for the smallest category of female small business owners (Goffee and Scase, 1985). However, these statistics have changed with the increase in younger women entrepreneurs, who tend to be single and without children, reflecting the age-linked model of women's career development (Mavin, 2000). As motherhood impinges on women's ownership of assets, their access to resources and the realization of capital (Brush et al., 2009), this change is likely to have a significant impact on women's entrepreneurship in the future.

Caputo and Dolinsky (1998) also found that being married to an entrepreneur was a key factor in determining the entrepreneurial activity of women, and that there was a positive correlation between the financial success experienced by entrepreneurial spouses and the women's decision to become entrepreneurially active. Other positive correlations to women entrepreneurs were access to the husband's knowledge and experience relating to setting up a business and help from the husband in arranging and providing childcare (ibid.). In addition, Catalyst (1998) found that women in dual career relationships had increased freedom to make career choices because their spouses had full-time employment. They were also more inclined to take risks, particularly career risks, for example, starting their own business, because of the freedom they had relating to their spouses' employment status. Thus, women who have financial and human resources available in the household have greater role flexibility, which can both motivate and support women's entrepreneurship (Caputo and Dolinsky, 1998).

In addition, women who have entrepreneurial parents are much more likely to pursue their own business ventures than those who do not (Martin, 2001), although they are much less likely to 'inherit' a business, or work in 'family enterprises' than men (Martin and Martin, 2002). Previous research suggests that business owners, particularly early-stage entrepreneurs, benefit substantially from the instrumental and emotional support of family members (Bird and Brush, 2002). A lack of family support can place early-stage entrepreneurs at a serious disadvantage and for women this can be especially destructive if they have heavy family responsibilities. It has been found that a lack of family support can result in women entrepreneurs working significantly fewer hours than men, which has a negative impact on growth and profitability (Shelton, 2006). Furthermore, while family and friends are seen by some women as an important and useful source of support, for others they can be unsupportive and damaging (Fielden and Hunt, 2011).

It is well recognized that educational levels influence entrepreneurial activity and that there is a positive relationship between the educational attainment of women and new enterprise start-up rates (e.g., Kovalainen et al., 2002; Davidsson and Honig, 2003). This form of human capital is a critical component of entrepreneurial activity, not just as a resource in its own right (Carter et al., 2006) but also because it can be used to acquire other forms of business resources, such as physical capital and financial capital (Brush et al., 2001). However, the type of education is also important in determining the degree of human capital available to women entrepreneurs. Typically, women have been less likely to gain education in business disciplines, particularly in emerging economies (e.g., China, India and South Africa) with a minority holding degrees in business, engineering or technical disciplines (McClelland et al., 2005). In contrast, in innovation economies the situation has changed dramatically, with more women today seeking degrees in traditionally male-dominated areas of management and professional qualifications (Fernandes and Cabral-Cardoso, 2003). For example, in the UK the proportion of women pursuing social administration and business degrees stood at only 10 per cent in 1973 (Davidson and Burke, 2004), but more recently that figure has risen to over 50 per cent (Davidson and Burke, 2011). In Australia today, more women graduate in business compared to males and this has been the case since 1995 (Wood, 2010). Furthermore, Wilson et al. (2007) found that access to entrepreneurial education is 'especially important in fuelling the pipeline of aspiring women entrepreneurs' (p. 398) because of the strong role education plays in developing an individual's perceptions of their entrepreneurial ability

and increasing entrepreneurial career intentions. Entrepreneurial education is important for all potential business owners but for women,
raising self-belief is the key to unlocking their entrepreneurial potential.

Work experience is another important source of human capital and
Moore (1999) refers to an individual's prior working experience as an
'incubator', whereby the entrepreneur can obtain valuable training and
skills such as finance, marketing and networking. By acquiring such skills
in this way, entrepreneurs can increase their ability to attract relevant and
required resources, which can enable them to make improved decisions
regarding the resources they may need to make the business a success
(Haynes, 2003). These findings were echoed by Bosma et al. (2004) who
found that prior industrial experience substantially improved small firms'
prospects for survival, profitability and growth.

Importantly, research has found that domain-specific human capital,
that is, education and experience, has a moderate effect on the formation
of entrepreneurial growth expectations (Manolova et al., 2007). However, unlike men, the growth aspirations for women-owned enterprises
are driven by factors other than human capital or the ability to secure
financial capital (Coleman, 2007). It appears that human capital has a
positive impact on the profitability of women-owned firms but not on
their growth rate. This highlights that the relationship between influencing variables is not a straightforward one and that such interactions are
not gender-neutral.

WOMEN ENTREPRENEURS: ASPIRATIONS AND MOTIVATIONS

The rise in enterprise creation has seen an increase in studies examining the
major motivating factors relating to women's entrepreneurial activity.
These have generally looked at the reasons why women are 'pushed' or
'pulled' into entrepreneurship (Van der Boon, 2005). Table 4.2 shows the
motivational factors of women entrepreneurs based on a compilation of
findings from seven different countries: the UK, US, Australia, India,
Singapore, Holland and New Zealand (Fielden and Davidson, 2005). It is
important to note that there is no one set of factors that influence women's
entrepreneurial activity, rather it is a combination of different factors
dependent on the individual. Age, domestic circumstances, education,
socioeconomic group, employment history, previous personal income,
culture and geographic location, all influence the weight of each factor
(ibid.).

Table 4.2 Push/pull factors influencing women entrepreneurs

Push factors	Pull factors
Lack of control	Control
Lack of independence	Independence
Lack of flexibility	Flexibility
Job dissatisfaction	Being one's own boss
Glass ceiling issues	Financial independence
Glass walls	'Making a difference'
Lack of challenge	Pursuing quality
Family influence	Realizing personal ambition
Not taken seriously	Self-determination
Lack of opportunities	Impacting on strategy
Dislike of boss	Achieving personal growth
Know you could do a better job than your superiors	Gaining recognition
	Need for self-actualization
Racism	Income generation
Limited education	Putting skills, experience and knowledge to use
Lack of role models	
Pay inequality	Fulfilling long-term dream
Occupational segregation	Achieving economic goals
Lack of affordable childcare	Life cycle stage
Discrimination	Sense of self-worth
Need for security	Autonomy
	Need for dominance
	Need for achievement

Source: Fielden and Davidson (2005, p. 266).

The development of the 'push–pull' framework has been very important in furthering our understanding of women's entrepreneurship as it demonstrates that, although there are similarities across national cultures, women entrepreneurs within those cultures are not homogeneous groups with regard to entrepreneurial motivations, that is, the degree to which they are influenced by the factors shown in Table 4.2. There is no one set of factors that dictate whether or not women enter into enterprise creation, rather it is a combination of factors dependent on individual characteristics. For example, women who cite 'push' factors are likely to be older, married, less well educated, be in full-time employment prior to business start-up, and have access to personal finance (Still, 2005). Also, women who start a business out of necessity frequently have less access to external finance and are less likely to be successful in their entrepreneurial ventures (Langowitz and Minniti, 2007). In contrast, those women who cite 'pull' factors are more likely to be younger, better educated and have more transferable business skills and knowledge (Carter et al., 2006). They are also more likely to pursue unexploited opportunities and are more likely to success- fully start a business (Langowitz and Minniti, 2007).

This has led to a distinction between the type and size of enterprises created by women: women in the 'push' category are more likely to create smaller enterprises, take fewer financial risks, employ few workers and experience lower levels of growth, whereas women in the 'pull' category are likely to take greater risks but experience greater growth (Fielden and Davidson, 2005). Furthermore, there are significant differences in how these women view their own identity, their families, their businesses and the wider business environment (Morris et al., 2006). Business growth is a deliberate choice for many women entrepreneurs and there is a strong link between high growth and business achievement. However, this is not always a sound long-term strategy, as highly optimistic business owners learn less from past experiences and take more risks, thus while they tend to be more financially successful they are also more susceptible to failure (Hmielski and Baron, 2009).

Two areas that appear to have the greatest impact on women's decisions to pursue their own business are the 'glass ceiling' (Mattis and Levin, 2010) and the need or desire for flexibility (Davidson and Burke, 2011). These may be perceived as push or pull factors depending on the individual woman and her circumstances, and are influenced by factors such as country, culture, or religion. However, it should be noted that while the impact of these issues may differ, they are a shared phenomenon experi- enced by women around the world. In today's business environment, despite women achieving greater numbers of business and professional degrees, they are still failing to reach top corporate management positions, which is still being attributed to the glass ceiling (Catalyst, 2003; Singh and Vinnicombe, 2009; Wood, 2009, 2010). Consequently, many of these women are leaving the corporate world to set up their own businesses (Terjesen, 2005). For example, a US study by Mattis and Levin (2010) found that of the women entrepreneurs who had left corporate careers to start their own business, nearly one-third (29 per cent) stated glass ceiling issues and dissatisfaction with their work environment as major reasons for wanting to set up their own business.

This increasing population of new women entrepreneurs who have corporate or management experience have been labelled as 'careerpreneur', 'modern' and/or 'second-generation' entrepreneurs (Moore and Buttner, 1997; Moore, 2000). Vinnicombe and Bank (2003) suggest that the main motivating factors for the increase of female ex-corporate entrepreneurs are pay inequalities and career frustration due to this glass ceiling and the promise of a more flexible lifestyle from entrepreneurship.

Women entrepreneurs can also be categorized as 'intentional' or 'corporate climbers' (Moore and Buttner, 1997). Intentional entrepreneurs are seen as 'born to be' entrepreneurs; these are women who have always intended to set up their own business and have merely worked in other businesses to gain experience (Mattis, 2004; Mattis and Levin, 2010). In contrast, corporate climbers have intended to stay in employment in their organization and have not necessarily considered setting up on their own, however they have made the decision to leave their careers because of negative factors in their organization/work environment, such as a lack of career progression, or to take full advantage of an unexpected business opportunity (Mattis and Levin, 2010).

Bruni et al. (2004) examined the personal and contextual factors that influence women's decisions to start their own business. They concluded that women entrepreneurs' motivations when setting up their own business were centred on the need for flexibility, specifically relating to their childcare responsibilities, and their negative experiences from previous employment. On the whole these negative experiences were centred on gender discrimination and childcare difficulties. As a consequence, many women decide to set up their own business to provide them with an opportunity to manage their dual responsibility of work and family (Feldman and Bolino, 2000; Orhan and Scott, 2001). Marlow and Strange (1994, p. 179) refer to this as an 'accommodation tactic', whereby women can create the flexibility that they need to balance their work and domestic responsibilities (Shelton, 2006). As Bruni et al. (2004) argue, women's businesses tend to be integrated rather than separated from their family roles and relationships.

Many women want to spend more time with their children and to have increased flexibility to combine work and home (Kovalainen et al., 2002). More recent UK research has found that there is a new breed of enterprising female entrepreneurs defined as 'kitchen table tycoons'; these are women who successfully juggle the roles of mother and business owner (London School of Economics [LSE], 2006). This research states that 'it is the act of having and raising children which makes mothers so well placed to identify gaps in the market' (ibid., p. 6). Over half of the mothers surveyed were running businesses relating to children's services or products; home-friendly businesses such as web design and marketing were also common.

WOMEN ENTREPRENEURS: CHALLENGES AND BARRIERS

Women entrepreneurs continue to encounter constraints, regardless of the degree to which they are motivated by push/pull factors. They face a 'multiple burden of disadvantage' (Marlow, 2002, p. 85), which frequently arises as a direct result of gender discrimination and social exclusion (Fielden et al., 2003). This is exacerbated by the fact that, in general, women are less likely than men to be expecting to start a business, to know an entrepreneur, to see good business opportunities, to think that they have the necessary skills to start a business, or to have access to an entrepreneurial mentor (Harding, 2004). Indeed, the importance and benefits of mentoring for women entrepreneurs in providing support, advice and networking opportunities are well documented (Woolnough et al., 2006; Fielden and Davidson, 2010; Wood and Davidson, 2011).

Theoretical work on women's entrepreneurship suggests that women are confronted with both situational and dispositional barriers and obstacles that can prevent them from starting or developing their business (Fielden et al., 2003). Dispositional barriers can include a lack of human capital and social capital, family/work life balance and domestic responsibilities, and a lack of networking activity (Harding et al., 2003). In contrast, situational barriers can be seen as external factors, including a lack of appropriate support and guidance (Schmidt and Parker, 2003), and limited access to finance (Marlow and Patton, 2005). This section will consider both types of barriers and how they impact on women's entrepreneurship.

Social capital may be defined as the benefits an individual derives from their personal and professional networks, and is an essential business resource that contributes to both survival and profitability (McGrath Cohoon et al., 2010). There is a wealth of research that emphasizes the importance of networks for entrepreneurs and the social capital that can be found in such networks (e.g., Rosa and Hamilton, 1994; De Carolis and Saparito, 2006). The benefit of those networks for entrepreneurs is an increased access to information and advice, as well as social support. Hoang and Antoncic (2003, p. 167), state that 'actors' differential positioning within a network structure has an important impact on resource flows, and hence, on entrepreneurial outcomes'.

Research has clearly demonstrated that networks can have a positive impact on business development and are undeniably effective for sharing and exchanging information (Langowitz and Minniti, 2007). Yet women's networking activity is significantly lower than that of men and gender differences are found in the forming, establishing and managing of networks (Carter et al., 2006, 2007). Women are frequently excluded from traditional networks or lack information about such networks (Verheul and Thurik, 2001; Hunt et al., 2006). As a consequence, many women have less access to networks that can provide developmental relationships and as a result it is more difficult for women to develop influential relationships that can provide access to targeted career progression opportunities (Kaplan and Niederman, 2006).

Furthermore, women are more likely to set up a business from home (Loscocco and Smith-Hunter, 2004). In Australia, home-based businesses are the fastest-growing sector of small business operations, with a 16 per cent annual growth rate, and account for over half (58 per cent) of all businesses (Australia Bureau of Statistics, 2002). As reported in Chapter 6, home-based working is often the only way women from certain religious backgrounds are allowed to work. For example, Iranian immigrant women in Los Angeles in the US often enter into business ventures as a way of improving their capacity to earn a living (Dallalfar, 1994). However, home-based businesses may considerably reduce networking opportunities for women.

It is essential that women have the opportunity to network and develop appropriate support groups with other women who are in the same position (Prowess, 2004). Networking is seen as an invaluable method of gaining business support and advice. It is also seen as a way in which women can gain necessary contacts and combat the feeling of loneliness and isolation that many women entrepreneurs face. Networking can provide women with an important opportunity to gain relevant business skills and discuss issues and problems (Sarason and Morrison, 2005). This connection with other entrepreneurs can influence the perception of entrepreneurial opportunities and reduce the fear of failure that is negatively associated with women's entrepreneurial propensity (Langowitz and Minniti, 2007). As a result, interacting with other entrepreneurs is significantly and positively correlated to entrepreneurial motivation and future success.

However, the barriers to women's successful networking appear to be around the structure and composition of networks, rather than a lack of motivation to be part of such forums. A key finding from the British Chamber of Commerce report (Harding et al., 2003) was that women preferred to work in clusters, not only to establish their business but also to maintain and expand their businesses. These clusters represented a number of women working together and accessing support from one another, similar to a networking group. This highlights the need for women to work collectively to share their ideas, solutions, experiences, aspirations and inspirations, rather than engaging in the traditional male model of net-working. Women prefer smaller, more intimate groups, where they feel less threatened (Fielden and Hunt, 2011).

Gender differences are also apparent in the forming, stabilizing and managing of networks (Carter et al., 2006) and women have different requirements from networks, tending to use them as sounding boards, unlike their male counterparts who tend to use networks to gain resources (Moore and Buttner, 1997). It may be that women actively avoid networks that reflect the social support needs of men, as they cannot provide the affirmative support required by women entrepreneurs. However, it is not only access that is an issue, as women's perception of the effectiveness of those relationships is also dependent on the degree of tangible support they provide (Fielden and Hunt, 2011). Hisrich (1989, p. 28) suggested that women should be encouraged to develop a 'girls' network' to parallel the 'old boys' network' that exists and learn to delegate family or indeed business responsibilities, to other individuals when necessary. However, Ahl (2006) argues that this does not address the fundamental issue, rather it is suggesting that the barriers that women face are indeed removable by individual action and that it is the women themselves who need to change rather than the structures.

Women's perceptions of support appear to have a greater effect on their success in entrepreneurial ventures than does actual support, regardless of what measures of success are applied (Pollard, 2001). Rodriguez (2001) concluded that both the provision and acceptance of support are essential for achieving successful entrepreneurial performance outcomes: if the right kind of support is available from the right source of support, that support will be received positively and performance outcomes will be enhanced (Viswesvaran et al., 1999). Findings also suggest that being a receiver of one-sided support, such as the type given in most traditional business advice settings, may be detrimental to women's well-being (Antonucci, 1990). Thus, while it is acknowledged that social support is important in the promotion of women's entrepreneurial activity, there is still a lack of clear understanding as to how such support interplays with personal factors to influence their entrepreneurial behaviour (De Carolis and Saparito, 2006).

It would appear that women entrepreneurs are frequently in greater need of relevant training and support than their male counterparts, as they have a lack of relevant sector-based business skill and knowledge (Brush et al., 2009). However, they are less inclined to access business support services such as enterprise agencies, and service providers acknowledge that the number of women who approach them for support remains low (Schmidt and Parker, 2003). This has been attributed to a lack of understanding and doubts about the relevance of the services being offered and a lack of confidence and trust in these agencies (Fielden et al., 2003). In addition, childcare responsibilities and ethnic barriers have also been identified as key barriers to accessing traditional forms of business support (Omar et al., 2007).

However, there is another important factor that may deter women from seeking advice and support from traditional sources. A report published by Prowess, *Bridging the Enterprise Gap* (2004), stated that women have different attitudes and characteristics and business support providers need to recognize this. One difference identified was the use of language and, in general, that women did not use or feel comfortable with words such as 'enterprise' and 'business'. Women tended to view them as unattainable and something that they were not particularly interested in aspiring to (ibid.). Entrepreneurship is strongly male-labelled (Sundin, 2002; Tillmar, 2007), and not all women want to be regarded as entrepreneurs, as the strong male connotations may threaten their own identity. Tillmar (2007) stated that men tend to better fit the profile of the entrepreneur as an individual who works nearly 24 hours a day, an image that is promoted extensively in the media. Therefore, it may be that for many women entrepreneurs it is the 'male = entrepreneur' stereotype that is influencing who they seek advice from, as they simply do not identify with the images such terminology provokes (Hunt at al., 2006).

Access to finance is critical during enterprise start-up and subsequent business performance and it has long been recognized that undercapitalization during enterprise formation and development will lead to underperformance during the life of the business (Carter and Marlow, 2003). Previous research has shown that women entrepreneurs often start their businesses with lower levels of overall capitalization and lower ratios of debt finance than men (Coleman, 2007). These differences have been attributed to a range of structural and sectoral differences. For example, as women are more likely to start businesses located in the service sector, they may need less start-up capital than those in manufacturing, where high initial capital investment is required. This would also explain why women entrepreneurs are significantly less likely to seek equity capital (i.e., shareholder investments) than men (Orser et al., 2006). However, even when controlling for the perceived level of financial capital needed to develop a business, men-led ventures attract higher amounts of financial capital than women-led ventures (Alsos et al., 2006)

Women entrepreneurs, particularly low-growth, tend to rely on their own savings rather than attempting to access external funding (Marlow and Patton, 2005). This reliance on personal funds is due to a variety of reasons. For example, women often lack the track record that banks and other funding sources require. They also have fewer personal finance resources than men and have reduced access to financial or advisory support that is usually dominated by male networks (Orser et al., 2006). The dominance of men in the supply side of the finance market has also been thought to have consequences for the evaluation of business information, perceptions of sectors and type of businesses pursued (Foss and Ljunggren, 2006).

A lack of human, social and financial capital have all been found to negatively impact on women's ability to accrue personal savings, generate credit, or engage with venture capitalists (Marlow and Patton, 2005). As a consequence, women are significantly more likely to secure funding from their family, friends or business partners than from external sources (Fielden et al., 2003; McGrath Cohoon et al., 2010). It has been suggested that the reluctance of women to gain capital from external sources may be a result of the dominance of men in the supply side of the financial sector (Alsos et al., 2006). Although direct gender discrimination as a consequence of this male dominance is difficult to prove, it is recognized that gender undoubtedly has an impact on such decisions (Carter et al., 2006). It may be suggested that increasing the number of women in the supply side would help to solve this issue but a recent study by Carter et al. (2007) has demonstrated that merely increasing the number of women involved in loaning finance to businesses is an over-simplification of the gender dynamic with the bank–entrepreneurial relationship. The impact of gender appears to have wide-reaching consequences when it comes to the inward investment in women-led businesses.

A main cause of conflict for women entrepreneurs centres on balancing family and work roles, as those with families are more inclined to face primary domestic responsibilities and ultimately to have their careers interrupted at some stage (Kovalainen et al., 2002). Women strive to create a balance between work and family life and this has been a significant motivator for women starting their own business (Fielden and Davidson, 2010). However, when establishing a business it is often necessary to work long hours, particularly during the initial stages of business formation. This conflict can cause many women to face an opportunity cost between business development and family life. Shelton (2006) commented that women business owners experienced greater role conflict than men when attempting to manage and balance work and family life. This is further exacerbated by the unequal division of domestic labour and the impact of domestic work and family issues continues to have a significantly greater impact on the working lives of women compared to men (Loscocco and Smith-Hunter, 2004; Brush et al., 2009). A Barclays Bank report (2000) found that 80 per cent of women business owners, compared with just 17 per cent of men, had responsibility for looking after children and dealing with childcare issues. The problems the women entrepreneurs face with regard to childcare impacts on their business development and on their ability to access business support due to the limited time available; a finding that has been replicated around the globe (Fielden and Davidson, 2010).

WOMEN ENTREPRENEURS: STORIES OF SUCCESS

The following case studies describe the experiences of three highly successful British women entrepreneurs, Merryn Myatt, Sarah Perris and Helen Colley. Sarah and Merryn have run their communication, media and training business in partnership for the last five years and Helen started her own 'Farmhouse Fare' business after leaving school. These successful but very different entrepreneurs have been chosen for two reasons. First, one is a business partnership and the other is a sole business ownership, which are the two main business types operated by women entrepreneurs. Second, they have quite different philosophies on what constitutes entrepreneurial success, which demonstrates the heterogeneous views of women entrepreneurs.

BOX 4.1 SARAH PERRIS AND MERRYN MYATT – MANAGING DIRECTORS OF PERRIS-MYATT

Sarah and Merryn are equal partners in a highly successful consultancy company that specializes in bespoke communication and media training for a wide range of public and private sector clients, as well as high-profile individuals. They met five years ago at a business lunch at which Merryn was presenting and arranged to meet up for a quick coffee a few months later. At that initial meeting they discovered just how much they had in common and after four hours they had lots of ideas as to how they wanted their business to look and operate. They knew straight away that they would be firm friends but, more importantly, that they shared the same objectives and the same approach to business. For them the key issue was operating a highly professional business while keeping a balance between work and life. As Merryn explained: 'The clients get 150 per cent of our attention when we are with them, but they are not 150 per cent of our lives'.

An important factor in their success is the similarity of their backgrounds. Merryn's father was in oil and she was raised in Bahrain and educated in England, whereas Sarah's father was a diplomat and she spent her formative years in India, Venezuela,

Honduras, Germany, as well as the Middle East. They are both educated at boarding school, have two children of similar ages, had successful careers, and were both made redundant from their previous jobs: Sarah from her position as Worldwide Communications Director for Bentley Motors and Merryn from her position as a BBC national news presenter.

Their career backgrounds were extremely complementary and they have developed their business to capitalize on their core skills. After leaving London University with an Honours degree in English, Merryn went to work as a trainee journalist, working on a variety of regional newspapers in the news, business, consumer and financial sectors. She then went on to enjoy a high-profile, award-winning and influential career as a newsreader, editor and programme-maker in national and regional news and current affairs. Sarah is a communications strategist with 20 years' corporate experience in both the automotive and aerospace industries and she has worked for many years at director level in a number of multinational organizations.

Merryn was already running her own business when she met Sarah. She feels she had been both 'pushed' due to family illness and being made redundant, and 'pulled', as she wanted to use her skills and experience in a different direction. Her business choice was influenced by her need for flexibility and minimal capital investment, a situation that Sarah also found herself in. She too was both 'pushed' and 'pulled' into running her own business, as a single mother she wanted to spend time with her daughters but still wanted to work at a professional level.

Having really strong, powerful networks was a key factor in the business's early financial success and they purposefully set out to break the mould as to what a professional consultancy firm should look like. Unlike many women entrepreneurs, Merryn and Sarah constructed their business so that they achieved a good level of financial return but have enough time for family, friends and importantly themselves. The business suits were sent to the charity shop and their emphasis is on informal, friendly but professional service. They feel that they provide a better service to their clients by being 'relaxed, happy and less stressed', which comes from the confidence of age, experience and being 'thick skinned'. When they were told by one business support agency that 'we cannot help people like you', that is, women, they just went somewhere else that would. They make sure they take holidays and family is a priority; they are not interested in 'ruling the world' and do not define success in financial terms.

Sarah is frustrated by the examples of women entrepreneurs that just mirror the male model of success, commenting that far too many young women entrepreneurs feel that unless they adopt this approach they will fail. As an ambassador for the UK government's Women in Enterprise programme and a business mentor for the Prince's (HRH Prince Charles) Trust, Sarah spends a great deal of time supporting young entrepreneurs. She feels that for many a lack of confidence means that they place too much emphasis on the views of others and do not listen to their own instinct, which is often telling them that the male model of success is simply not for them.

Business partnerships often have a poor survival rate because of the divergent interests of each entrepreneur but this is certainly not the case with Merryn and Sarah. Not only do they share the same entrepreneurial objectives and ethos but they also admire each other greatly. Sarah said that she was 'blessed to have met Merryn, she has made my life much better' and Merryn commented that because of Sarah she felt 'much happier and confident'.[1]

BOX 4.2 HELEN COLLEY – MANAGING DIRECTOR, FARMHOUSE FARE

Helen was brought up on a farm in the North of England, which meant that she was exposed to the reality of being self-employed from an early age. Being from a relatively poor financial background, from the age of ten Helen had part-time jobs so that she had her own money. This need for control was fuelled by her experiences at school where she was bullied and, as a consequence of which, she 'did not feel particularly good at anything and wanted to prove I was good at something'. On leaving college in 1984 Helen set up a corporate catering company from her parents' farm and in 2002 she launched Farmhouse Fare Ltd, making premium hot puddings and chilled desserts for supermarkets and specialist shops.

With little more than a tiny bank loan, her parents' farmhouse kitchen and a refrigerated van, she set about building the business.

Farmhouse Fare's delectable delights were based on the hearty and indulgent treats served up at the kitchen table of Helen's great-great-grandmother, Janet Anderson. One of the key elements of these puddings is that they were made by hand using the finest ingredients and traditional methods. Local hotels and restaurants were the first to take her products but it was not long before she was receiving orders from the major supermarkets, with one exception – Tesco – a situation that Helen tackled head on at a lecture at Manchester Business School in 2005, where Tesco CEO Sir Terry Leahy was a guest speaker. During the usual question and answer section Helen thought it would be the ideal opportunity to ask him why Tesco didn't stock her puddings. She took a deep breath, placed her hand in the air, and 'by luck or whether it was the rare sight of a lady's hand', he took her question. He was intrigued and invited Helen to send samples in for trial, which she sent straight to Sir Terry himself. He was clearly impressed and Tesco became a major stockist of Farmhouse Fare products. As a result in just four years the company employed over 120 staff and in 2006 Helen sold the business to Daniels Chilled Foods for £10 million.

As demonstrated above, entrepreneurial confidence has never been an issue for Helen, as she has always taken a pragmatic approach to business, stating that she has always had the attitude that she was 'just going to do it'. For her, business success has been producing the best product and selling it to everyone, yet her impressive achievements have never been enough to satisfy the drive to prove she is good enough, even after winning countless international awards, including Credit Suisse Entrepreneur of the Year 2006, winner of the California Raisins Innovation Awards 2006, winner of the Personality of the Year at the Food Manufacture Excellence Awards 2007, and finalist in the European Business Awards Entrepreneur of the Year 2007.

Despite all of this well-deserved recognition, Helen is very down to earth and totally grounded. Although she has a high standard of living she is not indulgent, preferring to treat herself to an expensive handbag rather than surrounding herself with more ostentatious displays of financial success. Perhaps it is her farming background but she does not judge business success in monetary terms, rather she views personal happiness and contentment as the true measures of success.

Although Helen has never doubted herself in business she does suffer from self-esteem issues at a personal level. She has become adept at giving the impression of being a confident businesswoman but she states that 'most of it is an act to cover up personal hang-ups'. She realized early on that she did not fit into the standard entrepreneurial mould; as she explains 'you cannot go to the pub like a man, and lots of women don't like successful women'. However, she learnt to accept that it was alright to be different and that being a woman has its advantages in terms of social communication.

Helen is married with three children and realized very early on that you cannot have it all and that she had to live by the choices she made. She was a very hard personal taskmaster, setting difficult goals and driving herself to the point of burnout. Eventually, she realized that she could not continue at the same pace and, although she still has the same work ethic, she has achieved a greater work–life balance. She acknowledges that she 'missed a huge chunk of the kids' lives' but is now making up for it and feels more in tune with them because of all she has been through.

Family have always been an integral part of her business success and she could not have achieved all she has without them. However, she recognizes that as a person you change as your business grows and that affects those around you. Her perception of success has also changed over time and, even though her goals have changed, they are just as challenging and difficult to achieve.[2]

WOMEN ENTREPRENEURS: SUMMARY

As this chapter shows, women entrepreneurs are an essential source of economic growth for countries worldwide, yet despite this, entrepreneurship continues to be viewed as a male mentality and an experience that is associated with the actions of men (Bruni et al., 2004). As a result, the success achieved by women entrepreneurs is attributed to their sometimes necessary rejection of traditional business practices, and their development of new entrepreneurial principles. Research indicates that women are more likely to be successful when entering new business ventures than men, their businesses are less likely to fail in the first year and more likely to expand, creating more job opportunities than businesses run by men (Carter et al., 2001).

Women entrepreneurs are a diverse group and it is important not to assume that they have homogeneous characteristics (Cohen and Jennings,

1995). Women's experiences are influenced by factors such as age, education, marital status, ethnicity and so on, which impacts on the type of business they enter into, their starting capital and the development and growth of the business. This means that some women entrepreneurs are the antipathy of the male model of enterprise, whereas others are more closely aligned. For example, high-growth women entrepreneurs appear to have more in common with men than they do with low-growth women entrepreneurs (Morris et al., 2006). The lack of similarity between these women is almost entirely due to differences in human capital, specifically education and previous business experience.

However, although women are not a homogeneous group, gender does appear to be an important factor in determining how small business owners themselves define and perceive success (Walker and Brown, 2004). As can be seen from the case studies presented above, success is not always based on the growth or financial profits of the company, even though these are generally the criteria applied to determining business success in the male model. Many women entrepreneurs do not seek to grow their businesses, rather remaining relatively small so that they retain the flexibility and work–life balance that motivated them to start their own business in the first place (Fielden and Davidson, 2010). Therefore, for women, success is a complex balance of factors that include both financial and non-financial criteria; the same factors are usually present for all women but it is the individual emphasis placed on each criterion that differs.

WOMEN ENTREPRENEURS: THE FUTURE

In the past, the external factors influencing women's entrepreneurship, that is, legal, societal, political and economic, appear to have had little impact on the level of women's entrepreneurial activity or their experience of entrepreneurship. Women have been constrained by domestic and family responsibilities, poor access to finance, exclusion from mentors and effective business networks and poor social and human capital. The degree to which women entrepreneurs have experienced these barriers has been contingent on cultural, religious and societal norms, which are country-specific. This has led to an image of women's enterprises being one of poor growth and financial underachievement.

However, this is no longer the whole picture and the image of women entrepreneurs is becoming increasingly diverse. For example, there has been an increase in the entry of women from corporate backgrounds into entrepreneurship and a rise in the number of young educated women who are choosing to start their own businesses rather than face the glass ceiling.

Corporate women are often highly educated, frequently holding business-based qualifications, for example, Masters in Business Administration, and have a wealth of senior-level business experience. Younger women are also usually well educated and tend to be single and choose not to have children, or postpone starting a family, in favour of their entrepreneurial goals. Both types of women have high levels of both social and human capital and are very successful in terms of the male financial model of business.

This increased diversity within women's entrepreneurship should not be taken as a sign that the entrepreneurial playing field between men and women is now equal. Gender is still a variable that impacts on an individual's experience of the world they live in and continues to be subjected to external influence beyond the control of women. This means that for the foreseeable future at least, gender is still on the entrepreneurial agenda.

NOTES

1. Source: personal interview with authors, April 2011.
2. Source: personal interview with authors, June 2011.

REFERENCES

Ahl, H. (2006), 'Why research on women entrepreneurs needs new direction', *Entrepreneurship Theory and Practice*, **30** (5), 595–622.
Allen, I.E., A. Elam, N. Langowitz and M. Dean (2008), *Global Entrepreneurship Monitor 2007*, Global Entrepreneurship Research Association, available at: http://www.gemconsortium.org; accessed 8 August 2011.
Alsos, G.A., E.J. Isaksen and E. Ljunggren (2006), 'New venture financing and subsequent business growth in men- and women-led businesses', *Entrepreneurship Theory and Practice*, **30** (5), 667–86.
Antonucci, T.A. (1990), 'Social support and social relationships', in R.H. Binstock and L.K. George (eds), *Handbook of Aging and the Social Sciences*, San Diego, CA: Academic Press, pp. 205–26.
Australia Bureau of Statistics (2002), 'Characteristics of small businesses', Catalogue No. 8127.0, Canberra: Australian Government Publishing Service.
Barclays (2000), *Women in Business – The Barriers Start to Fall*, London: Barclays Bank plc.
Bird, B. and C. Brush (2002), 'A gendered perspective on organization creation', *Entrepreneurship Theory and Practice*, **26** (3), 41–65.
Boon, M. van der (2005), 'Women into enterprise: a European and international perspective', in S.L. Fielden and M.J. Davidson (eds), *International Handbook of Women and Small Business Entrepreneurship*, Cheltenham, UK and Northampton, MA, USA: Edward Elgar, pp. 161–77.

Bosma, N., M. van Praag, R. Thurik and G. de Wit (2004), 'The value of human and social capital investments for the business performance of start-ups', *Small Business Economics*, **23** (3), 227–36.

Bruni, A., S. Gheradi and B. Poggio (2004), 'Doing gender, doing entrepreneurship: an ethnographic account of intertwined practices', *Gender, Work and Organization*, **11** (4), 406–29.

Brush, C.G., P. Greene and M. Hart (2001), 'From initial idea to unique advantage: the entrepreneurial challenge of constructing a resource base', *Academy of Management Executive: Special Issue on Strategic Management and Entrepreneurship*, **15** (1), 64–80.

Brush, C.G., A. de Bruin and F. Welter (2009), 'A gender-aware framework for women's entrepreneurship', *International Journal of Gender and Entrepreneurship*, **1** (1), 8–24.

Caputo, R.K. and A. Dolinsky (1998), 'Women's choice to pursue self-employment: the role of financial and human capital of household members', *Journal of Small Business Management*, **36** (3), 8–18.

Carter, S. and S. Marlow (2003), 'Professional attainment as a challenge to gender disadvantage in entrepreneurship', paper presented at the 48th International Small Business Conference, Belfast.

Carter, S. and S. Marlow (2007), 'Female entrepreneurship: theoretical perspectives and empirical evidence', in N. Carter, C. Henry, B.O. Cinneide and K. Johnston (eds), *Female Entrepreneurship: Implications for Education, Training and Policy*, London: Routledge, pp. 11–37.

Carter, S., S. Anderson and E. Shaw (2001), *Women's Business Ownership: A Review of the Academic, Popular and Internet Literature*, London: Small Business Service.

Carter, S., E. Shaw, F. Wilson and W. Lam (2006), 'Gender, entrepreneurship and business finance: investigating the relationship between banks and entrepreneurs in the UK', in C.G. Brush, N.M. Carter, E.J. Gatewood, P.G. Greene and M.M. Hart (eds), *Growth-oriented Women Entrepreneurs and their Businesses – A Global Research Perspective*, Cheltenham, UK and Northampton, MA, USA: Edward Elgar, pp. 373–92.

Carter, S., E. Shaw, W. Lam and F. Wilson (2007), 'Gender, entrepreneurship and bank lending: the criteria and processes used by bank loan officers in assessing applications', *Entrepreneurship Theory and Practice*, **31** (3), 427–44.

Catalyst (1998), *Women Entrepreneurs: Why Companies Lose Female Talent and What They Can Do About It*, New York: Catalyst.

Catalyst (2003), *Census of Women on the Boards*, New York: Catalyst.

Cohen, L. and P. Jennings (1995), 'Supporting transition: the role of support agencies in women's move from employment to self-employment', paper presented at 18th ISBA National Conference, Paisley.

Coleman, S. (2007), 'The role of human and financial capital in the profitability and growth of women-owned small firms', *Journal of Small Business Management*, **45** (3), 303–19.

Dallalfar, A. (1994), 'Iranian women as immigrant entrepreneurs', *Gender and Society*, **8** (4), 541–61.

Davidson, M.J. and R. Burke (eds) (2004), *Women in Management Worldwide: Progress and Prospects*, London: Ashgate.

Davidson, M.J. and R.J. Burke (eds) (2011), *Women in Management Worldwide: Vol. II*, London: Gower.

Davidsson, P. and B. Honig (2003), 'The role of social and human capital among nascent entrepreneurs', *Journal of Business Venturing*, **18** (3), 301–31.

De Carolis, D.M. and P. Saparito (2006), 'Social capital, cognition, and entrepreneurial opportunities: a theoretical framework', *Entrepreneurship Theory and Practice*, **30** (1), 41–56.

Delmar, F. (2003), 'Women entrepreneurship: assessing data availability and future needs', paper for the Workshop on Improving Statistics on SMEs and Entrepreneurship, Paris: OECD, 17–19 September.

Feldman, D.C. and M.C. Bolino (2000), 'Career patterns of the self-employed: career motivations and career outcomes', *Journal of Small Business Management*, **38** (3), 53–67.

Fernandes, E. and C. Cabral-Gardoso (2003), 'Gender asymmetries and the manager stereotype among management students', *Women in Management Review*, **18** (1/2), 77–87.

Fielden, S.L. and M.J. Davidson (eds) (2005), *International Handbook of Women and Small Business Entrepreneurship*, Cheltenham, UK and Northampton, MA, USA: Edward Elgar.

Fielden, S.L. and M.J. Davidson (eds) (2010), *International Research Handbook on Successful Women Entrepreneurs*, Cheltenham, UK and Northampton, MA, USA: Edward Elgar.

Fielden, S.L. and C.M. Hunt (2011), 'Online coaching: an alternative source of social support for female entrepreneurs during venture creation', *International Small Business Journal*, **29** (4), 345–59.

Fielden, S.L., M.J. Davidson, A. Dawe and P.J. Makin (2003), 'Factors inhibiting the economic growth of female small business owners', *Journal of Small Business and Enterprise Development*, **10** (2), 152–66.

Foss, L. and E. Ljunggren (2006), 'Women's entrepreneurship in Norway: recent trends and future challenges', in C.G. Brush, N.M. Carter, E.J. Gatewood, P.G. Greene and M.M. Hart (eds), *Growth-oriented Women Entrepreneurs and their Businesses – A Global Research Perspective*, Cheltenham, UK and Northampton, MA, USA: Edward Elgar, pp. 154–83.

Goffee, R. and R. Scase (1985), *Women in Charge: The Experience of Female Entrepreneurs*, London: Allen and Unwin.

Harding, R. (2004), *Global Entrepreneurship Monitor, United Kingdom 2004*, available at: http://tna.europarchive.org/20081112122150/http://www.london.edu/assets/documents/PDF/GEM_UK_Report_2004.Pdf; accessed 18 August 2011.

Harding, R., M. Cowling and M. Ream (2003), *Achieving the Vision: Female Entrepreneurship*, London: The British Chamber of Commerce.

Haynes, P.J. (2003), 'Differences among entrepreneurs: "Are you experienced?" may be the wrong question', *International Journal of Entrepreneurial Behaviour and Research*, **9** (3), 111–23.

Hisrich, R. (1989), 'Women entrepreneurs: problems and prescriptions for success in the future', in O. Hagan, C. Rivchun and D. Sexton (eds), *Women-owned Businesses*, New York: Praeger, pp. 3–32.

Hmielski, K.M. and R.A. Baron (2009), 'Entrepreneurs' optimism and new venture performance: a social cognitive perspective', *Academy of Management Journal*, **52** (3), 473–88.

Hoang, H. and B. Antoncic (2003), 'Network based research in entrepreneurship: a critical review', *Journal of Business Venturing*, **18** (2), 165–87.

Hunt, C., S.L. Fielden, M.J. Davidson and A. Dawe (2006), *Tailored E-coaching for Female Entrepreneurs: Findings from a Study Examining Female Entrepreneurs' Experiences of an E-coaching Programme in the North West of England*, Manchester: Manchester Business School.

Kaplan, D.M. and F. Niederman (2006), 'Career management concerns for women in IT', in E.M. Trauth (ed.), *Encyclopedia of Gender and Information Technology*, Hersey, PA: Idea Group Publishers, pp. 84–9.

Kelley, D., N. Bosma and J.E. Amorós (2010), *Global Entrepreneurship Monitor 2010 Global Report*, Global Entrepreneurship Research Association, available at: http://www.gemconsortium.org/download/1313921797356/GEM%20GLOBAL %20REPORT%202010rev.pdf; accessed 30 April 2011.

Kovalainen, A., P. Arenius and L. Galloway (2002), 'Entrepreneurial activity of women in the global economy: analysis of data from 29 countries', paper presented at the Babson Kauffman Entrepreneurship Research Conference, Boulder, Colorado.

Langowitz, N. and M. Minniti (2007), 'The entrepreneurial propensity of women', *Entrepreneurship Theory and Practice*, **31** (3), 341–64.

Lewis, P. (2006), 'The quest for invisibility: female entrepreneurs and the masculine norm of entrepreneurship', *Gender, Work and Organization*, **13** (5), 453–69.

London School of Economics (2006), 'Kitchen table tycoons identified as new brand of female entrepreneurs', available at: http://www2.lse.ac.uk/newsAnd Media/news/archives/2006/YellowPagesResearch.aspx; accessed 18 August 2011.

Loscocco, K. and K. Smith-Hunter (2004), 'Women home-based business owners: insights from comparative analyses', *Women in Management*, **19** (3), 164–73.

Manolova, T.S., N.M. Carter, I.M. Manev and B.S. Gyoshev (2007), 'The differential effect of men and women entrepreneurs' human capital and networking expectancies in Bulgaria', *Entrepreneurship Theory and Practice*, **31** (3), 407–26.

Marlow, S. (2002), 'Self-employed women – new opportunities, old challenges?', *Entrepreneurship and Innovation*, **2** (2), 83–91.

Marlow, S. and D. Patton (2005), 'All credit to men? Entrepreneurship, finance and gender', *Entrepreneurship, Theory and Practice*, **29** (6), 717–35.

Marlow, S. and A. Strange (1994), 'Female entrepreneurs: success by whose standards?', in M. Tanton (ed.), *Women in Management: A Developing Process*, London: Routledge, pp. 172–84.

Martin, C. and L.M. Martin (2002), *SME Ownership Succession – Business Support and Policy Implications – A Research Project Seeking to Demonstrate How to Support Enterprises at the Final Stage of the Ownership Lifecycle*, London: ACCA Report.

Martin, C.A. and Tulgan, B. (2001), *Managing Generation Y*, New York: HRD Press.

Martin, L.M. (2001), 'More jobs for the boys? Succession planning in SMEs', *Women in Management Review*, **16** (5), 222–32.

Mattis, M.C. (2004), 'Women entrepreneurs: out from under the glass ceiling', *Women in Management Review*, **19** (3), 154–63.

Mattis, M.C. and L. Levin (2010), 'United States of America', in S.L. Fielden and M.J. Davidson (eds), *International Research Handbook on Successful Women Entrepreneurs*, Cheltenham, UK and Northampton, MA, USA: Edward Elgar, pp. 216–30.

Mavin, S. (2000), 'Approaches to careers in management: why UK organisations should consider gender', *Career Development International*, **5** (1), 13–20.

McClelland, E., J. Swail, J. Bell and P. Ibbotson (2005), 'Following the pathway of female entrepreneurs', *International Journal of Entrepreneurial Behaviour and Research*, **11** (2), 84–107.

McGrath Cohoon, J., V. Wadhwa and L. Mitchell (2010), *The Anatomy of an Entrepreneur: Are Successful Women Entrepreneurs Different from Men?*, Kansas City, Missouri: Kauffman Foundation.

Moore, D.P. (1999), 'Women entrepreneurs: approaching a new millennium', in G.N. Powell (ed.), *Handbook of Gender and Work*, Thousand Oaks, CA: Sage, pp. 371–90.

Moore, D.P. (2000), *Careerpreneurs: Lessons from Leading Women Entrepreneurs on Building a Career within Boundaries*, Palo Alto, CA: David Black Publishing.

Moore, D.P. and E.H. Buttner (1997), *Women Entrepreneurs: Moving Beyond the Glass Ceiling*, Thousand Oaks, CA: Sage.

Morris, M.H., N.N. Miyasaki, C.E. Watters and S.M. Coombes (2006), 'The dilemma of growth: understanding venture size choices of women entrepreneurs', *Journal of Small Business Management*, **44** (2), 221–44.

Omar, A., M.J. Davidson and S.L. Fielden (2007), *Black and Minority Ethnic (BME) Small Business Owners: A Comparative Study Investigating the Problems, Experiences and Barriers Faced by BME Female and Male Entrepreneurs in North West England*, Report Centre for Equality and Diversity at Work, available at: http://www.train2000.org.uk/research-reports/pdfs/BME-report. pdf; last accessed 10 August 2011.

Orhan, M. and D. Scott (2001), 'Why women enter into entrepreneurship: an explanatory model', *Women in Management Review*, **16** (5), 232–43.

Orser, B.J., A.L. Riding and K. Manley (2006), 'Women entrepreneurs and financial capital', *Entrepreneurship Theory and Practice*, **30** (5), 643–65.

Pollard, R.P.F. (2001), 'The role of social support on the perception of success for women entrepreneurs', *Dissertation Abstracts*, 2001-95018-291.

Prowess (2004), *Bridging the Enterprise Gap*, Phoenix Development Fund/ European Social Fund, UK.

Rodriguez, T. (2001), 'The wind beneath their wings: the moderating effects of social support on the entrepreneur and entrepreneurial performance outcomes', *Dissertation Abstracts International Section: Humanities and Social Sciences*, **61** (7-A), 2806.

Rosa, P. and D. Hamilton (1994), 'Gender and ownership in UK small firms', *Entrepreneurship Theory and Practice*, **18** (3), 11–28.

Sarason, Y. and Y. Morrison (2005), 'Hispanic women entrepreneurs and small business owners in the USA', in S.L. Fielden and M.J. Davidson (eds), *International Handbook of Women and Small Business Entrepreneurship*, Cheltenham, UK and Northampton, MA, USA: Edward Elgar, pp. 148–60.

Schmidt, R.A. and C. Parker (2003), 'Diversity in independent retailing: barriers and benefits – the impact of gender', *International Journal of Retail and Distribution Management*, **31** (8), 428–39.

Shelton, L.M. (2006), 'Female entrepreneurs, work–family conflict, and venture performance: new insights into the work–family interface', *Journal of Small Business Management*, **44** (2), 285–97.

Singh, V. and S. Vinnicombe (2009), *Female FTSE Report*, Cranfield: Cranfield School of Management.

Still, L. (2005), 'The constraints facing women entering small business ownership', in S.L. Fielden and M.J. Davidson (eds), *International Handbook of Women and*

Small Business Entrepreneurship, Cheltenham, UK and Northampton, MA, USA: Edward Elgar, pp. 55–65.

Sundin, E. (2002), 'Foretagandets manliga pragling: Orsaker och konsekvenser', in C. Holmquist and E. Sundin (eds), *Foretagerskan: Om Kuinnor och Entreprenorskap*, Stockholm: SNS.

Syed, J. (2010), 'Pakistan', in S.L. Fielden and M.J. Davidson (eds), *International Handbook of Women and Small Business Entrepreneurship*, Cheltenham, UK and Northampton, MA, USA: Edward Elgar, pp. 117–31.

Taylor, S.R. and J.D. Newcomer (2005), 'Characteristics of women small business owners', in S.L. Fielden and M.J. Davidson (eds), *International Handbook of Women and Small Business Entrepreneurship*, Cheltenham, UK and Northampton, MA, USA: Edward Elgar, pp. 17–31.

Terjesen, S. (2005), 'Senior women managers' transition to entrepreneurship', *Career Development International*, **10** (3), 246–59.

Tillmar, M. (2007), 'Gendered small-business assistance: lessons from a Swedish project', *Journal of European Industrial Training*, **31** (2), 84–99.

Verheul, I. and R. Thurik (2001), 'Start-up capital: does gender matter?', *Small Business Economics*, **20** (4), 443–76.

Verheul, I., A. van Stel and R. Thurik (2004), 'Explaining female and male entrepreneurship at the country level', *ERIM Report Series Research in Management*, available at: http://papers.ssrn.com/sol3/papers.cfm?abstract_id=1265440; last accessed 9 August.

Vinnicombe, S. and J. Bank (2003), *Women with Attitude: Lessons for Career Management*, London: Routledge.

Viswesvaran, C., J.I. Sanchez and J. Fisher (1999), 'The role of social support in the process of work stress: a meta analysis', *Journal of Vocational Behaviour*, **54** (2), 314–34.

Walker, A. and A. Brown (2004), 'What success factors are important to small business owners?', *International Small Business Journal*, **22** (6), 577–91.

Watkins, J.M. and D.S. Watkins (1984), 'The female entrepreneur: her background and determinants of business choice – some British data', *Frontiers of Entrepreneurship Research*, Wellesley, MA: Babson College.

Wilson, F., J. Kickul and D. Marlino (2007), 'Gender, entrepreneurial self-efficacy, and entrepreneurial career intentions: implications for entrepreneurial education', *Entrepreneurship Theory and Practice*, **31** (3), 387–406.

Wood, G.J. (2009), 'Revisiting women managers and organisational acceptance', *Gender in Management: An International Review*, **24** (8), 615–31.

Wood, G.J. (2010), 'Australia', in S.L. Fielden and M.J. Davidson (eds), *International Handbook of Women and Small Business Entrepreneurship*, Cheltenham, UK and Northampton, MA, USA: Edward Elgar, pp. 10–25.

Wood, G.J. and M.D. Davidson (2011), 'A review of male and female Australian Indigenous entrepreneurs: disadvantaged past – promising future?', *Gender in Management*, **26** (4), 311–26.

Woolnough, H., M.J. Davidson and S.L. Fielden (2006), 'The experiences of mentors on a career development and mentoring programme for female mental health nurses in the UK NHS', *Health Service Management Research Journal*, **19** (3), 186–96.

5. Ethnic minority entrepreneurs

> [O]ne of the most challenging aspects of research on ethnic minority owned businesses has been the lack of existing data needed to define the size and attributes of the sector.
>
> (The National Panel of Employment, 2005, p. 51)

INTRODUCTION

In recent years, there has been a significant shift in the orientation of ethnic groups towards business ownership and the business expertise among ethnic minority entrepreneurs has grown substantially (Bates, 2006). Consequently, ethnic minority businesses (EMBs) have been the focus of growing interest from a variety of sources over recent years and this has produced considerable debate and controversy with regard to the scale of their activities and policy needs of these businesses (Department of Trade and Industry, 2007). In contrast to immigrant entrepreneurs reviewed in Chapter 6 who are defined as new settlers in their adopted country of residence, this chapter concentrates on ethnic minority entrepreneurs who were born in their country of residence, although they may retain strong links to their country and culture of origin. Comparatively little is known about the characteristics of ethnic minority entrepreneurs, what motivates them and what barriers they face.

In the US and UK, EMBs have grown at a rate three times faster than other businesses (Bates, 2006), representing approximately 7 per cent of the total business numbers, a figure expected to continue to rise due to the expectation that the ethnic minority population will double over the next 25 years (Ethnic Minority Business Forum [EMBF], 2001). According to figures compiled by Barclays, in 2005, 50 000 new businesses in the UK were identified as being owned by ethnic minority entrepreneurs, compared to only 32 000 businesses in 2000. Furthermore, business start-ups from the black and ethnic minority communities were three times more likely to turn in profits compared to non-minority-owned businesses (Bates et al., 2006). This has been attributed to the rising number of young ethnic minority entrepreneurs, who are more than twice as likely to run their own businesses compared to their non-ethnic minority mainstream contemporaries.

EMBF (2001) estimated that in 2005 ethnic minority-owned enterprises were contributing around £13 billion a year to the British economy. Moreover, in London alone it was estimated that ethnic minority-owned businesses employed well over half a million people, with a combined sales turnover of £90 billion (London Development Agency, 2004). Clearly from these figures there is a strong economic case for understanding entrepreneurial activities amongst the ethnic minority entrepreneurs, as ethnic minority-owned firms constituted an important segment of the small business ownership overall (Ram and Smallbone, 2003; Dana, 2007). However, there is a lack of comprehensive information on these populations and 'one of the most challenging aspects of research on ethnic minority owned businesses has been the lack of existing data needed to define the size and attributes of the sector' (National Panel of Employment, 2005, p. 51).

However, while the interest in such enterprises is increasing because of the significant growth in the area, few studies make an explicit distinction between ethnic minority entrepreneurs, where the emphasis is on the 'ethnic' aspect of the individual entrepreneur, and ethnic minority businesses that focus on ethnic products, ethnic market customers or on Indigenous ethnic business strategies: for example, information channels and Islamic banking (Greene et al., 1997; Van Delft et. al., 2000; Levent et al., 2003). Thus, this chapter will focus on ethnic minority entrepreneurs rather than EMBs.

ETHNIC MINORITY ENTREPRENEURS: GENERAL CHARACTERISTICS

The expertise and human capital among ethnic minority entrepreneurs has grown substantially in recent decades (Bates, 2006). However, the evidence available does not refer to different individual ethnic groups (e.g., Pakistani versus Indian), rather it refers to ethnic minorities as a whole. Although this enables us to compare the business performance of enterprises owned by ethnic minorities with the mainstream majority in demonstrating that parity has still not been achieved (Bates and Badford, 2007), it is unhelpful in expanding our knowledge about the diverse experience of entrepreneurs from the many different ethnic minority groups. When examining the characteristics and backgrounds of ethnic minority entrepreneurs, it is necessary and important to acknowledge that this group comprises many sub-groups. Often, in ethnic minority business research, there is the tendency to examine Asian cultures and dismiss the other ethnic minorities that are firmly embedded within a society, for example, African. This was highlighted by Raghuram and Strange (2001) who stated how they were constantly faced with success stories from the UK Asian business sector and soon became conscious of the invisibility of African Caribbean businesses and the relevant problems and barriers that they face; they viewed this as a minority within a minority. The tendency to focus on the successes of Asian businesses perhaps reflects the higher level of participation by this ethnic group in self-employment. The *Small Business Service Household Survey of Entrepreneurship* (2002) reported that as a proportion of the working population, a higher number of Asians were in self-employment when compared to the other ethnic communities. Further, the UK *Annual Local Area Labour Force Survey* revealed that over 60 000 Asians, including Bangladeshis, Indians, Pakistanis and other Asians, were self-employed (Office for National Statistics, 2004).

In many developed countries ethnic minorities are disproportionately represented in business ownership. For example, in the UK people from Pakistani and Chinese groups were more likely to be self-employed than those in other ethnic groups. One in five Pakistanis in employment were self-employed (21 per cent), as were just fewer than one in six Chinese (16 per cent), compared to around one in ten (12 per cent) of mainstream British people (ibid.). It is important to note that in the UK there is a higher proportion of Asian entrepreneurs compared to other ethnic communities, with fewer than one in ten people from a mixed or black ethnic group engaging in business ownership. As Rafiq (1992) points out, 'Culture is important in any discussion of entrepreneurship because it can determine the attitudes of individuals towards entrepreneurship ... and certain cultural institutions may facilitate or hinder entry into entrepreneurship' (p. 46). Ram et al. (2000, p. 188) note the influence of culture on the pathway of different ethnic groups into entrepreneurship. For example, Asian, Chinese and Indian entrepreneurs are most likely to emerge from advantaged situations, that is, have successful entrepreneurial role models, be better educated and have managerial experiences. In contrast, Pakistani and Bengali businesses appear to emerge from disadvantaged situations. 'Ethnicity is cross-cut by class background in this as in many other instances', which they reinforce by a further quote by Werbner (1998) who 'identifies a distinctive Pakistani ethos of self-sacrifice, self-denial and hard work that serves to fuel entrepreneurial activity' (ibid.).

In relation to ethnic minority entrepreneurs in the US, second-generation Chinese, Indians and Koreans were reported to be highly successful in entrepreneurial ventures (Jacoby, 2000), with Koreans having recently been reported to be 'entrepreneurially superior' as they have the highest proportion of self-employment, followed by Israelis and Palestinians (Bogan and Darity, 2008, p. 2008). Despite this breadth of literature, there appears to be a lack of consensus about the reasons certain ethnic groups in the US (particularly Asians) are more successful than others (Bogan and Darity, 2008). Certainly, it does appear that US-born residents of Asian origin are able to establish markedly higher levels of debt capital than African Americans (ibid.). However, some ethnic groups are reported less likely to be self-employed, with African Americans having the lowest rate of business ownership in the US amongst mainstream, Asian, Native American and Hispanic ethnic/racial groups (Fairlie, 2004). This suggests that some ethnic groups appear to face steep barriers in terms of becoming entrepreneurs – even if they were born in the host country. Certain ethnic groups become more successful that the 'local' population, possibly because of entrenched discrimination and negative stereotyping experienced by a particular ethnic group (Bogan and Darity, 2008).

Although culture is undoubtedly an important factor, there are other aspects of ethnicity that have a greater influence on individual ethnic minority entrepreneurs (Clark and Drinkwater, 2000). For example, attitudes towards entrepreneurship are also influenced by religion (Rafiq, 1992). Muslim and Sikh communities take a positive view of business ownership because both of the prominent figures in these religions were themselves entrepreneurs, and in the Hindu religion, the Vaishya caste (i.e., a social division based on occupation) specializes in business activities. In the UK, Clark and Drinkwater (2000) found a substantial collinearity between ethnicity and religion, with Christians and those who did not follow a religion under-represented in business ownership, compared to Muslims, Sikhs and Hindus, who were well represented. This potentially explains the comparatively low number of Chinese entrepreneurs, as in a 2001 survey, more than half (53 per cent) said that they had no religion (Office for National Statistics, 2004). For most ethnic groups younger people were less religious than older people, although this difference is not so pronounced among South Asians. This again may explain why one of the highest rates of business ownership is seen in young Asian males who have the highest religious commitment, where the association between ethnicity and religion is strong.

Another influencing factor is location, with many ethnic minority businesses often attached to settlement patterns, or enclaves (i.e., a concentration of individuals from the same ethnic background), which has resulted in most ethnic minority businesses being located in urban and inner city areas. Further, it has been suggested that the tendency for ethnic minority businesses to be concentrated in a few key sectors is related to specific ethnic resources, such as the availability of cheap family or co-ethnic labour, pooled savings and access to trusted networks (Basu, 1998; Fadahunsi et al., 2000). In the UK, these are predominately within the service sector and are significantly different from non-ethnic-owned enterprises, that is, 90 per cent compared to 70 per cent for non-ethnic-owned enterprises (National Panel of Employment, 2005). The overall business activities of ethnic minority entrepreneurs tend to be concentrated in industries such as transport and distributive sectors; the retail trade and hotels/restaurants account for 22 per cent of business activity among this group (Office for National Statistics, 2004). However, certain ethnic groups are concentrated in particular areas of entrepreneurship. For example, Bangladeshi and Chinese men and women are concentrated in the hotel and restaurant sector, whereas Indians and Pakistanis are still principally involved in retailing, especially in convenience grocery stores. Pakistani men are most likely to be in transport and communication, especially in taxi driving (McEvoy and Hafeez, 2006). Kloosterman et al. (1999) suggested that the reasons why ethnic minorities were concentrated in certain sectors is an interaction of complex factors, including internal ethnic resources, cultural background and external economic, legal and environmental influences.

Although the general trend has been for ethnic minority entrepreneurs to be concentrated in low financial value areas, the situation appears to be changing for second- and third-generation ethnic minority entrepreneurs, who tend to enter more profitable markets and professional services (Ram, 2003; Smallbone et al., 2007). Furthermore, and contrary to previous arguments, Clark and Drinkwater (2000) found that only one-fifth of ethnic minority-owned businesses in England and Wales provided 'specialist ethnic' goods or services, but there was a great deal of variation across ethnic groups with Chinese or Bangladeshis far more likely to supply ethnically niche goods. This break away from traditional areas of ethnic minority entrepreneurship is dependent on a number of factors, including education, networks and cultural ties (Fadahunsi et al., 2000). Networks provide an important comparison between immigrant and ethnic minority entrepreneurs. For those that have access to them, immigrant entrepreneurs have relied on informal networks within their own communities in order to mobilize resources and generate sales, but for ethnic minority entrepreneurs born in their country of residence their networks have become more mainstream and these have facilitated their competitive advantage in the wider market place.

Contemporary perspectives appear to be that individuals from different ethnic backgrounds who have been born and educated in the country of their birth (i.e., the host country of their immigrant parents) will have different attitudes, as well as experiences, from those of their parents. In some ethnic communities, entrepreneurs appear to have moved away from the more traditional business areas of their parents and may have become established in more professional areas that offer higher salaries and more status. These ethnic cohorts are often more highly educated, and hence enter into entrepreneurial ventures in ways different from those previously available to their immigrant parents or grandparents (Rusinovic, 2008).

Gender is another factor that influences ethnic minority entrepreneurship. Obtaining recent statistics on ethnic minority women entrepreneurs is a challenge in view of the limited empirical research over the years. Nonetheless, Owen (1995) reported that the proportion of self-employed ethnic minority women in Great Britain was substantially higher than their non-ethnic minority counterparts, that is, 8.2 per cent compared to 6.8 per cent respectively. According to the Global Entrepreneurship Monitor (GEM) (2005) *UK Executive Report*, with the exception of women from Indian, Pakistani and black African backgrounds, women from ethnic minorities are substantially more entrepreneurial than their non-ethnic female counterparts. The female total entrepreneurial activity (TEA) amongst non-ethnic people was 3.6 per cent, but was 2.5 times higher amongst women from mixed backgrounds (10.2 per cent), Bangladeshis (10.9 per cent), other Asians (10.3 per cent) and black Caribbeans (10.5 per cent). The most entrepreneurial grouping is that of 'other black' at 29.2 per cent (i.e., those of African ancestry) (Dawe and Fielden, 2005). Even so, Dawe and Fielden noted that it was not possible to accurately estimate how many ethnic minority women were in business. These women and their businesses are often invisible, as they are based in the home, and are separate to the non-ethnic community. Furthermore, many of the ethnic businesses operated by women have a male figurehead, especially in communities that do not allow women to mix with men.

ETHNIC MINORITY ENTREPRENEURS: ASPIRATIONS AND MOTIVATIONS

As outlined previously, the representation of ethnic minority businesses varies depending on the different ethnic minority groups. It must be noted, however, that this is not just a British phenomenon: ethnic minority participation in enterprises is similar throughout Europe and in the United States; there are many ethnic minority-owned businesses (Ram et al., 2000; GEM, 2005). It has been suggested that the reason Asian men enter into business is the lack of progress they make in employment, compared to their non-ethnic minority counterparts who can access upward mobility in employment. Many Asian workers hit a glass ceiling, which they cannot progress through to the higher echelons of management as their route is blocked, unlike their non-ethnic colleagues (Davidson, 1997). Recent literature (e.g., Fielden and Davidson, 2010) has put forward other reasons for this move by ethnic minorities into business ownership, including high unemployment levels, job dissatisfaction and avoidance of racial discrimination.

A British study conducted by Basu and Goswami (1999) on 118 ethnic minority entrepreneurs revealed that these entrepreneurs were driven by the same 'pull' and 'push' factors as non-ethnic minority entrepreneurs. Basu and Goswami (1999) found the main 'push' factors to be the inability to find employment, underpaid salaried work; discrimination in the labour market economy and redundancy. 'Pull' factors for these ethnic minority entrepreneurs were found to be a desire for independence, financial betterment, higher social status, greater personal control and previous business experience.

Nevertheless, the type of push and pull factors may differ between the different ethnic groups. An English study by Metcalf et al. (1996) for example, found that Indians were more financially motivated and attached more importance to autonomy and monetary rewards, whereas African-Asians and Pakistanis tended to view business ownership as a source of status. The influence of individual 'push/pull' factors was also affected by age, and a UK study on ethnic minority entrepreneurs has pointed to a generational difference in the motivation behind business start-ups (National Panel of Employment, 2005). Specifically, many ethnic-owned enterprises were established out of necessity, as an alternative to paid employment. These businesses tended to be less diverse in terms of their customer base and relied upon their ethnically based business connections and relationships (Greene et al., 1997; Bates et al., 2006). Gender is also a significant source of difference when looking at 'push/pull' factors for different ethnic groups. A study by Omar et al. (2007) found that achievement factors such as a lack of career progression were important for all genders but particularly so for those from Indian and South Asian backgrounds. In contrast, for black men and women 'push' factors, specifically a lack of employment, were significant motivators, whereas Asian men and women were far more motivated by a range of 'pull' factors. The greater number of motivating factors experienced by Asian business owners compared to African Caribbean business owners may explain the disparity in entrepreneurial rates between the two groups in the UK (Raghuram and Strange, 2001).

However, while most business motivators appear generic for men regardless of ethnic background, for women different ethnic and cultural influences appears to be much stronger. For example, women of different ethnic minorities have very different experiences and motivations with regard to owning their own business. According to Basu's (1998) UK research of Indians, Srinivasan's (1995) survey of Asians and Curran and Blackburn's (1993) account of African Caribbean and Bangladeshis, the main cause for entry into self-employment for women in these different ethnic groups tended to be derived from positive 'pull' factors that were similar to the reasons stated by entrepreneurs in general. However, for Pakistanis, the scenario may be different; these women were more likely to suffer from poorer employment prospects, discrimination and racism at work than other groups. Therefore, Pakistanis may be more motivated to set up their own business by negative 'push' factors (Basu, 1998).

It should also be noted that Omar et al.'s (2007) study of British women from Asian backgrounds (which included a high percentage of Muslim women), felt that they were under pressure from their husbands not to work with other men due to religious constraints. Furthermore, women from all Asian backgrounds felt that their husbands did not approve of them working with anyone (male or female) from a different cultural background. As with previous work (Dhaliwall, 2000) the 'glass ceiling' was cited as much more of an issue for UK Indian and black women than for Asian or Chinese women. The issue of blocked career paths may be reduced for South Asian women, as following in the traditions of the family held a greater importance (Omar et al., 2007). Furthermore, this may also be true of other Asian and Chinese women, again because of a more collectivist culture and/or sex role traditionalism (Rana et al., 1998; Omar and Davidson, 2001). For black women entrepreneurs in the UK, using their relevant experience to prove their value was a significant pull factor, which (as they tended to feel more isolated than other ethnic minority women) may be a means of bolstering self-efficacy (i.e., achievement beliefs) by viewing their personal experiences as entrepreneurial capital (Fielden and Davidson, 2005). Fielden and Davidson concluded that women entrepreneurs from other ethnic groups may have drawn on family experiences and support to develop and maintain self-efficacy rather than having to be self-supporting, which ultimately may impact on entrepreneurial success.

ETHNIC MINORITY ENTREPRENEURS: CHALLENGES AND BARRIERS

Compared to other entrepreneurs, ethnic minority entrepreneurs experience different constraints in the start-up and operation of their businesses. As with all other aspects of the experiences of ethnic minority entrepreneurs, ethnic background and gender are defining factors in terms of the challenges and barriers they encounter. Thus, this section will look at various factors for both men and women, as well as factors specific to women minority ethnic entrepreneurs.

In general, the process of raising external finances was difficult for many small businesses regardless of the owner's ethnic background (Basu, 1998), although Ram et al. (2001) have reported that African Caribbean businesses in the UK have less success in accessing bank loans. This inability to access reasonable cost finance is a major constraint for many ethnic minority entrepreneurs, who face additional barriers to those encountered by non-minority entrepreneurs (Ekanem and Wyer, 2007), particularly during business start-up. Their lack of a business track record and/or collateral means that they are frequently reliant on the financial support of family members, friends and/or acquaintances from within their ethnic community. Although this tends to be a cheaper form of finance than traditional banking services, they are often capped at low levels of financial support (ibid.). However, even when ethnic minority entrepreneurs do have seemingly impressive track records and personal resources, they face discrimination (Ram, 2003). The Bank of England (1999) claimed that this was not in fact discrimination on the part of the banks, maintaining that it was as a consequence of risk aversion by lenders because of failure rates and poor planning by ethnic minority businesses.

Kon and Storey (2003) claimed that this leads to 'discouraged borrowers', that is, 'a good firm, requiring finance, that chooses not to apply to the bank because it feels its application will be rejected' (p. 39). It is not actual discrimination, although this clearly does appear to take place, rather it is perceived discrimination based upon expectation of outcome that inhibits many ethnic minority entrepreneurs from pursuing formal financing for their businesses. This was also acknowledged by the Bank of England (1999) in its report, which stated that: 'whilst there is little documented evidence of ethnic minority businesses (EMBs) suffering discrimination by finance providers, there is evidence that some EMBs perceive they are treated adversely ... and perception may be more important than reality in this context' (p. 35).

Female ethnic minority entrepreneurs appear to be even more disadvantaged by financial constraints (Scott and Irwin, 2009). In the US, Inman and Grant (2005) revealed that compared to mainstream women in service-oriented business, ethnic minority women entrepreneurs had had less initial financial support and faced an even greater challenge in obtaining resources that were essential for their business operations. Mulholland (1997) argued that this was because of the androcentric nature of society; hence ethnic minority women entrepreneurs often face the 'double disadvantage' of both their gender and their ethnicity (Smith-Hunter and Boyd, 2004). The absence of 'culture-sensitive' financial services had resulted in the female business owners having to rely heavily on their families for financial support (Dhaliwall, 2000; Fielden et al., 2003). While such financial arrangements may have helped them to establish their businesses, there exists the possibility that such arrangements could limit the amount of capital these female business owners could inject into their businesses and hence reduce their business growth potential (Carter et al., 2001). Similar to their female non-ethnic counterparts, the problem of accessing external financing is actually related to the problem of lack of information on what financial services are offered by both public and private financial institutions (Fielden and Davidson, 2005). Scott and Irwin (2009) believe that this frequently means that ethnic minority women entrepreneurs are 'discouraged entrepreneurs' simply because of the discrimination and disadvantage they face.

A consistent finding of previous research on ethnic minority entrepreneurs is their low propensity to use mainstream business support agencies (Fadahunsi et al., 2000; Ram and Smallbone, 2001). Significantly, the low level of reported use of these support services was not because of lack of awareness of the existence of such services. Instead, a number of studies (ibid.) revealed that a lack of understanding about the types of support available, doubts about the relevance of what was offered, lack of confidence and trust in those delivering support and low ability to pay for such support, have all contributed to the above situation. Scott and Irwin (2009) refer to them as 'discouraged advisees', that is, those who do not approach potential sources of business advice because of their perceptions of such service. In 2002, the British Bankers' Association revealed that only 7 per cent of ethnic minority entrepreneurs surveyed in 2000 reported using public or quasi-public agencies for start-up advice, compared to 11 per cent of mainstream entrepreneurs. The National Panel of Employment (2005) noted that this trend was perplexing given the scale and coverage of the UK's business support infrastructure, identifying poor 'visibility' or lack of awareness of existing provisions as the most obvious causes of the failures of the current business support infrastructure (EMBF, 2005).

This situation is even worse for women ethnic minority entrepreneurs. In Omar et al.'s (2007) study of UK female black and ethnic minority entrepreneurs, they found that they had a low propensity to use mainstream business support agencies, as well as limited knowledge and information about the support services available for small businesses. According to Ram and Smallbone (2003), the low-level use of mainstream business support agencies by ethnic minority women entrepreneurs cannot be solely attributed to the lack of interest on the part of these business owners. For example, British women of South Asian, Chinese and Middle Eastern origins still appeared to have problems accessing mainstream business support services due to the fact that these were predominantly run by non-ethnics. Other barriers that further enhanced this problem included language, religious beliefs and the close nature of their local communities (Omar et al., 2007).

Religious discrimination, leading to reluctance to mix with other ethnic groups, has the potential to further isolate those from Asian backgrounds, and perceptions of persecution because of ethnicity have the potential to radically damage the business opportunities available to Asian men and women. Although this group have traditionally excelled in business ownership in the UK, particularly Asian men (Raghuram and Strange, 2001), increased suspicion linked to Middle East stereotypes of terrorism may have a serious impact on future growth for Asian businesses beyond their local communities. This issue has not been explicitly explored in previous research, but reflects changing attitudes and demonstrates that the picture with regard to ethnicity and different ethnic groups is not a static one. It is a fluid phenomenon that requires ongoing attention if appropriate support, advice and assistance is to be provided by government agencies. Mainstreaming should be an opportunity that all businesses can exploit regardless of background and gender, but if perceptions of Asian business owners are not addressed, these negative and destructive attitudes may seriously limit the potential market for such businesses.

The family is frequently mentioned in assessments of the apparent distinctiveness of ethnic minority business enterprises (Mingeone, 1999, Ram et al., 2001). Indeed, the family, in its various forms and guises, is said to account for the successes of some ethnic groups like that of the Asians and the lower level of small business operations in other ethnic communities (Boyd, 1990). According to Ram et al. (2001, p. 328): 'familial ideologies are also thought to imbue particular ethnic communities with "cultures" supposedly conducive to entrepreneurial activity'. The family, however, may act as a hindrance or a controlling factor for some ethnic minority women entrepreneurs. For example, the British Asian community, as the discussion above revealed, viewed women as subservient and in general, women were expected to fall into the role of 'housewives'. The family in such a community is so significant that there is an expectation within the community in general and the family specifically, for the wife not to work (Ram et al., 2001). This finding is in line with the findings of other studies (e.g., Mitter, 1986; Phizacklea, 1990; Ram, 1994) all demonstrating that the family can serve as an arena of exploitation, where the roles of women are subordinated. Rana et al. (1998) further revealed that while British Asian women tended to benefit from the extended family network, such networks had also resulted in a higher level of stress amongst these women. This prevailing culture has had a negative effect on women who have decided to work, as they feel pressurized by the family or made to feel guilty by family members who believe that they are putting work before their domestic and family duties. Furthermore, the burden of the extended family may often add to the long working hours these women put into their work; the nature of the extended family involves spending a great deal of time at weekends socializing and preparing for guests, thus ultimately leaving these women with little time to perform other domestic responsibilities or to rest (Rana et al., 1998; Dawe and Fielden, 2005).

Studies on ethnic minority women revealed that these women faced an even greater challenge than their mainstream female counterparts because of their gender and ethnicity (see Bell, 1990; Davidson, 1997). Davidson (1997) found that ethnic minority women live in a bi-cultural world and faced even greater role conflict, specifically: these women faced the double negative effects of sexism and racism. Few, if any, had role models and were more likely to feel isolated. They contended with stereotypical images based on gender and ethnic origin; had greater home/social/work conflicts, (particularly in terms of their role conflict with regard to the family and the black community) and were sometimes accused of 'selling out' to the white community. There are few studies that specifically look at ethnic minority women entrepreneurs but those that have, for example Henley (2007), found that gender and ethnicity were significant barriers in the transition to business ownership. According to Dhaliwall (2000), South Asian women are doubly disadvantaged and they engage in entrepreneurship as a response to blocked mobility (Ram and Jones, 1998; Smith-Hunter and Boyd, 2004).

The cultural restraints faced by many women from Asian backgrounds and the often 'hidden' nature of the contribution to business operation may go some way to explaining their feelings of isolation and not being taken seriously as a business owner (Dhaliwall, 2000; Dawe and Fielden, 2005). However, it appears that black women (i.e., of African ancestry) are perhaps the most disadvantaged in terms of lacking role models, emotional and instrumental support, and feeling that they are not recognized as business owners. In all of these aspects Dawe and Fielden (2005) found that British black women entrepreneurs reported the highest levels of disadvantage and they appear to be more 'invisible' than any other ethnic group. This invisibility does not have an obvious cultural basis, yet it is reflected throughout the academic literature and policy by its absence. The issue of isolation, a lack of credibility, an absence of role models, poor availability of suitable business support provision and a general lack of the same opportunities afforded to men from the same ethnic backgrounds needs to be addressed, but for black women it is an imperative.

ETHNIC MINORITY ENTREPRENEURS: STORIES OF SUCCESS

The following two case studies celebrate the success that can be achieved by ethnic minority entrepreneurs. These highly successful entrepreneurs have been chosen for two reasons. First, they are drawn from under-represented groups within minority ethnic entrepreneurship, that is, an Indian woman (GEM, 2005) and an African man (Raghuram and Strange, 2001). Second, they represent the second generation of business owners who have expanded beyond the confines of their ethnic communities, yet they hold on to their cultural heritage and background and integrate those values into their entrepreneurial ventures.

BOX 5.1 VINODKA (VIN) MURRIA – CHIEF EXECUTIVE OF ADVANCED COMPUTER SOFTWARE PLC[1]

Vin is the CEO of a stock market listed health care software acquisition company with a market value of £120 million, an impressive achievement for a company that launched less than two years ago. Professionally, she is one of the shining lights of the software sector in the UK and her 20-year career has spanned venture capital, private equity, chief executive and operational roles, with a strong focus on mergers and acquisitions. The Indian software entrepreneur is the eldest of five children. Her working life began just after she had finished her A levels at Coventry Comprehensive, when, with a place at university awaiting her, she went to work for her father, who was in danger of losing his corner shop. 'We would have been on the streets', she says. 'I spent a year of my life fighting with the banks, dealing with it, having to sell the business and sell the property so that we could pay the banks back and get out. That is what focuses you on cash, on management, on where the money is coming from'. Vin remembers clearly the day the bank manager came to visit. 'What was really galling was that the guy from Barclays came and had lunch with my parents first. If he had not done that, and just come and said he was pulling the plug … it was that that made me go: "You have got to be joking!"' The family moved to a smaller property in Coventry but Vin's father died shortly afterwards. 'He was ill anyway but I am convinced that it had an effect', she says. 'It was scary. If your back's against the

---

wall, what you do is fight. I don't give up. I fight bloody hard'. The experience galvanized an already steely work ethic, instilled in her by her parents.

Vin holds a first-class Honours degree in Computer Science (1982 to 1986) and an MBA (1993 to 1994) from London. She is an investor and adviser to a number of listed and unlisted companies, including Concateno Plc; a Director of Myratech.net plc and Computer Software Group; a Non-Executive Director and Member of Remuneration Committee of Mediasurface Plc; a Non-Executive Chairman, Member of Audit Committee and a Member of Remuneration Committee at Leeds Group Plc.

Vin joined Kewill Systems, the logistics software supplier, after university. Within a year of joining, at the age of 23, she was parachuted in to turn round newly bought Triffid Software and became Chief Operating Officer for European enterprise resource planning and e-commerce operations. The pattern she established in the early days at Kewill, acquiring companies and turning them round, has been repeated through her career. 'That was the start of the cycle', she says. 'I couldn't believe that anyone would put this much into me. Every year I rolled over to a different company'. As it was in logistics, Kewill was eventually converted to e-commerce stock and became caught up in the Internet bubble. However, Vin could sense that the bubble was now about to burst. She recalls a presentation that Kewill gave to the City at Deutsche Bank in March 2000: 'This room was heaving. People were talking about the price rocketing from £44 to £80. I remember thinking this was the same business I was in a year ago – and it hadn't changed'. She left the presentation, picked up the phone and sold all her stock. 'It was just that gut feel saying there is something not right here.'

Vin joined Elderstreet Investments Limited in 2002 to further support the firm's software application practice, with a focus on driving further investments where an understanding of the underlying operational business, market sector and financial issues was a tipping point between success and failure. She won admirers when she tore through the software industry at the helm of Computer Software Group (CSG). In the space of four-and-a-half years she acquired 16 businesses, led a £91 million management buyout backed by HG Capital and then rolled the business together with another and sold it on to Hellman and Friedman, the private equity group, for £500 million. Now she is at it again. Advanced Computer Software (ACS) does not have a name to set pulses racing, but with Murria as Chief Executive its potential has already caused a stir. After pulling together legal software providers at CSG, she raised £43 million for ACS in May 2010 with the intention of amassing software firms that supply the health service.

She gets up at 6 a.m. at her Surrey home, has a cup of tea and takes the train to London. 'I am buzzing from the minute I start. I am the only person on the train who smiles and talks', she says. Vin arrives at the Holborn office of Elderstreet by 8 a.m. 'Half my time is spent talking to the management teams and the rest is looking at acquisitions and where we should be going next'. Three times a week she is out with new businesses or investors and meets up to eight prospective acquisitions a month. 'You have got to keep yourself out there', she says. She rarely bothers with lunch and most nights she is home by 8 p.m.

Vin spends a lot of time with her husband, a university lecturer, and 14-year-old son, who wants to shadow his mother at work during the summer. 'He is brighter than me. I don't know where he gets it from.' She also has her own personal goals. After climbing Mount Kilimanjaro in 2008, she undertook a 60-mile trek across the Namibian desert in 2010 for the Fredericks Foundation. 'I don't know why I'm doing it. I must be mad.' She walks, cycles, runs and climbs to unwind, training with a former world champion pole vaulter on Saturday mornings. Vin also finds time to support the PS Foundation, which pays for the education of children in Amritsar and Delhi, the cities her family trace their roots back to. She founded the charity when a year off between jobs took her back there, 'You always end up back in the same community. My mother showed me where I was born, and I have to tell you that even now it is a mud hut. I looked round and realized there were kids who didn't have a hope in hell of getting an education. That could so easily have been me. Yet how do you change it? In India, if you educate a child, you save the family. It is really as basic as that.' She takes only a £15 000 nominal salary as ACS Chief Executive. The amount saved by the company in not paying her a full rate is paid to her charity and a slug of her £13 million stake in the business has also been pledged to the charity: she does not ask anyone else to contribute to the charity. 'I could not sit there and shake a tin. My bottom line is: this is what I want to do, it makes me feel fantastic and I am prepared to put my money behind it.'

In her career Vin has picked up plenty of advice – some of it about why she would fail. 'Someone said, "You are Asian, you are female and you are young". Well, I've managed to fix one of those things', the 46-year-old says. With such an impressive career and commitment to her roots she seems to have fixed a great deal more than just the age problem. Vin has successfully overcome any barriers she has faced and in recognition of her many achievements Vinodka Murria was awarded Asian Businesswoman of the Year in 2010.[2]

BOX 5.2 OZWALD BOATENG – FASHION DESIGNER

Ozwald was born in 1968, in London. His parents were originally from Ghana, and came to London in the 1950s. The family, which included his two older siblings, lived in the Muswell Hill area of North London, but his parents divorced when he was eight. In Ghana his mother had worked in the fabric business, and took in custom work as a seamstress in England. Ozwald recalled that as a five-year-old, his mother made him a purple mohair suit that quickly became his favourite outfit. His father, once headmaster of a school in Ghana, was a strict but not authoritarian parent. He once remarked in an interview with Celia Walden for the *Mail on Sunday* that 'On occasion, he would let us bend the rules. His good guidance meant that we never felt the need to break them'. He added, 'There is a unique formality bound up with Ghanaian tradition which I often think led me to what I do now'.

At the age of 16, he began dating a girl he met at a London technical college, where he was studying computer science at the time. 'She was incredibly artistic, she could paint, sculpt, design clothes, everything', he told John Walsh in another interview published in *The Independent*. 'She was doing this college fashion show, and asked me to help. I said, "I can't make clothes", but she showed me and for some reason it was easy'. He soon began making clothes for himself. 'There were always sewing machines around the house although I never went near them', he told Walsh, recalling his childhood. He was surprised by the reaction his self-made gear elicited. 'What stunned me was, when I wore them, people actually wanted to buy them'.

Soon Boateng had switched the focus of his studies to fashion design at Southgate College, and he began working out of a studio in London's East End selling his wares. He found the programme at

Southgate difficult at times. 'There was a conflict because it was very difficult being told what a product should be, as in my mind I was already doing it. I was asked to do things that I wasn't inspired by. Why create if you're not inspired to?' he recalled in an interview with Sam Phillips for *The Independent*. By the time he was 18, Boateng's clothes were selling at stores in the King's Road section of Chelsea, and in 1993 he opened a store on another trendy street, Portobello Road. He found his true calling, however, when he began haunting the austere but pricey tailor shops of London's Savile Row.

Ozwald saw himself as more than a tailor or designer, so he coined the term 'bespoke couturier' and switched the focus of his business to making custom suits for men. He made history as a tailor-turned-designer, showing his first line at the international menswear collections in Paris and attracted notice when he became one of the first-ever British tailors to stage a fashion show. 'Everybody said I was crazy', he told Phillips, referring to the 1994 London show. The publicity helped him find a backer for a ready-to-wear line and to open a more formal retail venture, a store just off the famed Savile Row, on Vigo Street, in 1995. Soon his ready-to-wear line was selling at Saks Fifth Avenue and Barneys New York in the United States.

The bright hues of Boateng's well-cut suits, shirts and other formal items earned him a devoted following, and his suits were worn by celebrities such as Mick Jagger, Seal, Herbie Hancock, Jamie Foxx, Laurence Fishburne, David Bowie, Jude Law, Will Smith, Keanu Reeves and Robbie Williams. They were also worn by actors in the films *Tomorrow Never Dies* and *Lock, Stock and Two Smoking Barrels*. Between 1996 and 1997, sales soared 150 per cent worldwide.

In early 1998, however, a looming financial crisis in Asia caused two large orders from Hong Kong and Japan to be cancelled, and Boateng lost his backer. His ready-to-wear business went into receivership in the spring of 1998, but he saved it by entering into a deal with British department store chain Debenhams to design a moderately priced line of men's clothing. 'It was mind-blowing for me that my bad news would generate so much media', he told Phillips in *The Independent*. 'The media were very sad but also very positive about my creativity. ... It was good to see how many people I'd touched with my work. That was a really tough scenario, but the media gave me the ability to overcome the situation.'

In 1999 he suffered another setback when his entire collection was stolen, and in 2001 found himself in an unusual battle with US rapper and actor Sean 'P. Diddy' Combs over scheduling concerns at the New York spring menswear collection shows. His Bryant Park event was scheduled for 7 p.m., while Combs's 'Sean Jean' line was going to be shown at 8 p.m. Combs's representatives, however, overwhelmed by the media attention surrounding the rap mogul, asked that all invitees be seated by 7 p.m. – which meant that many important buyers and tastemakers would miss Boateng's collection as they ended up being locked outside the show hall. Representatives from both sides met, and peace was made.

Despite his flamboyant wares, Boateng has remained an accepted presence among the more staid Savile Row tailors. When his store opened, many brought him welcome gifts. 'I think they respect what I've done. I've brought an enormous amount of public awareness to the street, and they respect my style. On the Row, they don't say, "Oh, there's that wacky guy from down the road". They say, "I see, that's nice, he's done that".'

In June 2006, the Sundance Channel began airing a reality television series called *House of Boateng*, which follows Boateng's efforts to launch his bespoke couture line in the United States. He was also named one of the 100 Great Black Britons by *The Voice* newspaper and the Greater London Authority, and received the Order of the British Empire in the 2006 Queen's New Year's Honours.[3]

ETHNIC MINORITY ENTREPRENEURS: SUMMARY

The experiences of ethnic minority entrepreneurs are complex and are influenced by a range of factors including cultural, religious and community factors. However, it is clear that these factors differ significantly between ethnic groups and influence attitudes towards entrepreneurship, the sectors in which entrepreneurs work and their interactions with ethnic communities and mainstream businesses. It must also be acknowledged that ethnic minority entrepreneurs frequently have different issues than those encountered by non-minority entrepreneurs. For example, existing British government business support services have failed to cater for the needs of ethnic minority entrepreneurs (National Panel of Employment,

2005). According to this review (which is the latest available), it appears that even though the government had spent over £1.8 billion on business advice services, it had treated ethnic minority entrepreneurs as a homogeneous group and failed to take account of their different and diverse needs.

It is clear that ethnic minority entrepreneurs do encounter varying degrees of discrimination, particularly in relation to accessing business finance, compared to non-ethnic minority entrepreneurs. However, it is women ethnic minority entrepreneurs who are the most disadvantaged and who face the greatest social, cultural and personal barriers in business ownership, facing the double negative of gender and ethnicity: these variables interact to produce varying impacts and issues. Women ethnic minority entrepreneurs may share similar issues of prejudice and discrimination as men but they do not necessarily experience those issues in the same way. It is important to note that the interface between gender and racial discrimination is not a clear one and may vary across situations (Omar et al., 2007) and there are some instances when racial discrimination will be the dominant factor and others where gender will be the key factor.

ETHNIC MINORITY ENTREPRENEURS: THE FUTURE

According to Smallbone et al. (2005), cultural diversity offered by ethnic and immigrant populations can be seen as providing a rich competitive advantage through the mechanism of 'the positive relationships between diversity, creativity and innovation' (p. 51). This combination of factors and skills can contribute to highly successful entrepreneurial ventures. Furthermore, the position of ethnic minority entrepreneurs has been constantly changing over the last few decades, with increasing numbers and sizes of ethnic-owned businesses. There has also been a move away from businesses that only supply niche products to local ethnic communities, with businesses targeting much more mainstream markets. This is due in part to the sheer numbers of ethnic minority entrepreneurs but also to culture shifts within ethnic groups. Compared to their immigrant fore-fathers, second- and third-generation ethnic minority entrepreneurs are not constrained to the same degree by the same religious and cultural barriers as their parents, a situation that is likely to continue as future generations move even further away from their cultural ties and become more integrated into mainstream society. Therefore, future generations of ethnic minority entrepreneurs are likely to be even more prolific and successful than their predecessors, entering more and more diverse sectors and markets. For most countries, ethnic minority entrepreneurship is becoming a key factor in their economic success and one that needs to be nurtured and encouraged if the potential of their contribution is to be realized.

In addition, future research can add to this understanding in several key areas. One fruitful area seems to be an exploration of whether an ethnic minority business venture that has successfully negotiated the start-up phase actually prohibits other members of the family from developing their own human capital – which would allow them to move toward setting up their own business ventures (Sequeira and Rasheed, 2004). Furthermore, certain questions arise from the research into the second or third generation of the initial 'immigrant' family. As educational qualifications and language proficiency will not be the impediments that they may have been for the first-generation immigrants to the host country, one needs to question whether the younger ethnic minority generations will be required to participate in the established business of their parents, or grandparents, or will they be free of this expectation and have the ability to compete on their own merits to achieve their own entrepreneurial venture? Possibly, there may be flexibility in allowing the younger generation to set up links in the greater community, thus allowing an expansion beyond the immigrant enclave that may have previously been impossible (ibid.).

NOTES

1. Plc is a limited liability company that sells shares to the public in the United Kingdom.
2. Sources: adapted from the following: interview with James Ashton, 'My prescription for the NHS', available at: http://business.timesonline.co.uk/tol/business/industry_sectors/health/article6690050.ece; both accessed 13 August 2011.
3. Sources: adapted from the following: a report by Carol Brennan 'Boateng, Ozwald 1968', *Contemporary Black Biography*, **28**, March 2011 from Encyclopedia.com, available at: http://www.encyclopedia.com/doc/1G2-2873700012.html; last accessed 13 August 2011.

REFERENCES

Bank of England (1999), *The Financing of Ethnic Minority Firms*, London: Bank of England.
Barclays Bank (2005), *Black and Minority Ethnic Business Owners: A Market Research Perspective*, London: Barclays SME Research Team.
Basu, A. (1998), 'An exploration of entrepreneurial activity among Asian small businesses in Britain', *Small Business Economics*, **10** (4), 313–26.
Basu, A. and A. Goswami (1999), 'South Asian entrepreneurs in Great Britain: factors influencing growth', *International Journal of Entrepreneurial Behaviour and Research*, **5** (5), 251–75.
Bates, T. (2006), 'The urban development potential of black-owned businesses', *Journal of the American Planning Association*, **72** (2), 272–91.

Bates, T. and W. Badford (2007), 'Traits and performance of the minority venture-capital industry', *The Annals of the American Academy of Political and Social Science*, **613**, 95–107.

Bates, T., W.E. Jackson III and J.H. Johnson Jr (2006), 'Advancing research on minority entrepreneurs', *The Annals of the American Academy of Political and Social Science*, **613**, 10–17.

Bell, E.L. (1990), 'The bicultural life experience of career-oriented black women', *Journal of Organisational Behavior*, **11** (6), 459–78.

Bogan, V. and W. Darity Jr (2008), 'Culture and entrepreneurship? African American and immigrant self-employment in the United States', *The Journal of Socio-Economics*, **37** (5), 1999–2019.

Boyd, R. (1990), 'Black and Asian self-employment in large metropolitan areas: a comparative analysis', *Social Problems*, **37** (2), 258–74.

Carter, S., S. Anderson and E. Shaw (2001), *Women's Business Ownership: A Review of the Academic, Popular and Internet Literature*, London: Small Business Service.

Clark, K. and S. Drinkwater (2000), 'Pushed out or pulled in? Self-employment among ethnic minorities in England and Wales', *Labour Economics*, **7** (5), 603–28.

Curran, J. and R. Blackburn (1993), *Ethnic Enterprise and the High Street Bank*, Kingston-upon-Thames, UK: Kingston Business School.

Dana, L.-P. (2007) (ed.), *Handbook on Ethnic Minority Entrepreneurs*, Cheltenham, UK and Northampton, MA, USA: Edward Elgar.

Davidson, M.J. (1997), *The Black and Ethnic Minority Woman Manager: Cracking the Concrete Ceiling*, London: Paul Chapman.

Dawe, A.J. and S.L. Fielden (2005), 'The experiences of Asian women entering business start-ups in the UK', in S.L. Fielden and M.J. Davidson (eds), *International Handbook of Women and Small Business Entrepreneurship*, Cheltenham, UK and Northampton, MA, USA: Edward Elgar, pp. 120–32.

Department of Trade and Industry (2007), 'New ethnic minority business taskforce launched by DTI', available at: http://www.ethnicnow.com/channels/government-politics/press-release/14/1255/new-ethnic-minority-business-task-force-launched-by-dti.html; accessed 10 August 2011.

Dhaliwall, S. (2000), 'Asian female entrepreneurs and women in business – an exploratory study', *Enterprise and Innovation Management Studies*, **1** (2), 207–16.

Ekanem, I. and P. Wyer (2007), 'A fresh start and the learning experiences of ethnic minority entrepreneurs', *International Journal of Consumer Studies*, **31** (2), 144–51.

Ethnic Minority Business Forum (EMBF) (2001), *Annual Report 2000–2001*, London: EMBF.

Ethnic Minority Business Forum (EMBF) (2005), *EMBF: The Way Forward 2005–2008*, London: EMBF.

Fadahunsi, A., D. Smallbone and S. Supri (2000), 'Networking and ethnic minority enterprise development: insights from a North London study', *Journal of Small Business and Enterprise Development*, **7** (3), 28–40.

Fairlie, R.W. (2004), 'Recent trends in ethnic and racial business ownership', *Small Business Economics*, **23** (3), 203–18.

Fielden, S.L. and M.J. Davidson (eds) (2005), *International Handbook of Women and Small Business Entrepreneurship*, Cheltenham, UK and Northampton, MA, USA: Edward Elgar.

Fielden, S.L. and M.J. Davidson (eds) (2010), *International Research Handbook on Successful Women Entrepreneurs*, Cheltenham, UK and Northampton, MA, USA.

Fielden, S.L., M.J. Davidson, A.J. Dawe and P.J. Makin (2003), 'Factors inhibiting the economic growth of female-owned small businesses in North West England', *Journal of Small Business and Enterprise Development*, **10** (2), 151–66.

Global Entrepreneurship Monitor (GEM) (2005), *UK Executive Report*, available at: http://www.gemconsortium.org/download/1313749712121/GEM_2005_Report.pdf; accessed 20 August 2011.

Greene, P., C. Brush and T. Brown (1997), 'Resource configurations in new ventures: relationships to owner and company characteristics', *Journal of Small Business Strategy*, **8** (2), 25–40.

Henley, A. (2007), 'Entrepreneurial aspirations and transition into self-employment: evidence from British longitudinal data', *Entrepreneurship and Regional Development*, **19** (3), 253–80.

Inman, K. and L.M. Grant (2005), 'African American women and small business start-up: backgrounds, goals and strategies used by African American women in the initialization and operation of small businesses', in S.L. Fielden and M.J. Davidson (eds), *International Handbook of Women and Small Business Entrepreneurship*, Cheltenham, UK and Northampton, MA, USA: Edward Elgar, pp. 105–19.

Jacoby, T. (2000), 'Second-generation question mark', *American Enterprise*, **11** (8), 32–6.

Kloosterman, R.C., J.P. van der Leun and J. Rath (1999), 'Mixed embeddedness, migrant entrepreneurship and informal economic activities', *International Journal of Urban and Regional Research*, **32** (2), 253–67.

Kon, Y. and D.J. Storey (2003), 'A theory of discouraged borrowers', *Small Business Economics*, **21** (1), 37–49.

Levent, T.B., E. Masurel and P. Nijkamp (2003), 'Diversity in entrepreneurship: ethnic and female roles in urban economic life', available at *Social Science Research Network Electronic Paper Collection*, http://papers.ssrn.com/sol3/results.cfm; accessed 30 April 2011.

London Development Agency (2004), *London Business Survey 2004*, London: LDA.

McEvoy, D. and K. Hafeez (2006), 'The changing face of ethnic minority entrepreneurship in Britain', paper presented at the 4th Interdisciplinary European Conference on Entrepreneurship Research, University of Regensburg, 22–24 February.

Metcalf, H., T. Modood and S. Virdee (1996), *Asian Self-employment: The Interaction of Culture and Economics in England*, London: Policy Studies Institute.

Mingeone, E. (1999), 'Introduction: immigrants and the informal economy in European cities', *International Journal of Urban and Regional Research*, **23** (2), 109–11.

Mitter, S. (1986), 'Industrial restructuring and manufacturing homework', *Capital and Class*, **27** (9), 37–80.

Mulholland, K. (1997), 'The family enterprise and business strategies', *Work, Employment and Society*, **11** (4), 685–711.

National Panel of Employment (2005), 'The employment, self-employment and business growth of ethnic and faith minority groups', available at: http://www.dwp.gov.uk/publications/publications-archive/national-employment-panel/#e; accessed 30 April 2011.

Office for National Statistics (2004), *Annual Local Area Labour Force Survey*, available at: www.statistics.gov.uk; accessed 30 April 2011.

Omar, A. and M.J. Davidson (2001), 'Women in management: a comparative cross-cultural overview', *Cross Cultural Management: An International Journal*, **8** (3/4), 35–67.

Omar, A., M.J. Davidson and S.L. Fielden (2007), *Black and Minority Ethnic (BME) Small Business Owners: A Comparative Study Investigating the Problems, Experiences and Barriers faced by BME Female and Male Entrepreneurs in North West England*, Report for Centre for Equality and Diversity at Work, available at http://www.train2000.org.uk/research-reports/pdfs/BME-report.pdf; accessed 14 August 2011.

Owen, D. (1995), *Ethnic Minority Women and Employment*, Manchester: Equal Opportunities Commission.

Phizacklea, A. (1990), *Unpacking the Fashion Industry*, London: Routledge.

Rafiq, M. (1992), 'Ethnicity and enterprise: a comparison of Muslim and non-Muslim-owned Asian businesses in Britain', *New Community*, **19** (1), 43–60.

Raghuram, P. and A. Strange (2001), 'Studying economic institutions, placing cultural politics: methodological musings from a study of ethnic minority enterprise', *Geoforum*, **32** (3), 377–88.

Ram, M. (1994), *Managing to Survive: Working Lives in Small Firms*, Oxford: Blackwell.

Ram, M. (2003), 'Paving professional futures', *International Small Business Journal*, **21** (1), 55–69.

Ram, M. and T. Jones (1998), *Ethnic Minorities in Business*, Milton Keynes: Small Business Research Trust Report.

Ram, M. and D. Smallbone (2001), *Ethnic Minority Enterprise: Policy in Practice*, London: Small Business Service.

Ram, M. and D. Smallbone (2003), 'Policies to support ethnic minority enterprise: the English experience', *Entrepreneurship and Regional Development*, **15** (2), 151–66.

Ram, M., G. Barrett and T. Jones (2000), 'Ethnicity and enterprise', in S. Carter and D. Jones-Evans (eds), *Enterprise and Small Business Principles, Practice and Policy*, Harlow, Essex: Pearson Education Ltd, pp. 192–208.

Ram, M., T. Abbas, B. Sanghera, G. Barlow and T. Jones (2001), 'Making the link: households and small business activity in a multi-ethnic context', *Community, Work and Family*, **4** (3), 327–48.

Rana, B., C. Kagan, S. Lewis and U. Rout (1998), 'British South Asian managers and professionals: experiences of work and the family', *Women in Management Review*, **13** (6), 221–32.

Rusinovic, K. (2008), 'Moving between markets? Immigrant entrepreneurs in different markets', *International Journal of Entrepreneurial Behaviour and Research*, **14** (6), 440–54.

Scott, J.M. and D. Irwin (2009), 'Discouraged advisees? The influence of gender, ethnicity and education in the use of advice and finance by UK SMEs', *Environment and Planning C: Government Policy*, **27** (2), 230–45.

Sequeira, J.M. and A.A. Rasheed (2004), 'The role of social and human capital in the start-up and growth of immigrant businesses', *Ethnic Entrepreneurship: Structure and Process (International Research in the Business Disciplines)*, **4**, 77–94.

Small Business Service (2002), *SBS Household Survey of Entrepreneurship*, Shef-
field: Small Business Service.
Smallbone, D., M. Bertotti and I. Ekanem (2005), 'Diversification in ethnic minor-
ity business: the case of Asians in London's creative industries', *Journal of Small
Business and Enterprise Development*, **12** (1), 41–56.
Smallbone, D., J. Kitching and R. Athayde (2007), 'Ethnic diversity, entrepreneur-
ship and competitiveness in a global city', paper presented at the ICEEM
International Colloquium, The University of Bradford School of Management,
Bradford, 22–23 March.
Smith-Hunter, A.E. and R.L. Boyd (2004), 'Applying theories of entrepreneurship
to a comparative analysis of white and minority women business owners',
Women in Management Review, **19** (1), 18–28.
Srinivasan, S. (1995), *The South Asian Petite Bourgeoisie, An Oxford Case Study*,
Aldershot: Avebury.
Van Delft, H., C. Gorter and P. Nijkamp (2000), 'In search of ethnic entrepreneur-
ship opportunities in the city: a comparative policy study', *Environment and
Planning C: Government and Policy*, **18** (4), 429–50.
Werbner, P. (1998), 'Taking and giving: working women and female bonds in a
Pakistani immigrant neighbourhood', in S. Westwood and P. Bhachu (eds),
Enterprising Women, Ethnicity, Economy and Gender Relations, London: Rout-
ledge, pp. 145–62.

6.   Immigrant entrepreneurs

[A] pattern of skilled immigrants leading innovation and creating jobs and wealth, has become a nationwide phenomenon ... We estimate, based on an analysis of the World Intellectual Property Organization (WIPO) patent databases, that foreign nationals residing in the U.S. were named as inventors or co-inventors in 24.2% of international patent applications filed from the U.S. in 2006.

(Wadhwa et al., 2007, p. 4)

INTRODUCTION

An immigrant is defined as 'a person who comes to a country where they were not born in order to settle there'.[1] In the past, immigrant workers were forcibly brought into a country to fulfil various labour needs, and as such, they are not a new phenomenon. For example, since early colonization of the Asia-Pacific region, Asian workers have been utilized as indentured workers in plantations. Such forced movements of workers occurred in an era where Asian men were seen as exploitable workers who were expendable; Asian women were seen as *their* subordinates (Toro-Morn and Alicea, 2004), and this description provides a lucid picture of where immigrant males and females were placed on any existing societal ladder. More recently, there has been a huge growth in the mobility of people who choose to immigrate to seek a better life, for themselves and their families. 'Push' or 'pull' factors, such as religious or political persecution on the one hand, or on the other, perceived economic opportunities elsewhere, influence large-scale immigration to diverse countries in the world (Sequeira and Rasheed, 2004).

However, according to Pio (2007), the host country may lack the ability and 'political' will to adequately manage the range of ethnic minority immigrants from diverse countries. Minority ethnic migrants are frequently treated as 'the other', and as such, are seen as inferior secondary citizens; exclusionary practices are commonplace, effectively controlling numbers of immigrants deemed to be 'appropriate' and limiting entry of those deemed to be 'inappropriate' into a country (ibid.). There is a recognition that subtle exclusionary practices continue and therefore government initiatives and legislation are frequently aimed at reducing discrimination to immigrant groups (ibid.).

Immigrant populations are capable of contributing significantly to the economic growth of the host country through entrepreneurial activities. This is exemplified by UK data that highlighted that immigrants from Commonwealth countries 'have created the most companies proportionately of any immigrant group in Europe. More immigrants work for themselves than for others in Britain' (Echikson et al., 2000, p. 3). This is a telling statistic, and could explain why many governments are keen to continue the flow of immigrants to their countries.

Immigrant entrepreneurship provides a mechanism to integrate immigrants into the mainstream of the host society, and it is often perceived as a comfortable form of socioeconomic self-help. In many countries, entrepreneurship has been seen as an economic solution to alleviate the high numbers of unemployed immigrants after initial entry into the host country (Rath and Kloosterman, 2000). Certainly, there is a recognition that a reduction of welfare dependence can occur through self-employment, as well as an increased equality that can be achieved for minority populations through entrepreneurial ventures (e.g., Shinnar and Young, 2008). Fascinatingly, an immigrant does not need to become assimilated into a country in order to be a successful entrepreneur. According to early research, economic success for the immigrant entrepreneur does not necessarily entail an acculturation into the host country, as many businesses may start up by catering for established ethnic clientele in the first instance. It is only at a later stage that the immigrant entrepreneur may consider expanding into the mainstream market place (Dallalfar,1994).

Despite the harsh reality that many immigrants face when taking up residence in a host country, the numbers of immigrants continue to swell the populations of host nations. New Zealand offers a useful illustration of how the demographics of a country can be changed significantly when numbers of immigrants from various countries take up residence in a host country. In 2007, the population of New Zealand was estimated to be approximately 4 000 000, with 67.6 per cent making up the New Zealand European population (*Pākehā*)[2]; 14.6 per cent being Indigenous Maori, 9.2 per cent being of Asian origin (Indian and Chinese predominantly) and 6.9 per cent originating from the Pacific islands (Pio, 2007). In the UK, London, one of the most culturally diverse cities in the world, offers an interesting case study because of the proportions of immigrants who have taken up residence there. In 2005, more than 29 per cent of the population in London was described as ethnic minority, and 9 per cent of this group were classified as Asian. Indian immigrants made up 5.6 per cent of this cohort, followed by people from other Asian countries, Bangladesh and Pakistan (Smallbone et al., 2005).

The United States has long been a magnet for immigrants from around the world and there is a deeply entrenched philosophy that 'Immigrant entrepreneurship is a way of "making it" in America' (Bonacich, 1987, p. 446). There is wide acceptance that 'Self-employment is a vital facet of the United States economy' (Bogan and Darity, 2008, p. 1999), and that significant political clout is held by small business owners (Bogan and Darity, 2008). Estimates of the immigrant population in the US vary widely; one estimate is a figure of over 30 million, which would equate to approximately 11 per cent of the population overall (Sequeira and Rasheed, 2004). Another estimate places the figure much higher at nearly 60 million, which is approaching one-fifth of the overall population (Jacoby, 2000). Obviously, it is difficult to obtain exact figures when the legal status of the immigrant may be unclear. This is an important consideration; once legal status has been obtained, this will have a direct effect on the ability of the immigrant to generate wealth (Echikson et al., 2000).

Recently, there has been a recognition of the importance of the role of the immigrant entrepreneur in the United States. In their report entitled *America's New Immigrant Entrepreneurs* Wadhwa et al. (2007) concluded that 'a pattern of skilled immigrants leading innovation and creating jobs and wealth has become a nationwide phenomenon' (p. 4). A growing proportion of immigrants to the US are taking key roles in entrepreneurial ventures, such as companies in the Silicon Valley where 24 per cent of the technology businesses over a 20-year period were run by Chinese and Indian engineers (Wadhwa et al., 2007). These authors presented the following statistics to illustrate the significant role played by immigrant entrepreneurship in the field of engineering and technology in the US between 1995 and 2005:

- Nationwide, $52 billion in sales was generated by these immigrant-founded companies; 450 000 workers were employed in 2005.
- The industry fields of software and innovation/manufacturing-related services account for 80 per cent of immigrant-founded companies in the US.
- Twenty-five per cent had at least one foreign-born key founder.
- Twenty-six per cent of all immigrant-founded companies have Indian founders.
- In California and New Jersey more than a third of companies have been founded by immigrants (39 per cent and 38 per cent respectively).

- Immigrants from Cuba, Brazil, Columbia, Venezuela and Guatemala set up 35 per cent of the companies in Florida.
- In New Jersey, 47 per cent of all immigrant-founded businesses were set up by Indian immigrants (Wadhwa et al., 2007, p. 4).

Previous research has tended to utilize perspectives drawn from the fields of sociology, anthropology and economic geographers (Rath and Klooster-man, 2000). There has also been a prime focus on the ethnocultural characteristics of the immigrant entrepreneur (ibid.), particularly examining the way certain groups of immigrants appear to be more entrepreneurial than others (Kloosterman and Rath, 2001). For example, early research into Korean immigrants in the US found that over one-third of adult Korean immigrants were small business owners and/or managers at that time (Kim and Hurh, 1985). Chinese and Turkish immigrants are also believed to show a particular proclivity for entrepreneurial business ventures (Rath and Kloosterman, 2000). In addition, some studies report that more immigrants become self-employed than do native-born citizens, with some ethnic groups such as Bulgarian, Israeli and Korean immigrants to the US outstripping the local residents by more than 50 per cent (e.g., Lunn and Steen, 2000). Clearly, some ethnic immigrant groups appear to be more successful than others in taking up entrepreneurial ventures.

The self-employment of Asian immigrants is reported to be above that of whites born in the US as well as non-whites, and had even surpassed the self-employment rates of white immigrants to the US in 2008 (Bogan and Darity, 2008). Chinese, Indian and Korean second-generation immigrants are reported to be highly successful in entrepreneurial ventures in the US (Jacoby, 2000), with Korean immigrants having recently been reported to be 'entrepreneurially superior' as they have the highest proportion of self-employment, followed by Israelis and Palestinians (Bogan and Darity, 2008, p. 2008). Furthermore, when Asian immigrants become engaged in an entrepreneurial venture, there appears to be a tendency for self-employed African American 'natives' to be displaced (Fairlie and Meyer, 2003).

While the US has been a magnet for immigrant populations for several hundred years, in recent decades, European countries have been allowing immigrants to take up residence, and self-employed immigrants are also dramatically increasing in numbers in these countries. For example, in the Netherlands, 3.3 per cent of self-employed entrepreneurs were immigrants in 1987, with a sharp increase in this number ten years later to 7.4 per cent (Rath and Kloosterman, 2000). Dramatic increases in the numbers of immigrants over the past four decades have been observed and in the largest four cities in the Netherlands the population is made up of almost 40 per cent immigrants (Rusinovic, 2008). The proportions of immigrants classi-fied as 'non-Western' who had become entrepreneurs had increased sharply over the three-year period from 1999 to 2002 (an increase of 31.5 per cent) (ibid.). In contrast, the number of native Dutch-born entrepreneurs increased by only 3.2 per cent (ibid.).

Two of the early theoretical frameworks that have been useful in further-ing understanding of immigrant entrepreneurs are the 'disadvantage theory' and the 'cultural theory of entrepreneurship' (Kim and Hurh, 1985). The 'disadvantage theory' encapsulates the perspective that many immigrants may be disadvantaged by inadequate language skills, educa-tional qualifications, unemployment or discrimination experienced from the host country, and therefore these factors encourage self-employment (ibid.). On the other hand, the 'culture theory' puts forward the proposition that some groups of immigrants may have the propensity to engage in entrepreneurial business ventures because of their cultural and ethnic background (ibid.). In both theoretical perspectives, the entrepreneurial activity is seen as a collective enterprise, rather than an individualistic venture (ibid.). An examination of the characteristics of the immigrant entrepreneur can serve to further a deeper understanding of the important phenomenon of immigrant entrepreneurship.

IMMIGRANT ENTREPRENEURS: GENERAL CHARACTERISTICS

While there is a recognition that immigrants may become successful in business through utilizing the established ethnic resources already existing in a host country, individual characteristics are also considered to be important in either pushing or pulling people into considering a business venture of their own. For example, most immigrant business owners are married (Shinnar and Young, 2008), and this is seen as a facilitator of a successful business venture. The resource of having family members to perform as reliable and trustworthy (often unpaid) workers (Kim and Hurh, 1985; Bonacich, 1987) may be instrumental in a successful start-up phase of the business. According to Rath and Kloosterman (2000), the majority of immigrant entrepreneurs are located in the retail, wholesale and restaurant sectors, where barriers to entry are relatively small.

In the past, immigrant entrepreneurs were seen as people who lacked educational qualifications and financial resources. Many early migrants fitted this description and looked for lower-status positions, such as unskilled labouring. Currently, education, gender and age are considered to be very important factors in an individual immigrant entering self-employment (Shinnar and Young, 2008). In reality, immigrants may be well educated and highly employable; for example, they may be employed as technically qualified and experienced workers, or as managers with prior experience in senior positions. Indeed, the highly skilled immigrant has created an awareness that a completely different immigrant entrepreneur is increasingly seen, particularly in countries with advanced economies. Some immigrants arrive in the host country with proficiency in English, independent financial capital and impressive educational qualifications (Jacoby, 2000). In fact, the high proportion (60 per cent) of Indian immigrants to the US who hold a four-year college qualification is much higher than the figure for native-born Americans (25 per cent) (ibid.). Therefore, there are increasing numbers of very highly skilled immigrant entrepreneurs coming out of countries that are less developed and with emerging economies (Kloosterman and Rath, 2001). As mentioned previously, both China and India provide Silicon Valley with highly specialized workforces who have become very important in software development and so on. Such growth in suitably qualified immigrant entrepreneurs is likely to continue, and to become a significant source of highly skilled labour (ibid.).

For decades it has been recognized that education is strongly correlated with successful immigrant entrepreneurship (e.g., De Freitas, 1991). Having a higher educational qualification makes it more likely that immigrants will become self-employed, particularly if those qualifications are received in the host country. This allows easier access to the mainstream job market – research by Olson et al. (2000) illustrates this phenomenon clearly. These authors reported that Hispanic immigrant entrepreneurs were more likely to have an undergraduate degree or higher when compared with Hispanic employees in the US workforce as a whole. Furthermore, Asian and African American entrepreneurs were more likely to have held a graduate degree when they began their business ventures when compared with the national US working population (Bergman, 2005). In terms of age, early research has established that older immigrants are more likely to take up a business venture, compared to younger people. This may have to do with the skills and abilities accumulated over time in previous employment, and also the capacity to access finance (De Freitas, 1991).

An early investigation on a specific population of immigrants provides an opportunity to test out the generalizability of these research findings. In an early study, Kim and Hurh (1985) reported on the characteristics of their sample of 100 Korean immigrants in Chicago, who had started their own business ventures on average 2.7 years after arriving in the US. Most of the group were male (89.4 per cent), with females making up 10.6 per cent of the sample. The average age of respondents was 39.8 years, with a range between 21 and 50. The majority of the respondents were married (90.4 per cent), with most of this group having young children (92.9 per cent). On average, this group of immigrants had been in the US for just over eight years, and had been in their own business on average for 5.4 years, working approximately 58.1 hours per week. This group often employed other Korean immigrant workers; sometimes this was seen as a 'win–win' situation, but on other occasions, was seen as problematic because of the poor pay and long hours offered to employees (ibid.).

Small business ventures for this group were a direct result of the perceived limited employment opportunities in the host country. Of interest was the fact that more than half of the participants in the study had reported completing their education to college level *prior to their emigration* (ibid.). The importance of family was emphasized by almost three-quarters of the respondents who relied on family savings for the initial capital for their entrepreneurial venture. This group of Korean entrepreneurs continued to maintain close ethnic and social ties with their families and relatives in Chicago (ibid.). Furthermore, the working wives of the male small business owners were believed to play significant roles in the operation of the business venture through their managerial support and their unpaid labour (ibid.). Therefore, the immigrant entrepreneur in the US at this time was likely to be male, married with children, and be close to 40 years of age. These individual characteristics are considered to act as conducive 'pull' factors for immigrants contemplating self-employment (Shinnar and Young, 2008).

IMMIGRANT ENTREPRENEURS: ASPIRATIONS AND MOTIVATIONS

There are many motivators for the immigrant entrepreneur who decides to start up their own business. Many nascent entrepreneurs hold the view that positive outcomes will derive from the business venture, which they often see as the best option available to them because of the few opportunities they perceive in the mainstream business world (Shinnar and Young, 2008).

Both 'pull' and 'push' factors have been examined in an attempt to understand the motivations of those who consider starting up their own business. As outlined in Chapter 1, 'pull' factors refer to the element of choice and the potentially positive outcomes of self-employment, whereas 'push' factors are seen as offering an explanation for those who become self-employed because there are no other perceived options (ibid.). This latter perspective is often considered to be very relevant for immigrants, particularly on initially taking up residence in a new country. Push factors have been mentioned as a significant motivator by 40 per cent of the sample in one study into Hispanic immigrant entrepreneurs in Las Vegas (ibid.).

However, 'pull' factors are also evident in motivating immigrant groups to consider self-employment through perceived higher income possibilities. Olson et al. (2000) have reported that Hispanic immigrants in the US who become self-employed earned 33 per cent more than other Hispanic immigrants who remained on wages as an employee. In addition, flexibility to work around family requirements, enhanced status and upward mobility, and a chance at becoming independent were also seen as important motivators (Shinnar and Young, 2008). Certainly, high proportions of Korean business owners in the US have reported that they were motivated to start up a business venture in an attempt to offset the barriers they experienced to access other occupations (Bogan and Darity, 2008).

Additionally, one of the specific pull factors for immigrant entrepreneurs is the ethnic enclave where they may reside (Shinnar and Young, 2008). Enclaves are described as metropolitan areas where businesses operate and are owned by earlier immigrants from the same home country, or where those who are direct descendants of earlier immigrants may be concentrated. Such enclaves are often facilitators of entry into self-employment and business ownership because they provide a ready source of workers, as well as potential customers (ibid.). Ethnic enclaves are made up of firms that may be geographically close to each other, share some economic interdependence, as well as provide a source of employment for ethnic employees (Light and Karageorgis, 1994). Therefore, ethnic enclaves provide economic advantages both for the self-employed as well as for workers, and they 'function as a result of reciprocal relationships that are restricted by norms and trust' (Sequeira and Rasheed, 2004, p. 80).

In addition, the strong ties and networks that may operate in an ethnic community can become a very beneficial resource in a business start-up for the newly arrived immigrant. These ties 'can be a key determinant of successful start-up and continued business development and growth' (ibid., p. 78). For the immigrant entrepreneur, having strong ethnic connections is seen as a facilitator when contemplating setting up in business. Such connections may reduce business costs, and be a source of advice, training, supply of materials, customers and possibly investment capital (Light and Gold, 2000).

However, paradoxically, some of the benefits that can be accrued by the immigrant entrepreneur through setting up business in an ethnic market can also be seen as a barrier, especially when the potential for growth of the business is contemplated (Rusinovic, 2008). This is because an ethnic market is usually made up of many immigrant entrepreneurs who may be producing and selling similar services or products for a relatively small group of customers, who may have limited purchasing power (ibid.). Therefore, while setting up business in the ethnic market may provide initial benefits to the nascent immigrant entrepreneur, when business growth is contemplated, the same benefits can be seen in the light of a barrier to expanding into the mainstream market of the general population (Barrett et al., 2003; Rusinovic, 2008).

In general, the disadvantages often experienced by immigrant populations can act to strengthen group cohesion and heighten solidarity. This can act to create critical resources from which the immigrant entrepreneur may draw (Sequeira and Rasheed, 2004). Examples of these resources include informal credit, shared expertise and previous business knowledge as well as some degree of training (Sequeira and Rasheed, 2004). The ethnic identity of the immigrant provides a passport to access these resources, hence eliminating many of the start-up costs that would otherwise have to be negotiated. In addition, effective role models and mentors, possibly from the ethnic enclave, are considered to be an important driver and motivator for newly arrived immigrants considering owning their own businesses (Shinnar and Young, 2008).

In relation to gender, as illustrated throughout this book, previous research has reported that a greater proportion of men will be self-employed (Fielden and Davidson, 2010), and that men may have different motives for taking up a business venture compared to women. Research carried out in New Zealand (Pio, 2007) provides more insight into the motivation of female immigrant entrepreneurs. Three distinct categories of motivation were found in a comparative study of 45 Indian female entrepreneurs who were interviewed. It is noted in this sample that 17 women were ethnic Indian born in New Zealand and the remainder were immigrants who had been in New Zealand less than five years (22 women) or between five and 25 years (six women). First, one group were motivated to start a business venture in order to help them through a particular financial difficulty. Another group embraced entrepreneurship as they had an interest in working in an entrepreneurial manner. Finally, another group of women went into business because such a choice was seen as the norm in their particular castes (ibid.).

Other motivators are evident in the early research of Dallalfar (1994) in the US. Iranian immigrant women in Los Angeles were motivated by a desire to earn a living in a culturally and socially acceptable manner, such as running a small business from their home base. Such ventures were very capable of becoming highly profitable businesses, with the benefit of requiring low initial set-up costs (ibid.). For this group of entrepreneurs, such business ventures created the possibility to establish strong social networks through friendship and kinship. Interestingly, such a possibility was not seen as suitable for male Iranian immigrants. According to Dallal-far (1994), 'work settings that are located in the home either facilitate the possibility of business entry or deter such business opportunities, depending on gender' (p. 550).

One interesting perspective is that some immigrant populations hold a view that they are 'in exile', and this may well motivate them to create strong networks that will support and nurture them through the difficulties of trying to start a life in a new country. Such a perspective by immigrant groups can paradoxically create a motivator for those wishing to start up a business venture: 'We have here items that I know Iranians in exile like myself need and nostalgically long for' (ibid., p. 555).

IMMIGRANT ENTREPRENEURS: CHALLENGES AND BARRIERS

Despite the magnet of perceived economic opportunities, immigrants face unique challenges when endeavouring to enter labour markets that are established in host countries (Heilbrunn and Kushnirovich, 2008). In a general sense, the barriers and constraints experienced by immigrant entrepreneurs are often common to other small businesses, including those run by a native-born business owner (Smallbone et al., 2005). Common elements can include a lack of management expertise or professional business skills, financial constraints and the cost of suitable business premises. However, the immigrant entrepreneur may experience loss in both the human and social capital they may have accrued in their home country, as well as their network of business contacts (Shinnar and Young, 2008).

Other barriers specific to the immigrant entrepreneur may also include difficulties arising from attempting to break out of the market niche of the established ethnic cohort in an attempt to enter the mainstream market. Lack of access to appropriate business support agencies is also an impediment to business for the immigrant entrepreneur (Smallbone et al., 2005). Immigrant groups frequently report experiencing general discrimination, that education and previous training experiences are not being recognized, lower wages, minimal promotional opportunities and language barriers (Shinnar and Young, 2008). Indeed, language barriers are a particular problem for those immigrants who have not had the opportunity to learn the language of the host country prior to arrival (Rowley, 2004).

In addition, having access to the necessary resources is often difficult for immigrant entrepreneurs, although there is a recognition that 'resources shape the opportunities for immigrant businesses' (Heilbrunn and Kushnirovich, 2008, p. 694). Certainly, the inability to obtain bank loans or finance from other lending bodies is a common theme in much of the literature on immigrants wishing to become nascent entrepreneurs (e.g., Dallalfar, 1994; Weber, 2006, cited in Shinnar and Young, 2008). According to Kushnirovich (2009), this is an important hurdle for immigrant entrepreneurs, as the ability to obtain financial support is a key factor in the scope of immigrant businesses' start-up potential.

Immigrant entrepreneurs are also considered to be disadvantaged because of their lack of knowledge about business practices and legislation specific to their host country (Mitchell, 2003). At the individual level, these difficulties appear to be experienced by the majority of immigrants. Other barriers can arise through the high cost that may have to be invested to maintain social capital (Adler and Kwon, 2002). Barriers can also arise through unrealistic expectations of immigrants who hope to achieve success through the success of the business ventures of established ethnic entrepreneurs or who become totally embedded in the ethnic enclave (Sequeira and Rasheed, 2004). Of interest is the finding by Heilbrunn and Kushnirovich (2007) that immigrant entrepreneurs often have similar barriers to face as Indigenous entrepreneurs, however, immigrant entrepreneurs may find the barriers more difficult to deal with because of their perception of being outsiders in the host country. Future research exploring these dynamics could further enhance an understanding of how the immigrant entrepreneur may best achieve optimal success.

The external economic environment may also create difficulties for the entrepreneurial immigrant (Collins, 2003), and some of these difficulties can be exacerbated by discrimination, both overt and covert. Discrimination can take many forms. For example, in an organizational setting, problems can arise where employers hold a view that they are unable to incorporate certain workers into a workplace because of a question of 'fit' with other workers in their workplace. Asian Americans were reported to suffer discrimination in this way, as many were considered to be effectively excluded from higher-paying jobs, characterized by promotion opportunities and tenure of employment in early research (Yoon, 1997).

Barriers caused by subtle discriminatory practices were also reported by female Indian immigrants in New Zealand (Pio, 2007). First, because of a belief that qualifications received in another country were not as valid as those received in the host country, immigrant women considered that their competence and skills were being questioned. Second, New Zealand migrants were reported to be receiving preferential treatment if they were white and had a name that was similar to names commonly found in the host country (ibid.). According to Dunstan et al. (2004), preference continues to be given to white rather than non-white migrants to New Zealand. Therefore, barriers may be experienced by the immigrant minority group when employers appear to be reluctant to employ people who are seen as different, or 'the other' (Pio, 2007). Sequeira and Rasheed (2004) concur that discrimination does occur, reporting that immigrants can be excluded from job opportunities available to native-born citizens in the general labour market, resulting in unemployment as well as under-employment.

One of the primary barriers to immigrant entrepreneurs may well be the discrimination they experience through the erroneous stereotypical perceptions held by a majority of the native population of the country; these views revolve around unemployment and crime, both often believed to be caused by the influx of immigrants into a country (Echikson et al., 2000). It appears that discrimination is a significant barrier for many immigrants wishing to enter into entrepreneurial ventures (Smallbone et al., 2005; Shinnar and Young, 2008). The discrimination experienced by many immigrants creates significant barriers to the nascent entrepreneur, and because of experiences of this kind, Pio's (2007) New Zealand female immigrant entrepreneurs described the first two years of their new life in their adoptive country as 'hell'.

However, paradoxically, discrimination against some groups has an advantageous impact on the entrepreneurial ventures of others. For example, in the US, both overt and covert discrimination against African American people who set up their own business ventures was believed to have helped Korean immigrant entrepreneurs become established (Bogan and Darity, 2008). Ironically, some of the motivators for immigrants to become self-employed flow directly from the barriers they experience. According to Dallalfar (1994), it is the commonly experienced disadvantages that motivate the immigrant to consider self-employment. Despite the challenges and barriers, stories of phenomenal success have arisen from humble beginnings, and two illustrations are set out in the following case studies of immigrant entrepreneurs.

IMMIGRANT ENTREPRENEURS: STORIES OF SUCCESS

The following two case studies exemplify the success that is possible for immigrant entrepreneurs, despite enormous hardship and obstacles. First, the story of Tan Le illustrates a journey that has taken her from a refugee to Australian of the Year. The second case study traces the phenomenal success of Frank Lowy who arrived in the host country as a 'penniless immigrant' and is now described as the richest person in Australia.

BOX 6.1   TAN LE, 'YOUNG GLOBAL LEADER' (WORLD ECONOMIC FORUM) AND 'MOST INFLUENTIAL WOMAN IN TECHNOLOGY, 2010'

Tan Le was four years old when she arrived in Australia from Vietnam with her family. Despite the language difficulties she encountered, she was an excellent student and enrolled in a Law and Commerce degree at Monash University at the age of 16. She completed this four years later at the age of 20. Before she commenced her university studies, Tan was very actively involved in community service, joining the Vietnamese Community of Footscray Association, which was established to provide training and find employment for Vietnamese immigrants in Australia. She was also instrumental in setting up a counselling and refuge service for Vietnamese women.

In addition, Tan has played a key role in promoting multiculturalism in Melbourne, getting the community behind her to raise money for charities, as well as working with the *Vietnamese Weekly* newspaper to provide assistance to Vietnamese Australians entering into business ventures. More recently, Tan has moved into the area of technology entrepreneurship. She co-founded SASme in 2000, a telecommunication software company that pioneered Short Message Peer to Peer (SMPP) platforms to telecommunication carriers and content aggregators in Australia. The company grew from a modest beginning to employing a team of 35 people based in Australia, Asia and Europe. Tan is also the co-founder of Emotiv Systems, founded in 2003, an Australian neuro-engineering company that developed cutting-edge interface technology for digital media, where inputs can be taken directly from the brain. Emotiv Systems is a pioneer and world leader in this field, and Tan Le's vision is to revolutionize human–computer input in a similar way to the graphic user interface of 20 years ago. Researchers and developers are already working with this technology in 70 countries around the world.

In 1998, Tan was voted as one of Australia's 30 most successful women under 30 years of age. In the same year, she became the Young Australian of the Year. Since 2001, she has also been an Ambassador for the Status of Women. In 2009, Tan was awarded the accolade of 'Young Global Leader' by the World Economic Forum, and was named the 'Most Influential Woman in Technology' in 2010 by *Fast Company* magazine. This impressive list of achievements paved the way for Tan to be invited to the UK as a Special Visitor and guest of the British High Commission and Foreign Commonwealth Office. In addition, she was made a Goodwill Ambassador for Australia in Asia, and she is also a patron of the Australian Youth Ambassadors for Development Program.

Currently, she serves on a number of prominent boards, including the Australian Citizenship Council, the National Committee for Human Rights Education in Australia, the Centre for the Mind, RMIT Business in Entrepreneurship, as well as Plan International Australia. She is highly sought after as an inspirational speaker, particularly when she outlines her vision for the future of young Australians in the new millennium.[3]

BOX 6.2 FRANK LOWY, FOUNDER OF THE LOWY INSTITUTE FOR INTERNATIONAL POLICY AND CO-FOUNDER OF WESTFIELD HOLDINGS; COMPANION OF THE ORDER OF AUSTRALIA

Frank Lowy was born in Czechoslovakia and lived in Hungary during World War II. He spent time in a detention camp in Cyprus and in Palestine, before moving to Israel. In 1952, he joined his family who had settled in Australia after leaving Europe, as a 'penniless immigrant'. His first business was delivering small goods and deli sandwiches, but in 1953, he met John Saunders, a Hungarian immigrant, and they became business partners, creating the Westfield Group. Westfield, described as a vertically integrated shopping centre group, manages all aspects of shopping centre development from design and construction through to leasing, management and marketing.

The Westfield Group has enjoyed phenomenal success over the past 60 years, which is believed to be underpinned by creating value through intensive management at an operational level and through a strategic development programme. This continually improves the quality of the portfolio, generating income and capital growth for investors.

It is now the world's largest listed retail property group and has interests in, and operates, a global portfolio of 119 high-quality regional shopping centres in Australia, New Zealand, the United Kingdom and the United States. Westfield manages 23 700 retailers as tenants, across more than 10 million square metres of retail space. The combined value of the shopping centres is valued at more than $61 billion.

Frank Lowy is also well known for his philanthropy, setting up the Lowy Institute for International Policy in 2003 to mark the 50th anniversary of his arrival in Australia. The Institute is described as an international policy 'think tank' focusing on foreign affairs. The aim is to open up ideas and dialogue on international developments, with a particular emphasis on Australia's role on the world stage. The objectives of the Institute are broad, and encompass economic, strategic and political agendas. The overall goal of the Institute is to achieve two specific key outcomes. First, there is a desire to generate distinctive research that drives fresh policy options to inform Australia's international policy. Second, wider discussion about Australia's role in the world is promoted through accessible and high-quality forums, debates, seminars, conferences and lectures.

Frank's philanthropy has been acknowledged internationally. He was awarded the Woodrow Wilson Award for Corporate Citizenship in 2005, and in 2007 he received the Henni Friedlander Award for the Common Good at Bowdoin College in Brunswick, Maine, United States. In addition, Frank has been awarded a Companion of the Order of Australia, and has served on various boards in Australia, including the Reserve Bank of Australia. More recently, Frank has become involved in promoting the Football Federation Australia, and has worked tirelessly to promote acceptance of soccer in Australia. He has enjoyed some success in this area; Australia is now a member of the Asian Football Confederation and Frank is a member of the FIFA board. The *Los Angeles Times* has reported that Westfield is now 'the largest owner of shopping centres in California and the world', and the personal worth of Frank Lowy has been estimated at A$6.3 billion, making him the richest person in Australia. Memories of detention camps in Cyprus and Palestine must seem a lifetime away.[4]

IMMIGRANT ENTREPRENEURS: SUMMARY

Enhancing an understanding of immigrant entrepreneurship is obviously of key importance to all countries, be they classified as host or home countries. In summary, the immigrant entrepreneur is capable of contributing significantly to the host countries' economies. Many immigrant groups embrace entrepreneurial activity with great commitment and desire and despite difficult beginnings and debilitating challenges and barriers, many enjoy considerable success. The immigrant entrepreneur is most likely to be male, married with children and be close to 40 years of age. These characteristics have been reported in much cross-cultural research, and are considered to be important 'pull' factors in motivating immigrants considering self-employment. Ethnic ties are of the utmost importance, as is being located in the established ethnic enclave – especially in the start-up phase of the new business venture. Family links are valued, providing essential social and economic support, as well as the necessary resources for staffing the business.

Increasingly, immigrants arrive in the host country with educational qualifications obtained in the home country. The highly educated – often graduates – who may now form a new generation of immigrants, have followed patterns to entrepreneurial start-up and growth that are different from the patterns followed by the earlier immigrants. The new arrivals may also take advantage of venture capital and other 'public offerings' (Sequeira and Rasheed, 2004) and therefore, an understanding of their experiences of facilitators and barriers will be a useful addition to existing knowledge in this area.

Finally, it is acknowledged that there are huge differences in the economic success achieved by certain immigrant communities. Research that examines the diverse immigrant populations and their business successes or failures could provide further insights into the facilitators for the entrepreneurs from different immigrant communities who take up entrepreneurial ventures in their adopted countries (ibid.).

IMMIGRANT ENTREPRENEURS: THE FUTURE

With the ageing population worldwide, long-range planners have predicted that immigrants will continue to play a key role in economic growth in the future (Echikson et al., 2000; Desiderio and Salt, 2011). Certainly, the need to retain a dynamic workforce to offset the natural decline caused by the ageing population is recognized; a UN study estimated that 40 million immigrants will be required in the European Union (EU) by 2025 to address this shortfall (Echikson et al., 2000).

Immigrant workers can clearly contribute significantly to the economic growth of a country. A decade ago, immigrants in the EU reportedly earned in excess of $461 billion a year, which generated $153 billion in taxes (ibid.). In 2010, it has been estimated that although migrants constitute only 8 per cent of the population in the UK, they contribute approximately 10 per cent to the GDP (Migration Watch UK, 2010). In Western European countries, it has been shown that immigrant workers appear to have a propensity to set up business ventures at a greater rate than those of the native-born self-employed citizens (18 per cent and 7 per cent respectively) (Echikson et al., 2000) and also in the US (Fairlie, 2004).

Currently, there are few studies that focus on the area of immigrant women who become entrepreneurs in host countries although it is acknowledged that male and female immigrants may utilize ethnic and gender resources differently (Dallalfar, 1994); this will have a direct impact on the type of businesses they set up, and the way they go about running their business. This could be a rewarding area to explore in more depth. Certainly, many migrant women from ethnic minority groups have an overriding desire for improving the lifestyles of their families, and hence they are open to the challenges of finding an opportunity anywhere in the world (Pio, 2007). One of the universal problems they may face is that they are moving into an existing society that may need their services, but there may be resistance to them sharing a meaningful and equal place in the new home country (ibid.).

Despite this, many immigrant women embrace entrepreneurship consciously and deliberately, as they see it as an opportunity to obtain some of the privileges taken as a given in their host countries. For many immigrant women, entrepreneurship offers an avenue of earning a superior salary to the low-paid or devalued work they may be offered in their host country, or by male business owners (Dallalfar, 1994). Many immigrant entrepreneurial women report improvements in both their social, as well as economic positions, and see their lives, and the lives of their children, as being vastly improved. According to Pio (2007), ethnic immigrant women who embrace entrepreneurship have the capacity to create 'a power house for change' (p. 646). Therefore, further research into immigrant women entrepreneurs could provide a valuable added benefit both economically and socially at the micro (family) and macro (society) levels.

Finally, an exploration of the factors that assist immigrant entrepreneurs to move their business ventures into the wider community market may be of assistance to other entrepreneurs who wish to expand their market outside the established ethnic enclave (Sequeira and Rasheed, 2004). Some future projections could lay the foundations for strategic planning on immigration in countries that traditionally attract the largest immigrant population. For example, Asia currently has 60 per cent of the world's population, hence this may be the potential source of many future migrants in the world who will take up residence in a host country (Hugo, 2002). The question to be addressed is whether governments in advanced economic Western countries have planned for this eventuality. What steps have been taken to facilitate the entry of highly skilled and highly educated possibly Asian immigrants into the country, and the workforce – in particular the proportion who may take up self-employment or a larger-scale entrepreneurial venture? To maximize the potential of both male and female immigrants, governments need to question whether the provision of adequate childcare facilities has been considered, as this is typically catered for by ageing parents in Asian societies. Governments also need to continuously address what steps have been taken to integrate the increasing numbers of immigrants into the existing society in a host country, in order to minimize any racial discord, hostility, discrimination or prejudice.

Clearly, government policies need to be geared toward minority business development that are inclusive of immigrants and all existing ethnic groups in a host country (Fairlie, 2004). For the immigrant entrepreneur, this may go some way toward ensuring that any overt mechanisms of discrimination are not impacting on the businesses they own and operate. The contribution of the immigrant entrepreneur must not be underestimated; the host country is the beneficiary of a diverse, multicultural workforce, which is capable of contributing significantly to the national economy and enriching the lives of the mainstream population. More importantly, from an economic perspective, the immigrant entrepreneur has the capacity to 'contribute to expanding trade between the host country and their countries of origin' (Desiderio and Salt, 2011, p. 1).

NOTES

1. http://wordnetweb.princeton.edu/perl/webwn?s=immigrant; accessed 14 August 2011.
2. *Pākehā* is a Maori word for New Zealanders who are not of Maori origin.
3. Sources: adapted from the following: Young Australian of the Year Award, http://www.australianoftheyear.org.au/pages/page137.asp; accessed 8 December 2010; All American Talent and Celebrity Network; Emotiv Systems.
4. Sources: adapted from the following: about Westfield Group, http://westfield.com/corporate/about-westfield-group/history/Westfield_50th_Anniversary.html; about the Lowy Institute, http://www.lowyinstitute.org/AboutUs.asp; R. Vincent (2006) 'Deal to open up shopping malls', *Los Angeles Times*, http://articles.latimes.com/2006/feb/18/business/fi-mall18; accessed 15 August 2011.

REFERENCES

Adler, P. and S. Kwon (2002), 'Social capital: prospects for a new concept', *Academy of Management Review*, **27** (1), 17–40.

Barrett, G., T. Jones and D. McEvoy (2003), 'United Kingdom: severely constrained entrepreneurialism', in R. Kloosterman and J. Rath (eds), *Immigrant Entrepreneurs: Venturing Abroad in the Age of Globalization*, Oxford: Berg.

Bergman, M. (2005), 'Census Bureau provides first glimpse at the characteristics of U.S. business owners', available at http://www.highbeam.com/doc/1G1-128070426.html; accessed 14 August 2011.

Bogan, V. and W. Darity Jr (2008), 'Culture and entrepreneurship? African American and immigrant self-employment in the United States', *The Journal of Socio-Economics*, **37**, 1999–2019.

Bonacich, E. (1987), '"Making it" in America: a social evaluation of the ethics of immigrant entrepreneurship', *Sociological Perspectives*, **30** (4), 446–66.

Collins, J. (2003), 'Cultural diversity and entrepreneurship: policy responses to immigrant entrepreneurs in Australia', *Entrepreneurship and Regional Development*, **15** (2), 137–49.

Dallalfar, A. (1994), 'Iranian women as immigrant entrepreneurs', *Gender and Society*, **8** (4), 541–61.

De Freitas, G. (1991), *Inequality at Work: Hispanics in the U.S. Labor Force*, New York: Oxford University Press.

Desiderio, M. and J. Salt (2011), *Main Findings of the Conference on Entrepreneurship and Employment Creation of Immigrants in OECD Countries*, 9–10 June 2010, Paris.

Dunstan, S., S. Boyd and S. Crichton (2004), *Migrant's Experiences of New Zealand*, New Zealand Immigration Service, Wellington.

Echikson, W., K.A. Schmidt, H. Dawley and A. Bawden (2000), 'Unsung heroes', *BusinessWeek International Edition*, 28 February 2000, available at: http://elibrary.ru/item.asp?id=6332821; accessed 10 December 2010.

Fairlie, R.W. (2004), 'Recent trends in ethnic and racial business ownership', *Small Business Economics*, **23** (3), 203–18.

Fairlie, R.W. and B.D. Meyer (2003), 'The effect of immigration on native self-employment', *Journal of Labor Economics*, **21** (3), 619–50.

Fielden, S.L. and M.J. Davidson (eds) (2010), *International Research Handbook on Successful Women Entrepreneurs*, Cheltenham, UK and Northampton, MA, USA: Edward Elgar.

Heilbrunn, S. and N. Kushnirovich (2007), 'Immigrant and Indigenous enterprises: similarities and differences', *International Journal of Business Performance Management*, **9** (3), 344–61.

Heilbrunn, S. and N. Kushnirovich (2008), 'The impact of policy on immigrant entrepreneurship and businesses practice in Israel', *International Journal of Public Sector Management*, **21** (7), 693–703.

Hugo, G. (2002), 'Introduction. The Japan Institute of Labour', in *Migration and the Labour Market in Asia: Recent Trends and Policies*, Paris: OECD, pp. 7–16.

Jacoby, T. (2000), 'Second-generation question mark', *American Enterprise*, **11** (8), 32–36.

Kim, K.C. and W.M. Hurh (1985), 'Ethnic resources utilization of Korean immigrant entrepreneurs in the Chicago minority area', *International Migration Review*, **19** (1), 82–111.

Kloosterman, R. and J. Rath (2001), 'Immigrant entrepreneurs in advanced economies: mixed embeddedness further explored', *Journal of Ethnic and Migration Studies*, **27** (2), 189–202.

Kushnirovich, N. (2009), 'Policy for supporting business minorities: a study of women and immigrant entrepreneurs', *International Journal of Management and Enterprise Development*, **7** (4), 394–408.

Light, I. and S. Gold (2000), *Ethnic Economies*, San Diego, CA: Academic Press.

Light, I. and S. Karageorgis (1994), 'The ethnic economy', in N.J. Smelser and R. Swedberg (eds), *The Handbook of Economic Sociology*, Princeton, NJ: Princeton University Press, pp. 647–71.

Lunn, J. and T.P. Steen (2000), 'An investigation into the effects of ethnicity and immigration on self-employment', *International Advances in Economic Research*, **6** (3), 498–520.

Migration Watch UK (2010), 'Economic contribution of A8 migrants', available at: http://www.migrationwatchuk.org/Briefingpaper/document/14; accessed 7 December 2010.

Mitchell, B. (2003), 'The role of networks among entrepreneurs from different ethnic groups', *The Small Business Monitor*, **1** (1), 78–86.

Olson, P.D., V. Zuiker-Solis and C. Montalto (2000), 'Self employed Hispanics and Hispanic wage earners: differences in earnings', *Hispanic Journal of Behaviour Sciences*, **22** (1), 114–30.

Pio, E. (2007), 'Ethnic minority migrant women entrepreneurs and the imperial imprimatur', *Women in Management Review*, **22** (8), 631–49.

Rath, J. and R. Kloosterman (2000), 'A critical review of research on immigrant entrepreneurship', *International Migration Review*, **34** (3), 657–81.

Rowley, T. (2004), 'Entrepreneurship means adaption', available at: http://www.matr.net/print-12097.html; accessed 4 August 2010.

Rusinovic, K. (2008), 'Moving between markets? Immigrant entrepreneurs in different markets', *International Journal of Entrepreneurial Behaviour & Research*, **14** (6), 440–54.

Sequeira, J.M. and A.A. Rasheed (2004), 'The role of social and human capital in the start-up and growth of immigrant businesses', *Ethnic Entrepreneurship: Structure and Process International Research in the Business Disciplines*, **4**, 77–94.

Shinnar, R.S. and C.A. Young (2008), 'Hispanic immigrant entrepreneurs in the Las Vegas Metropolitan Area: motivations for entry into and outcomes of self-employment', *Journal of Small Business Management*, **46** (2), 242–62.

Smallbone, D., M. Bertotti and I. Ekanem (2005), 'Diversification in ethnic minority business: the case of Asians in London's creative industries', *Journal of Small Business and Enterprise Development*, **12** (1), 41–56.

Toro-Morn, M. and M. Alicea (eds) (2004), *Migration and Immigration: A Global View*, Westport, CT: Greenwood Press.

Wadhwa, V., A. Saxenian, B. Rissing and G. Gereffi (2007), *America's New Immigrant Entrepreneurs*, School of Information, University of California, Berkeley.

Yoon, I.-J. (1997), *On My Own: Korean Business and Race Relations in America*, Chicago: The University of Chicago Press.

7. Lesbian, gay and bisexual (LGB) entrepreneurs

The challenges that remain are not just centred on public attitudes. New research for the Commission indicates that homophobia still significantly impacts on the lives of LGB men and women and remains entrenched within institutions and communities.

(Equality and Human Rights Commission, 2009, p. 9)

INTRODUCTION

It was only just over two decades ago in 1990 that the World Health Organization removed homosexuality from its list of mental diseases. Nevertheless, in the United Nations, 86 member states still class consensual same sex among adults as a criminal offence, six provinces have legal provisions to punish homosexuality with imprisonment and seven still use the death penalty as a punishment (IDAHO-UK, 2009). Hence, it is not surprising that sexual orientation occupational research, and in particular, entrepreneurial research, has tended to remain a taboo subject until very recently and has been both sporadic and sparse (Ward et al., 2006; Davies, 2010). Willsdon (2005) also proposed that a reason why LBGs as a minority group have been largely ignored by researchers is that unlike many of the other minority entrepreneurs included in this book such as black and ethnic minorities, homosexuality can be easily concealed. Varnell (2001) is cited by Galloway (2007) and highlights the economic importance of LGBs as part of this research category:

> [B]lack entrepreneurship has been studied as contributing to material prosperity and social equality ... The same is true of women's businesses ... but no one, either economists nor anyone else, seems to have studied gays and lesbians ... (as a result) we are probably underestimating the importance of gay entrepreneurs and how we could help them. (Galloway, 2007, pp. 271–2)

To date, there are no official statistics of the exact numbers of LGBs in the population in different countries and estimates vary. In the UK for example, it has been established that LGBs make up 1.7 million in the workforce

(Stonewall, 2009), 150 000 university students (Valentine et al., 2009) and between 2 and 10 per cent of the total population (Galloway, 2007). In the US, around 6 per cent of the population identifies itself as either gay or lesbian and it has been estimated that there are between 16 and 20 million LGBs aged over 18 years of age (Schindehutte et al., 2005).

It is important to note that recent authors such as Schindehutte et al. (2005) and Davidson (2011) have emphasized the multidimensional nature involved in identifying oneself as gay and highlighted how this has generally been ignored by researchers in the past. Consequently, Schindehutte et al. (2005, p. 29) defined being gay in terms of spiritual (in relation to one's purpose and meaning), the way one behaves, attitudinal, ways of feeling (i.e., emotions), cognitive issues of an individual's life and identity and the way one defines oneself.

Furthermore, Iwasaki and Ristock (2007) point out that researchers should acknowledge the various complexities of potentially discriminatory, oppressive layers facing different LGB individuals. For example, black, disabled lesbians may be subject to homophobia, gender discrimination and exclusion from both black and disabled communities (ibid.).

Anti-discrimination legislation protecting LGBs varies throughout the world, with Australia and European countries being the most progressive (IDAHO-UK, 2009). Davies (2010) mentions how this therefore makes it challenging to generalize research from one country to another or indeed, within countries. In the US, for example, there is no legal protection regarding discrimination against LGBs in the workplace in 28 out of 50 states (Herek et al., 2009). The European Union (EU) in 2000 required EU member states to legally protect employers from discrimination based on their sexual orientation through an Employment Directive. This was followed in the UK in 2003 by the Employment Equality (Sexual Orientation) Regulations, and the Equality Act (Sexual Orientation) Regulations 2007, which also made it illegal to discriminate against LGBs in the provision of services, facilities and goods (Pillinger, 2008). The recent UK Equality Act (2010) codified all aspects of anti-discrimination law and further helped to secure greater anti-discriminatory practices against LGBs (Davies, 2010).

Nevertheless, in spite of the introduction of protective anti-discrimination legislation related to sexual orientation in certain countries, there is a continual body of research indicating that LGBs still face potentially high levels of discrimination in the workplace. This includes high levels of occupational stress, isolation, homophobia, harassment and bullying and evidence suggests LGBs often experience major fears about disclosing their sexual orientation at work (Bendl and Fleischmann, 2008). Indeed, the UK Equality and Human Rights Commission (EHRC), in their recent report entitled: *Beyond Tolerance: Making Sexual Orientation a*

Public Matter, proposed: 'The challenges that remain are not just centred on public attitudes. New research for the Commission indicates that homophobia still significantly impacts on the lives of LGB men and women and remains entrenched within institutions and communities' (EHRC, 2009, p. 5).

However, on a more optimistic note, recent evidence particularly from the US, Europe (including the UK) and Australia, indicates that an increasing number of LGBs are setting up new businesses. According to Willsdon (2005) this may well be a result of more and more LGBs leaving corporate jobs since the emergence of the gay liberation movement in the 1970s and may be indicative of the opportunities to be open about one's sexuality. Furthermore, Willsdon proposes that in the UK the formation of such trade publications as the *Gay to Z Directory* with over 5000 gay/lesbian-friendly businesses listed and LGB groups such as the Gay Business Association with over 200 members, means that LGB entrepreneurs have at last become visible and cannot be ignored.

Moreover, similar LGB associations exist in the US, including the National Gay and Lesbian Chamber of Commerce, which actively supports LGB entrepreneurship (Haynes, 2010). It should be pointed out that the word 'gay' is sometimes used by researchers in the field when referring to all LGBs (both male and female). Furthermore, while it is acknowledged that transsexual entrepreneurs undoubtedly also face numerous (often unique) discriminatory challenges, an absence of any significant studies on this minority group, unfortunately, prevents their inclusion in this chapter.

LGB ENTREPRENEURS: GENERAL CHARACTERISTICS

In his review of the early history of gay entrepreneurs in the US, Varnell (1999) described how LGBs engaged in more and more entrepreneurial activity in the early 1920s and into the 1930s. This often involved the holding of gay dances and the ownership of speakeasies and restaurants. Protection from both public and police harassment and hostility towards these gay establishments was often secured by either hiring police and/or paying the police 'protection money' (ibid.). Ironically, gay entrepreneurship thrived even more with the end of prohibition when the State Liquor Authority cracked down on the gay presence in bars (defined by police as 'disorderly') and many bar owners were closed down for illegally serving gays. According to Varnell, (ibid., p. 2): 'The syndicates, which developed during prohibition, had enough money, political clout and inside police contacts to provide protection for the bars and their patrons; and the syndicates cared little about public opinion. The famed Stonewall Bar itself was a syndicate-owned bar.'

Almost a century later from the pioneering US gay entrepreneurs in the early twentieth century, precise estimates of the number of LGB entrepreneurs are still sketchy. Schindehutte et al. (2005) suggested that in the US, taking into account that around 18 per cent of LGBs are self-employed totalling around 2 million people, this accounted for 10.4 per cent of all US businesses. Furthermore, there are indications that the percentages are growing annually with Hamar (2010) estimating 1.2 million gay-owned businesses in the US, with around 29 000 of them belonging to local Gay Chambers of Commerce.

Recent US surveys of Internet users have consistently found that LGB populations are twice as likely as their heterosexual counterparts to have graduated from college, be professional/managerial and have annual household incomes of over $250 000 (GLBT Market Demographics, 2010). Indeed, the increasing value of the 'pink dollar/pound' is now an important part of marketing strategy for businesses (large and small) throughout the world. In the UK for example, major brands such as Pepsi, Heinz, Lloyds TSB and IKEA have all launched advertising campaigns specially aimed at appealing to gay consumers (Costa, 2010). In the US the LGB population combined spending has been estimated to be around $732 billion (*San Diego Gay and Lesbian News*, 2010). In the UK, the gay market has been estimated to be worth £70 billion (Galloway, 2007) and in the Irish LGB population of only 195 000, they spend over 33 million euros on beauty products/services and over 60 million euros on fashion annually (Kidney and Cooney, 2009). Furthermore, it has been assessed that there are a staggering 25 million gay people living in Latin America and they spend billions of US dollars alone on leisure travel every year (Merco Press, 2010).

Galloway (2007) makes the point that much of the previous LGB entrepreneurial research has tended to assume that these businesses have 'inside knowledge' and are catering predominantly for the lucrative gay market and quoted the example of a well-known British gay entrepreneur, Ivan Massow (featured later as a case study):

> There is much evidence that gay entrepreneurs can be best placed to exploit the gay market, as their ability to see and realise opportunities within it are enhanced by their inclusion in and understanding of, the culture. A famous example of this is the multi-millionaire gay entrepreneur Ivan Massow, who for various reasons, chose not to cater for those of non-traditional orientation. (Galloway, 2007, p. 27)

However, there is much discussion in the literature that there is a lack of evidence that gay people, by virtue of being gay, somehow comprise a single community and as with every other minority group, individual identity is multidimensional (Davidson, 2011). According to Galloway (2007), this notion is expounded in Queer Theory: 'Queer Theory rejects the idea of "one community", such as feminists or gay people, comprising a homogeneous ideological group, claiming that the labelling of the group is the majority's construction in order to classify those apparently ideologically opposed to the prevailing power system' (p. 275).

Galloway (2007) further substantiates this theory by referring to Wilson (1997) who identified two separate very different types of 'gay culture', that is, 'flamboyant' and 'closet'. Moreover, in relation to gay entrepreneurs, both Levin (1998) and Schindehutte et al. (2005) reported two separate groups. One was described as entrepreneurs who were gay and independent and wished to be differentiated from heterosexual society and fit in with their own community, and another described as gay entrepreneurs who aspired to be more accepted by the heterosexual society.

Research findings also indicate that while the early pioneer gay entrepreneurs often catered specifically for the gay market, this is certainly not the case today. In her large-scale survey of 700 gay business owners in the UK, Levin (1998) reported that only 15 per cent catered exclusively for the gay market but 45 per cent admitted to targeting their business at the gay community and commonly mentioned the rewards they gained from a feeling of being able to contribute to the LGB community. In the US, Schindehutte et al. (2005) found that two-thirds of gay entrepreneurs depended on growth of trade with the non-gay community.

When analysing the profiles of gay entrepreneurs compared to their heterosexual female and male counterparts, Willsdon's (2005) study, of 68 predominantly male UK homosexuals, revealed some interesting similarities and differences when comparing his data to a much earlier heterosexual entrepreneurial study carried out by Watkins and Watkins (1984). In terms of business operation areas, only 25 per cent of male heterosexual entrepreneurs in Watkins and Watkins' UK study, and 61 per cent of heterosexual women, were involved in service-related businesses compared to 88 per cent of homosexual entrepreneurs (Willsdon, 2005). Furthermore, compared to their heterosexual counterparts, homosexual entrepreneurs in Willsdon's study set up business at an average age of 32 years (exactly the same as heterosexual females) but at a younger age than their male heterosexual counterparts (i.e., average 39 years) (see Watkins and Watkins, 1984).

In her more extensive survey of 700 UK LGB entrepreneurs, Levin (1998) found that a high 70 per cent had started enterprises in the same industries they had had previous experience in (average eight years). Interestingly, 20 per cent of Levin's (1998) entrepreneurs were still working with their current gay partner and 23 per cent with an ex-partner. Not surprisingly, both male and female LGB business owners are much less likely to have a family and children compared to their heterosexual counterparts (Kidney and Cooney, 2009).

One of the most comprehensive profiles of the business and personal characteristics of LGB entrepreneurs is provided by Schindehutte et al.'s (2005) US survey of 344 gay entrepreneurs. Similar to other LGB business owner studies (e.g., Willsdon, 2005), a low percentage were bisexual (5 per cent) and the majority were male (74 per cent), Caucasian (94 per cent), highly educated (69 per cent college or postgraduate degrees) and working predominantly in the private sector (98 per cent) (Schindehutte et al., 2005). Almost three-quarters of their sample were aged between 36 and 55 years of age and owned a high percentage of the total equity in their business. Thirty-nine per cent were sole owners, just under a third had had previous employment in small business and the majority of businesses generated sales revenues of less than $5 million (ibid.).

To date, we still know little about the personality and personal backgrounds of LGB entrepreneurs. An interesting US study by Di Bernardo (2007) compared female and minority homosexual entrepreneurs to male and non-minority entrepreneurs to ascertain whether there were differences in the 'Big Five' personality factors (Goldberg, 1990) – neuroticism, extraversion, openness, agreeableness and conscientiousness. Referring to the gender inversion hypothesis, Di Bernardo (2007) initially predicted that there would be personality differences:

> With respect to the study of personality and the homosexual population, there has been recent research to support their gender inversion hypothesis, which is that gay men's traits tend to be somewhat feminized and that lesbian's traits tend to be somewhat masculinized (Kite and Deaux, 1987; Lippa, 2005; Looy, 2005). As a result of this data, this study expected that the gender inversion hypothesis would contribute to differences in several of the personality dimensions of homosexual male and homosexual female entrepreneurs. (Di Bernardo, 2007, p. 8)

Nevertheless, contrary to the initial hypothesis, Di Bernardo found no significant differences for any of the personality dimensions between male and female LGB entrepreneurs and minority and non-minority LGB entrepreneurs. In relation to personal backgrounds and experiences, Willsdon (2005) concluded that the majority of his UK (predominantly male) gay entrepreneurs had had a weak relationship with their fathers, supporting previous earlier findings on male heterosexual entrepreneurs (e.g., Kets de Vries, 1977). Furthermore, just over a third of Willsdon's (2005) LGB entrepreneurial respondents appeared 'marginalized' and reported feeling isolated from their heterosexual peers. Over a third had suffered some form of homophobic abuse during childhood and only 9 per cent had dared to be open about their sexuality at school, with almost 20 per cent waiting until they became entrepreneurs before being open about their homosexuality (ibid.).

Similar to their heterosexual counterparts (see Fielden and Davidson, 2010), Schindehutte et al. (2005) discovered that LGB entrepreneurs were often likely to have had an entrepreneurial parent (32 per cent) as well as being influenced in their entrepreneurial vocation by entrepreneurial role models (27 per cent). With role models (including parents as entrepreneurs) providing inspiration and vocational aspirations for LGB business owners, the next section investigates these motivational issues more fully.

LGB ENTREPRENEURS: ASPIRATIONS AND MOTIVATIONS

A number of studies that have investigated the degree to which 'push' factors (e.g., discrimination in the workplace) versus 'pull' factors (e.g., social reasons) motivate LGB individuals to take on the risks associated with business creation have revealed various (and sometimes conflicting) insights. Similar to many of the minority entrepreneurs reviewed in this book, for LGBs one would predict that push factors would be particularly important, given the societal barriers confronting them. Indeed, Schindehutte et al. (2005, p. 31) proposed that these push factors could include such barriers as: 'job discrimination, perceived inappropriateness of certain occupations for gays and lesbians (e.g. military; childcare), homophobia, fear of AIDS and societal stigma'. In his literature-based arguments reviewing the motivations for LGBs, Galloway (2007) also isolated push factors as being predominately negative and included 'harassment in employment' (pushed into self-employment as a means of avoiding the homophobic work culture) and 'discrimination in employment' (pushed into entrepreneurship in order to escape career discrimination).

However, these propositions that negative push factors are the greatest motivation factors were not borne out by Schindehutte et al.'s (2005) analysis of responses from their 314 (predominantly male) LGB entrepreneurs. They found the most common motivators for starting ventures were related to 'freedom', 'ability to do what I want to do', 'helping people' and 'making a living'. The least important motivators on the other hand included 'limited opportunities with established companies', 'get rich' and 'prejudice/discrimination/social hostility'. As mentioned previously, Schindehutte et al. (2005) identified two distinct groups within their LGB entrepreneurial population and there were some differences between them in terms of business motivations. 'Identifiers' often viewed starting a new enterprise as a sort of 'coming out' process, felt more isolated and viewed prejudice facing LGBs' business as significant. They also strongly identified with the LGB community in terms of acting as entrepreneurial LGB role models as well as supporting LGB networks and events. On the other hand, 'independents' were much more likely to believe their sexual orientation was a non-issue in entrepreneurship, or that LGB entrepreneurs faced unique obstacles (ibid.). Indeed, independents' motivating factors for setting up enterprises were very similar to entrepreneurs in general. Schindehutte et al. (2005, p. 38) summarized their findings by stating:

> While fully committed (the 'independents') to their gay identity, this identity may be less central to their sense of self. They do not feel stigmatized to the extent that they must live their lives apart from mainstream society ... the identifiers might be considered gay entrepreneurs, while the independents could be characterized as entrepreneurs who are gay.

Willsdon (2005) concluded that UK homosexual entrepreneurs were generally motivated by many of the same factors as entrepreneurs in general. He maintained that any prior glass ceiling issues had had little influence on having 'pushed' these gay entrepreneurs into business ventures and nor had previous homophobic experiences in the workplace (ibid.). Almost all had been 'pulled' into entrepreneurship by positive factors such as the attractions of being independent and setting up on their own, and the majority (83 per cent) had entered from past employment. The most common reason quoted by a third of the LGB respondents was linked to presented economic opportunities, which Willsdon (2005) points out is a similar 'pull' factor for the majority of non-minority entrepreneurs. Moreover, Galloway (2007) summarized the 'pull' factors for LGB entrepreneurs as being divided into two main categories. The first related to 'career choice' (enabling entrepreneurship to provide opportunities to pursue interests), and the second linked to 'ideology' (starting firms for ideological reasons such as providing gay community services rather than for good business reasons).

Despite some conflicting findings in the literature and an emphasis on positive 'pull factors' as major motivational forces, Kidney and Cooney (2009) still conclude that the past and present homophobia towards LGB individuals undoubtedly has an influence on the motivations and aspirations of the LGB entrepreneur compared to their heterosexual counterparts. These authors emphasize that research indicates that gay entrepreneurs have a strong need to feel they are in control of how they are perceived and that supporting one's lifestyle is a particularly high motivator combined with needs for personal and professional growth, freedom and personal satisfaction (Kidney and Cooney, 2009).

LGB ENTREPRENEURS: CHALLENGES AND BARRIERS

From the review so far, it is not surprising that all the recent evidence to date indicates that having started their own business, LGBs are much more likely to be confronted with a series of barriers not encountered by their heterosexual counterparts. These obstacles are predominantly associated with homophobic attitudes and behaviours ranging from difficulties with suppliers to hiring employees (Kidney and Cooney, 2009). As mentioned early in Chapter 1, there are also many countries where homophobic oppression (sometimes linked with religious doctrines) is of a magnitude that prevents LGB entrepreneurs from ever 'coming out' and being open about their sexual orientation. In China for example, in 1997, homosexuality was a criminal offence and in 2001 it was considered a mental illness (Sweeney, 2010). In his recent report on the situation in China, Sweeney (ibid.) described how the Chinese police had cancelled a gay pageant shortly before it was due to be opened, as well as postponing the opening of a gay bar in Dali. In reference to the prospect of an LGBT (lesbian, gay, bisexual and transgender) resort opening in China in the future, Sweeney concluded it would be unlikely, as even if funding was available for gay entrepreneurs, their target market would be afraid to buy gay-specific products.

Even in the more liberal US, over three-quarters of Schindehutte et al.'s (2005) LGB entrepreneurial respondents agreed to some degree that having to deal with homophobia and discrimination was a business issue for them. These authors summarized in rank order the areas isolated as being of greatest difficulty to include: 'obtaining suppliers/vendors, obtaining licences and approvals, marketing and advertising, obtaining premises, hiring employees and obtaining business loans from banks' (ibid., p. 32). In terms of the final obstacle concerning bank loans, this was also confirmed by Willsdon's (2005) UK LGB entrepreneurial study where only 42 per cent used banks to set up their businesses, with half relying solely on their own funds. Interestingly, Willsdon (2005) concluded that LGB entrepreneurs were very similar to their female heterosexual counterparts in relation to their financial business support profiles (see Chapter 4). Indeed, evidence of discriminatory practice from banks appears to still continue, as illustrated in Carpentier's (2010) recent account of the US Citibank shutting down a gay entrepreneur's bank account over a blog's content:

Jason Goldberg is the CEO of a company called 'Fabulis', which is developing a website, iPhone app and social media application targeted at gay men. His company – which is at least his third start-up – is funded by investors including *The Washington Post* and the venture capitalist Allen Morgan, and they just launched their beta version this month. You would think he would be the kind of customer Citi would want – but Citi decided otherwise after a compliance officer reviewed his site and decided that a social networking application for gay men was 'objectionable'. (Carpentier, 2010)

While the banks later reinstated the account and maintained their employees were 'in the wrong', Carpentier (2010) points out that the bank still failed to state that they themselves were wrong in the first instance to have suspended Goldberg's account without notification.

Certainly, one of the continuing unique dilemmas facing a significant proportion of LGB entrepreneurs is whether they should 'out' themselves when interviewing job candidates (Levin, 1998; Kidney and Cooney, 2009). In a recent article in *The Wall Street Journal* (2010) on the topic, some gay entrepreneurs such as Eileen Kessler, owner of a marketing communications firm in Washington, DC, believed it would be unprofessional to raise the topic at interview. Other gay entrepreneurs, however, reported examples of new recruits having left abruptly once they realized the owner or owners were gay and maintained it would have been cost beneficial to have 'outed' themselves from the start. A number of alternative compromise procedures were also proposed, including suggestions from diversity consultants that LGB business owners should emphasize the culture of their firm during recruitment interviews, indicating that diversity and inclusiveness is taken seriously (ibid.).

In terms of business success, over half (61 per cent) of Schindehutte et al.'s (2005) LGB business owners did not believe that if people were unaware of their sexual orientation, then their business would be more successful. Their LGB respondents isolated the most important measures of business success as being:

customer loyalty (89%), and sales growth (80%) followed by an ability to give back to the gay community (59%), employee satisfaction (54%), and achieving personal wealth (40%). While 13.5% of the entrepreneurs indicated that they sought rapid growth for their ventures, the majority (72.3%) were interested in moderate growth, with 14.2% seeking limited or no growth. (Schindehutte et al., 2005, p. 34)

It should also be emphasized that there have also been many positive factors associated with LGB entrepreneurship. Undoubtedly, it offers a comfortable working environment (particularly for younger gay entrepreneurs) to work in and be open about their sexuality without fear of homophobia from work colleagues (Levin, 1998). This was reinforced by Kidney and Cooney (2009) who referred to earlier research by Guasp and Balfour (2008), which illustrated that if LGBs felt they could be themselves in the workplace, they then performed more productively.

Schindehutte et al. (2005) also reported a number of positive attributes revealed by their LGB entrepreneurs, related specifically to their sexual orientation. For example, over three-quarters of their respondents maintained the realities and adversities associated with being gay had helped them face the demands and creativity required to run a business venture as well as providing inside knowledge when marketing and selling to LGBs. Furthermore, a high 73 per cent agreed that they were making a political statement in society by being openly gay, 68 per cent maintained that being a business owner helped counteract negative stereotypes associated with their sexuality and over half purported that their business often served as a surrogate family (ibid.).

Nevertheless, like numerous other researchers in the field, Schindehutte et al. conclude that overall, the challenges and barriers potentially facing LGB entrepreneurs often outweigh the advantages and include examples of: 'homophobic investors and suppliers, reluctance of mainstream companies to publicize their ties to a gay business concern, discrimination in advertising, difficulties with insurance coverage as a result of the AIDS crisis, and legal complications when gay couples jointly own a business' (p. 32).

LGB ENTREPRENEURS: STORIES OF SUCCESS

The following case studies include stories from two high-profile British gay entrepreneurs who utilized their business skills to fill gaps they identified in the market. Ivan Massow was one of the first entrepreneurs in the UK to target the 'pink pound' as well as provide an important financial service to LGBs at a time in the 1990s when they were being discriminated against because of the AIDS scare. Vicky Reeves launched her web solutions company at the age of 24 after realizing that there was need for a business that was able to deliver web projects from start to finish. Both of these highly successful entrepreneurs have actively acted as role models for aspiring gay business owners.

BOX 7.1 IVAN MASSOW – BRITISH ENTREPRENEUR (FINANCE) AND FILM MAKER

Ivan Massow is a well-known gay multi-millionaire businessman, entrepreneur and more recently, a film maker. During his life he has experienced a lot of loss. The son of a policeman whom Ivan has described as abusive, he was born Ivan Field in Brighton in 1967. At the age of 12, his mother gave him up for adoption on her remarriage with the hope of giving him a better life. He took the surname 'Massow' from his new (bachelor) adoptive, businessman father, who in later life rejected him after Ivan 'came out' as gay. As an adult, Ivan's long-term male partner committed suicide.

Ivan left school at 15 with only a few qualifications. He was severely dyslexic and began his career in the financial services in the early 1980s, remaining a 'closeted homosexual'. During this period of his working life, at a time when HIV rates were on the increase, he saw how gay men were being discriminated against when they applied for financial services. Indeed, premiums for gay men could be as high as 600 per cent more than their heterosexual counterparts, whatever their circumstances. Furthermore, gay men requiring insurance and mortgages were not only required to detail their sexual practices but had to have HIV tests, which in itself prejudices all applications in the future.

Hence, in 1990, Ivan 'came out' and started his own financial services business, 'Massow Financial Services', based in a squat in London, and catered specifically for gay men and women. At first, he was unable to get financial backing for his new venture but armed with his knowledge of the financial services sector, he managed to 'manipulate the system' and offer avenues for gay individuals to secure insurance and mortgages at the same rates as their heterosexual counterparts. He also became a well-known Conservative and campaigned against homophobia whilst befriending high-profile politicians such as William Hague and Michael Portillo, as well as ex-Prime Minister Baroness Thatcher (with whom he acted notoriously as her official companion at the Conservative Party Conference in 1999).

Ivan Massow was one of the first gay entrepreneurs in the UK to recognize the potential of the pink pound and according to McLean in his *Guardian* article profiling Massow, Ivan had: 'arguably done more than anyone else to make gay mainstream'. Describing his main motivations behind the creation of his first business, Ivan commented: 'When I started Massow's, it was a crusade because I thought people were being treated unjustly. I thought it would be a way of creating pressure through consolidated economic power. If it caught on, it could change the way gay people were viewed by society. I thought it was really important that business saw the gay community as a useful area to exploit, and what maybe is exploitation if the glass is half empty, is respect, consideration and eventual mainstream acceptance, if the glass is half-full'.

In 1999, he merged Massow's with its main competitor Rainbow Finance and gave up 30 per cent of his company, taking a less active role. However, within two years, he returned to the business, saving it from collapse and turning it round back into profitability. Ivan eventually sold the business to his employees for £100 as a 'thank you' to his loyal staff who had weathered the unsuccessful merger as well as a failed partnership with Zurich Life (which was later settled in court).

Ivan has continued to be a gay activist and support gay charities. He is a former Chairman of the Institute of Contemporary Arts and has also continued his interest in politics. Having left the Conservative Party (mainly because of their lack of support in scrapping Section 28[1]), he re-joined the Conservatives again and had an unsuccessful attempt at becoming Mayor of London. In 2010 he was placed on the Approved Conservative Candidate List and repeatedly maintains that he is most proud of being: 'the man who changed the Tories' attitude to gays'.

Between 2006 and 2008, Ivan left the UK to live in Barcelona and then Los Angeles, where he wrote, produced and directed the documentary-style film *Banksy's Coming for Dinner* starring Joan Collins. He has referred to his new film-making ventures as a 'retirement hobby' and on his return to residency in the UK, explained that his time overseas was a period that included therapy for past traumas and that he 'needed to get away, get back to basics, make things right'. Even his new 'hobby' venture has proved an enormous success, with his film about the artist Banksy being acclaimed by both audiences and critics.

In an interview in *The Times* in 2004, Ivan Massow reflected on his 'unlikely' successes in the business world, taking into account his disadvantaged childhood, by saying: 'It's amazing really. I'm a kid with no qualifications who didn't know how to get on. I could have been a junkie at 16. Those opportunities don't come to someone of my background'.[2]

BOX 7.2 VICKY REEVES – FOUNDER AND MANAGING DIRECTOR OF CHAMELEON NET

After graduating from the University of Hertfordshire with an Honours degree in Computer Science Vicky Reeves worked for a variety of large companies including iCAT, e Commerce (part of Intel) and Alcatel. She then launched her company 'Chameleon Net' in 1998 from her spare bedroom in London. She saw a 'hole in the IT market' and a need to set up a company that could deliver web projects from start to finish, that is, from design to development through to support and hosting as well as e-marketing. Vicky now employs around 25 people and her clients include UNICEF, Cable and Wireless, Sporting Index, Telehouse Europe and Hilton International.

When asked about how she went about starting her business, she recalled: 'I didn't really have an awful lot of experience. I was 24 when I started the business, so I didn't really have a huge amount of commercial experience either. So, I didn't really know where to turn to, so I started trying to talk to organizations like Business Link, which were useful and I also spoke to a lot of my friends' dads and colleagues and some people I knew in the industry and just sort of asked around as much as possible'.

Vicky maintained that her initial start-up phase of her business was: 'definitely scary'. However, she started preparation for her new venture whilst still working in full-time employment and contracted her first client (for a £5000 fee) before resigning from her job. Even so, like many new entrepreneurs, she soon realized that even though she didn't come from a sales background, she needed to learn how to sell in order to secure more clients. Vicky also emphasized the importance of cash flow in order to ensure her business grew: 'cash flow is really, really important in a business and it's still important now with, you know, our overheads being over £100 000 a month. We need to make sure that there's always cash coming in, so there's a constant, you know, battle to make sure that your clients pay you on time and the bigger the corporations, normally the longer it takes them to pay, so you do have to budget that in. So that's certainly one of the key things'.

Today, Vicky has divided her employees into those who specifically specialize in sales and the continual marketing and securing of new clients, and those who concentrate on the development and delivery of the IT operations and websites. She also places great emphasis on team building within her staff and creating an amicable working culture in which employees also socialize together. Vicky maintains she gets a lot of satisfaction from being able to control the strategic direction of the company, as well as the feeling of achievement seeing the success of the websites that Chameleon Net develops for its clients. In particular, she is extremely proud of the websites they have designed for UNICEF, which resulted in online donations increasing by over 300 per cent. When asked what advice she would offer to other aspiring, young entrepreneurs, Vicky emphasized the importance of learning how to network: 'I think my advice would be that networking is the most important thing that I've learnt in business since the start of the company, because it's all about networking and who you know to be able to get business'.

Indeed, she maintains she has never ever thrown away a business card and that it's really vital to maintain contact with people. Vicky also advocates that when taking the risk of beginning a new business venture, one should ensure you are as secure and stable as possible. She believes you need drive, focus, enthusiasm and lots and lots of passion and ensure you are well prepared before letting go of your day job.

Between 2008 and 2010, she advised the UK government on its support of small business as member of the Small Business Forum headed by Peter Mandelson. Vicky has also been the recipient of numerous prestigious awards in acknowledgment of her business success. These have included the 'Best Women in Technology Award' (businesses under 250 employees) at the 2005 'BlackBerry Women and Technology Awards', the 'Female Entrepreneur of the Year' finalist at the Fast Growth Business Awards 2008 and the 'European Women of Achievement Award' (all of these awards being great PR for her company).

In addition, in 2005 she won the 'Young Entrepreneur of the Year Gay and Lesbian Award', which was presented to her at London's Savoy Hotel. She later reflected on this award and its importance in encouraging gay people like herself who aspire to become entrepreneurs: 'It is slowly becoming easier for women, gay or straight, to succeed in the business world. Awards like this are fantastic in helping raise the profile of minority groups. Plus, with all the glitz and glamour, it was great fun collecting the award – it felt a bit like a "*Heat* magazine" moment'.[3]

LGB ENTREPRENEURS: SUMMARY

It is evident from the material reviewed in this chapter that unlike other minority entrepreneurs featured in this book, LGBs are not only likely to have experienced some types of discrimination and prejudice (often from an early age) but may also be subject to legal proceedings (or worse) if they reveal their sexuality. In many countries, homosexuality is against the law and even punishable by death (IDAHO-UK, 2009). Moreover, even in the US, more than half of the states still have no anti-discrimination laws relating to LGBs in the workplace (Herek et al., 2009). It is of little surprise therefore, to discover that research into LGB business owners has only really taken hold in the last decade or so and tends to be restricted to countries that have introduced legislation aimed at protecting LGBs against homophobic practices (Davidson, 2011).

Undoubtedly, the numbers of LGB entrepreneurs are increasing (albeit that many are still being forced to 'stay in the closet' and hide their sexual orientation) and they make a huge contribution to the global economy and their local communities (including LGB communities) (Resources for Gay and Lesbian Entrepreneurs, 2010). While LGB business owners often seem to have similar catalysts and motivations to set up business ventures to their heterosexual counterparts, they often have different demographic profiles and also face unique challenges and barriers. Compared to heterosexual entrepreneurs, LGB business owners tend to be more highly educated, are more likely to be professional, be childless, have higher financial business turnovers (once established) and are more likely to support and cater for the LGB community (although not exclusively so) (Galloway, 2007; GLBT Market Demographics, 2010). Like heterosexual business owners, the majority of LGBs are male, Caucasian, work in the private sector, are likely to have had an entrepreneurial parent and have similar personality characteristics (Schindehutte et al., 2005; Di Bernardo, 2007; Fielden and David-son, 2010).

While the majority of LGB entrepreneurs have reported experiencing homophobic discrimination and prejudice at some periods throughout their lives (including in their previous work environment), 'push' factors associated with homophobia when deciding to start their business ventures were not the main motivators (Schindehutte et al., 2005). Similar to the heterosexual self-employed (particularly females), evidence suggests that LGB entrepreneurs were much more likely to be influenced by 'pull' factors such as freedom and personal and financial independence (Willsdon, 2005).

Even so, Kidney and Cooney (2009) make the point that many researchers conclude that gay entrepreneurs may not always be aware of negative influences and that discrimination can be subtle and go unrecognized. Certainly though, many LGB business owners do indeed recognize that homophobia can be a significant business issue. This appears to be acknowledged as more of a potential problem for 'identifiers' (i.e., those LGBs who consider themselves to be 'gay' entrepreneurs) compared to 'independents' who want less attention to their sexuality and to be treated just like other business owners (Schindehutte et al., 2005). Furthermore, dilemmas about 'coming out' (including when employing 'non-gay' employees), are all potential stressors and strains unique to LGB entrepreneurs (Kidney and Cooney, 2009).

While discriminatory experiences from a young age may affect LGB business owners in a negative way by instilling feelings of distrust, disappointment and isolation, Kidney and Cooney (2009) also conclude that it could conversely result in gay individuals being more innovative and creative. In their review, these authors summarized the following eight unique and significant factors attributable to gay entrepreneurs: innovativeness, the area of gay employment, scepticism, affinity with the gay community (including marketing opportunities), self-protection, market demographic, social interaction and unconventional family models (leading to enhanced freedom and financial flexibility).

LGB ENTREPRENEURS: THE FUTURE

To date, while globally the challenges facing LGB entrepreneurs undoubtedly outweigh the advantages, there have been positive changes over the past few years with the introduction of stronger anti-discrimination legislation in many Western countries and positive changes in societal attitudes towards gays (Davidson, 2011). In the US and the UK, there is also evidence of an increasing number of programmes and networks being set up to support the LGB entrepreneurial community. For example, the new non-profit networking group for US gay entrepreneurs, 'Start Out', reported on their November (2010) event and their invited (role model) speaker Chip Conley (founder of 'Joie de Vivre', a boutique chain worth over $220 million). Conley addressed such questions as 'How do you come out of the closet in your business?' and 'How do you handle investors who might be uncomfortable with your vocal support of gay rights?' (Sorkin, 2010). Reporting on this conference, Sorkin concluded:

> In fact, the last decade has seen a flowering of affinity groups for gays in business. MBA candidates can get connected through 'Out for Business' clubs at their universities and the annual 'Reaching Out' conference, which brought more than 900 attendees to the West Peachtree Plaza in downtown Atlanta in October.

Other recent networks and resources for LGB business owners in the US include the 'National Gay and Lesbian Chamber of Commerce', *Echelon* (a gay magazine for LGBT business professionals), and 'Gay Franchise.com' (an online franchise directory with a list of franchisors that support LGB entrepreneurs) (Resources for Gay and Lesbian Entrepreneurs, 2010). Moreover, the continual development of online social networks such as Facebook, Twitter and LinkedIn, can also prove very beneficial for LGB entrepreneurs, both now and in the future. Klein (2010) for example, reported on a new LinkedIn for LGBT entrepreneurs entitled 'dot429' (429 spelling 'gay' on the telephone keypad). Although, in the past, there have been some concerns that such networks may brand LGB entrepreneurs in a sort of business ghetto, 'dot429' maintains it is unique in that it solicits both gay members and allies from the non-gay community, as well as advocating face-to-face networking (ibid.).

Interestingly, the utilization of the UK 'Business Link's Diverse Business Confidence Index' aimed at identifying how the recession was affecting London's small business by sector, business type and business ownership (deaf and disabled, gender, black, Asian and minority ethnic [BAME] and LGBT), revealed that the future looked particularly good for LGBT entrepreneurs (Queer UK, 2009). Despite the economic recession, compared to their heterosexual counterparts, LGBT business owners were more optimistic about growth and viewed the key drivers to growth as being related to seeking opportunities in new markets as well as launching new products and services (Queer UK, 2009).

However, in the final analysis, there is clearly an urgent need for more research into the multidimensional complexities of LGB entrepreneurship. For example, LGB entrepreneurial literature is still void of any comprehensive data on BAME entrepreneurs, lesbian entrepreneurs, LGB entrepreneurs from different religious backgrounds (e.g., Muslims), disabled LGB entrepreneurs, bisexual entrepreneurs and transsexuals, as well as large-scale cross-cultural studies. Galloway (2007) asserts that future research in the LGB entrepreneurial minority offers unique challenges for researchers, which will richly enhance our comprehension of the diversity of the entrepreneurship phenomenon. In the words of Galloway (2007, p. 279):

> Continued silence with regard to the study of gay entrepreneurship amongst the wider academic community will not only maintain the status quo in which gay entrepreneurship is held at the margins of socioeconomic life, but also could potentially comprise a missed opportunity for economic advantage within UK society generally.

NOTES

1. An amendment to the Local Government Act 1988 that stated a local authority 'shall not intentionally promote homosexuality or publish material with the intention of promoting homosexuality' or 'promote the teaching in any maintained school of the acceptability of homosexuality as a pretended family relationship'. Its existence caused many groups to close or limit their activities or self-censor. For example, a number of LGB student support groups in schools and colleges across Britain were closed due to fears by council legal staff that they could breach the Act (see http://en.wikipedia.org/wiki/Section_28).
2. Sources: adapted from the following: 'Ivan Massow: the never-ending Tory', *The Times Online*, 17 June 2009, www.timesonline.co.uk/tol/news/politics/article6506425.ece, accessed 21 March 2011; 'Out, proud and very rich', Gareth McLean, *The Guardian Online*, 26 October 2000, http://www.guardian.co.uk/world/2000/oct/26/gayrights. garethmclean, accessed 15 August 2011; Ivan Massow, http://en.wikipedia.org/wiki/Ivan_ Massow, accessed 15 August 2011.
3. Sources: adapted from the following: http://www.chameleon.eu/Page/Vicky-Reeves-Profile; http://www.preludegroup.co.uk/?p=1308; http://www.lgf.org.uk/vicky-reeves; http://www.linkedin.com/in/vickyreeves; all accessed 17 August 2011.

REFERENCES

Bendl, R. and A. Fleischmann (2008), 'Diversity management discourse meets queer theory', *Gender in Management: An International Review*, **23** (6), 382–94.

Carpentier, M. (2010), 'Citibank shuts down gay entrepreneur's bank account over blog's content', available at: http://washingtonindependent.com/77696/citibank-shuts-down-gay-entrepreneurs-bank-account-over-blogs-content; accessed 15 August 2011.

Costa, M. (2010), 'Pink pound's value rises in mainstream markets', available at http://www.marketingweek.co.uk/analysis/features/pink-pound%E2%80%99s-value-rises-in-mainstream-markets/3020077.articles; accessed 15 August 2011.

Davidson, M.J. (2011), 'The dark side of the rainbow: a research model of occupational stress and lesbian, gay and bisexuals (LGBs) in the workplace', in S. Groschl (ed.), *Diversity in the Workplace*, London: Gower.

Davies, G.S. (2010), 'A diversity integrative model of the factors affecting lesbian, gay and bisexual career choice intentions', MSc dissertation, University of Manchester, Faculty of Humanities, Manchester, UK.

Di Bernardo, E.M. (2007), 'The personality characteristics of homosexual entrepreneurs: an examination of gender and minority differences', PhD dissertation, Capella University, USA.

Equality and Human Rights Commission (EHRC) (2009), *Beyond Tolerance: Making Sexual Orientation a Public Matter*, Manchester: Equality and Human Rights Commission.

Fielden, S.L. and M.J. Davidson (eds) (2010), *International Research Handbook on Successful Women Entrepreneurs*, Cheltenham, UK and Northampton, MA, USA: Edward Elgar.

Galloway, L. (2007), 'Entrepreneurship and the gay minority. Why the silence?', *Entrepreneurship and Innovation*, **8** (4), 271–80.

GLBT Market Demographics (2010), available at: http://www.gaydays.com/Advertising/gay-and-lesbian-market-demographics.html; accessed 16 November 2010.

Goldberg, L.R. (1990), 'An alternative "description of personality": the Big Five factor structure', *Journal of Personality and Social Psychology*, **59** (6), 1216–29.

Guasp, A. and J. Balfour (2008), *Peak Performance: Gay People and Productivity*, London: Stonewall.

Hamar, M. (2010), 'Bilerico project building a network of gay entrepreneurs', available at http://www.bilerico.com/2010/06/building_a_network_of_gay_entrepreneurs.php; accessed 16 November 2010.

Haynes, D. (2010), 'What to watch: entrepreneurs, gay and lesbian contractors convene', available at http://www.washingtonpost.com/wp-dyn/content/article/2010/11/12/AR2010111205870.html; accessed 15 August 2011.

Herek, G.M., J.R. Gills and J.C. Coogan (2009), 'Internalized stigma among sexual minority adults: insights from a social psychological perspective', *Journal of Counselling Psychology*, **56** (1), 32–43.

IDAHO-UK (2009), 'International day against homophobia and transphobia', available at: http://www.idaho.org.uk/; accessed 18 August 2011.

Iwasaki, Y. and J.L. Ristock (2007), 'The nature of stress experienced by lesbians and gay men', *Anxiety, Stress and Coping*, **20** (3), 299–319.

Kets de Vries, M.F.R. (1977), 'The entrepreneurial personality: a person at the crossroads', *Journal of Management Studies*, **14** (1), 34–57.

Kidney, E. and T.M. Cooney (2009), 'How do gay entrepreneurs differ?', Irish Academy of Management Conference Proceedings, Galway, Ireland, 2–4 September.

Kite, M.E. and K. Deaux (1987), 'Gender belief systems: homosexuality and the implicit inversion theory', *Psychology of Women Quarterly*, **11** (1), 83–96.

Klein, K.E. (2010), 'A LinkedIn for LGBT entrepreneurs', available at: http://www.businessweek.com/smallbiz/content/jul2010/sb20100729_117892.htm; accessed 16 November 2010.

Levin, S. (1998), *In the Pink: The Making of Successful Gay- and Lesbian-owned Businesses*, New York: Haworth Press.

Lippa, R.A. (2005), *Gender, Nature and Nurture*, New Jersey: Lawrence Erlbaum.

Looy, H. (2005), 'The nature of gender: gender identity in persons who are intersexed or transgendered', *Journal of Psychology and Theology*, **33** (3), 166–78.

Merco Press (2010), 'More than 25 million gays live in Latin America and spend billions travelling', available at: http://en.mercopress.com/2010/11/03/more-than-25-million-gays-live-in-latin-america-and-spend-billions-travelling; accessed 15 August 2011.

Pillinger, J. (2008), *Extending Equality – Report of European Trade Union Confederation*, Brussels: ETUC.

Queer UK (2009), 'Gay entrepreneurs buck recession', available at: http://www.queeruk.net/2009/07/23/gay-entrepreneurs-buck-recession-trend/; accessed 15 August 2011.

Resources for Gay and Lesbian Entrepreneurs (2010), available at: http://www.gaebler.com/help-for-Gay-entrepreneurs.htm; accessed 16 November 2010.

San Diego Gay and Lesbian News (2010), 'America's gay buying power projected at $743 billion in 2010', available at: http://sdgln.com/news/2010/07/20/america-s-gay-buying-power-projected-743-billion-2010; accessed 16 November 2010.

Schindehutte, M., M. Morris and J. Allen (2005), 'Homosexuality and entrepreneurship – implications of gay identity for the venture-creation experience', *Entrepreneurship and Innovation*, **6** (1), 27–40.

Sorkin, R.A. (2010), 'Building a network of gay entrepreneurs', available at http://dealbook.nytimes.com/2010/05/20/building-a-network-of-gay-entrepreneurs; accessed 16 November 2010.

Stonewall (2009), *Bisexual People in the Workplace: Practical Advice for Employees*, London: Stonewall.

Sweeney, P. (2010), 'Gay investment consulting in China', available at: http://www.chinaeconomicreview.com/en/node/28646; accessed 15 August 2011.

The Wall Street Journal (2010), 'Should gay owners out themselves?', available at: http://online.wsj.com/article/SB10001424052702303720604575169910619381720.html; accessed 15 August 2010.

Valentine, G., N. Wood and P. Plummer (2009), *The Experience of Lesbian, Gay and Bisexual and Trans Staff and Students in Higher Education*, London: Equality Challenge Unit.

Varnell, P. (1999), 'Gay consumer clout in the early 20th century', available at: http://www.igfculturewatch.com/1999/11/30/gay-consumer-clout-in-the-early-20th-century; accessed 16 November 2010.

Varnell, P. (2001), *What Gay Entrepreneurs Contribute*, Chicago: Free Press.

Ward, J., D. Winstanley and K. Hill (2006), 'Don't frighten the horses: emotive issues in researching sexual orientation at work', *International Journal of Work Organisation and Emotion*, **1** (4), 305–11.

Watkins, D.S. and J. Watkins (1984), 'The female entrepreneur: her background and determinants of business choice, some British data', *International Small Business Journal*, **2** (4), 21–31.

Willsdon, J. (2005), 'Homosexual entrepreneurs: different but the same', *Irish Journal of Management*, **26** (1), 107–21.

Wilson, N.L. (1997), 'Queer culture and sexuality as a virtue of hospitality', in R. Goss and A.A. Strongheart (eds), *Our Families, Our Values: Snapshots of Queer Kinship*, New York: Haworth Press, pp. 21–35.

8.   Disabled entrepreneurs

> Disabled people are probably better qualified to start and run their own business, having already overcome, or able to deal with their disability within their normal day-to-day living. Starting a business may seem daunting but when you are doing something that you really enjoy, it couldn't be easier.
>
> (Albert Thompson, MD of Action Casualty Simulations [ACS])]

INTRODUCTION

It has been estimated that around 600 000 000 people, that is, approximately 10 per cent of the world's populations, have a disability. According to Disabled World (2010):

> A disability is a condition or function judged to be significantly impaired, relative to the usual standard of an individual or group. The term is used to refer to individual functioning, including physical impairment, sensory impairment, cognitive impairment, intellectual impairment, mental illness and various types of chronic disease.

Moreover, disabled individuals constitute 20 per cent of the world's poorest persons in both developing and developed countries (Stein and Stein, 2007; De Klerk, 2008). In both the US and the UK, 18 per cent of the population has a disability and in the UK there are 10 million disabled, also constituting 18 per cent of the working population (US Census Bureau, 2006; Labour Force Survey, 2009). Certainly, percentage rates of the disabled in the workforce vary between countries. In Ireland for example, employment rates of disabled individuals aged 15 to 64 years with disability health problems are comparatively high at 37.1 per cent compared to 67 per cent of non-disabled (Cooney, 2008). In Canada on the other hand, employees of 'prime working age' between 25 and 54 years with mental or physical disabilities constitute only 9 per cent of the workforce and of those working, a third earn below $20 000 per annum (Anderson et al., 2009). Furthermore, in the US, individuals with disabilities with full-time jobs earned about 22 per cent less than their non-disabled counterparts.

Clearly, disabled employees tend not only to earn less than the non-disabled, but are less likely to be part of the workforce. For example, in the UK only half of disabled people of working age are in employment compared to 80 per cent of the non-disabled of working age (Labour Force Survey, 2009). The UK employment rate for those with a work-limiting disability is 38 per cent for females and 43 per cent for males (Jones and Latrielle, 2006). Moreover, the employment rate of the disabled has been shown to be very dependent on the type of impairment, with the lowest employment rates of all impairment categories in the UK being individuals with mental health problems (only 20 per cent) (Shaw Trust, 2006; Cooney, 2008). In the US, Jones and Latrielle (2006) also point out that the disabled are twice as likely as the non-disabled to be employed as independent contractors, on temporary contracts or as part-timers.

It is interesting to note that in a number of developed countries, the education gap between the disabled and non-disabled is relatively small compared to the income/employment gap. In Canada for example, 57 per cent of the general population have completed post-secondary education compared to 46 per cent of individuals with disabilities (Social Development Canada, 2005). Furthermore, in the UK, while more than twice the number of disabled of working age have no qualifications compared to the non-disabled, more than 76 per cent of disabled people with a higher education qualification were in employment compared to 90 per cent of non-disabled (Labour Force Survey, 2006). Indeed, Anderson et al. (2009) propose that this relatively closer education gap lends support to the contention that the full potential of the disabled has not been realized in the market place. In a recent survey of disabled British employees, only 1 in 20 maintained they required support to do the job although many maintained they needed more understanding and support from their colleagues and managers in terms of stress management, the need to take breaks, flexible working hours and flexibility to take time off sick (Williams et al., 2008). According to Cooney (2008, p. 120), other issues that can influence a disabled individual's willingness or ability to join the labour market can include: 'the severity of the disability, access to and within a potential workplace, beliefs about the likelihood of facing discrimination, and the trade off between employment income and benefit receipts' (Smith and Twomey, 2002 cited in Cooney, 2008).

Explanations for the disadvantaged position of disabled employees compared to their non-disabled counterparts have included the structure of the differing benefit schemes/regimes, employer discrimination and the degree and strength of disability discrimination legislation (which obviously varies from country to country) (Schur, 2003; Jones and Latrielle, 2006). Cooney (2008) highlighted the particular reluctance of small and medium-sized enterprises (SMEs) to employ disabled individuals, based on the report by the European Foundation for Improvement of Living and Working Conditions (2006). These reasons were largely based on barriers linked to health and safety and insurance issues, lack of financial incentives, immunity from quotas and anti-discrimination legislation, and poor equal opportunity HR practices (Cooney, 2008). Similar to many of the other minority groups featured in this book, due to the lack of opportunities in the job market, it is not surprising to find that compared to the non-disabled entrepreneurial population, a higher proportion of people with disabilities (especially in the developed countries) turn to self-employment.

DISABLED ENTREPRENEURS: GENERAL CHARACTERISTICS

In the UK, recent statistics indicate that of those employed, 21 per cent of work-limited disabled men and 9 per cent of work-limited disabled women were classified as self-employed, compared to 17 per cent of non-disabled men and 6–7 per cent of non-disabled women who were self-employed (Jones and Latrielle, 2006). Certainly, over-representation of the disabled in self-employment, with men exhibiting higher incidences, is common in many countries. In the US, where small businesses dominate the economy, Angelocci et al. (2008) reported that twice as many individuals with disabilities are self-employed (predominately in home-based businesses), compared to non-disabled individuals. Another US survey of self-employed individuals with disabilities found the majority to be white (88 per cent) and male (66 per cent) (Holub, 2001).

In an in-depth comparative study in the UK, Jones and Latrielle (2006) categorized their sample into work-limited disabled and non-work-limited disabled and non-disabled. They found that the type of self-employment was fairly similar among the different disability groups. The exception to this was the male and female work-limited disabled, who were more likely than other disabled groups to classify themselves as 'working for self'. Furthermore, this group of disabled men were more likely to be sole operators (80 per cent) compared to 74 per cent of self-employed non-disabled men (ibid.). The US survey by Holub (2001) reported that some disabled entrepreneurs found niche markets that specifically provided for disabled individuals and some of these entrepreneurs had made efforts to employ people with disabilities.

A number of studies, including the Swedish study by Larsson (2006), have revealed that the majority of disabled entrepreneurs work part-time in their firm, which is in contrast to non-disabled entrepreneurs. What is also evident is that self-employment rates and severity of disability often increase with age (Boylan and Burchardt, 2002; Larsson, 2006). Similar to previous studies, Jones and Latrielle (2006) also found that their disabled self-employed sample (particularly the males) were older than their non-disabled counterparts. As a possible consequence, the disabled self-employed in all groups tended to have fewer dependent children (including pre-school age) and were more likely to work from home. In addition, consistent with other findings, they identified that the work-limited disabled in particular were less well qualified (especially in relation to university education) compared to the non-work-limited disabled and especially the non-disabled (ibid.). In summarizing the common characteristics of self-employed in both disabled and non-disabled individuals, similarities included: being older, being male, living in areas of high unemployment rates and having craft or vocational qualifications (Boylan and Burchardt, 2002).

When analysing the self-employment rates in the UK survey by type of impairment, Boylan and Burchardt (ibid.) found men with sensory impairments were the least likely to be self-employed whereas men and women with musculoskeletal impairments, and women with mental health problems, were more likely than other disabled individuals to be self-employed. These authors also found that both disabled self-employed men and women worked fewer hours than their non-disabled counterparts; 42.8 hours versus 48.6 hours and 29.5 hours versus 33.3 hours respectively (ibid.). What is evident is that in all countries globally, men and women with disabilities are much more likely to be unemployed. Moreover, the US Census Bureau (2006), in reference to this group, maintained that the evidence indicated that the risks associated with starting small business ownership was minimal compared with the possibilities of success.

DISABLED ENTREPRENEURS: ASPIRATIONS AND MOTIVATIONS

Cooney (2008) makes reference to Harper and Momm's (1989) suggestion that individuals with disabilities often make natural entrepreneurs, as having a disability can help instigate independent innovation and problem-solving abilities. Self-employment can provide entrepreneurs with disabilities with a wide range of employment benefits including better working conditions and hours, ability to increase income, ability to create one's own job and the opportunity to create a career path for unlimited future growth (Weiss-Doyel, 2001; Mathis, 2003). Furthermore, self-employment also offers freedom from disability and physical access-related barriers such as

inaccessible work environments, fatigue, geographical and transport problems, discrimination and prejudice in the workplace (particularly if the
business is home-based) (Mathis, 2003; Jones and Latrielle, 2006). Moreover, positive pull factors for starting a business were revealed by a survey
carried out by the US RTC Rural (Research and Training Center on
Disability in Rural Communities) (2003) in conjunction with the Disabled
Business Person's Association. The main reason quoted by disabled people
for starting a business venture was 'wanting to work for themselves' (56 per
cent), followed by 'identifying a product/service need' (48 per cent), 'wanting to make more money' (46 per cent), 'wanting to own a business' (46 per
cent), 'needing to create own job' (44 per cent), 'to accommodate a disability' (i.e., flexible working conditions and/or hours) (43 per cent), and finally,
'other jobs unavailable (15 per cent) (ibid.). Nevertheless, Jones and
Latrielle (2006) quoted a number of studies that emphasized the impact of
previous discrimination as a 'push' factor. These authors referred to a
particularly relevant study by Blanck et al. (2000), which investigated
Iowa's Entrepreneurs With Disabilities (EWD) programme designed to
help increase access to self-employment for the disabled. According to
Jones and Latrielle (2006, p. 5):

> These authors highlight the role of discrimination (either perceived or actual)
> and particularly in terms of hiring and firing, as a major motivation for disabled
> persons starting their own business, and conclude that self-employment affords
> increased employment opportunities for the disabled. Discrimination was also
> found by Schur (2003) to be more important as an explanation of higher
> self-employment rates among the disabled than for the other non-standard
> forms of employment that this group may enter.

When further examining the 'push' and 'pull' factors in relation to the
disabled entrepreneurs versus the non-disabled, Boylan and Burchardt
(2002, p. 90) highlighted some other differences:

> One important difference is in the reasons disabled people cite for entering
> self-employment: while both disabled and non-disabled people appreciate the
> flexibility some forms of self-employment bring, disabled people are less likely,
> on balance, to cite 'pull' factors for entering self-employment – especially those
> with low educational qualifications.

In this UK study, it is interesting to note that these authors also found few
differences in motivations across disability groups 'within' gender but
bigger differences being revealed 'between' genders. A higher percentage of
disabled women cited 'push' factors for becoming self-employed as being
due to family commitments (similar to non-disabled female entrepreneurs –
see Fielden and Davidson, 2010), whilst men were more likely to report

'push' factors related to being made redundant or the lack of local jobs (Boylan and Burchardt, 2002).

On a positive note, one of the few studies that has measured attitudes of disabled entrepreneurs (in the US), revealed that 91 per cent said they enjoyed operating their business, nearly three-quarters maintained that they were satisfied with their business and 56 per cent both describe their business as being successful and that their business had met or exceeded their expectations (Holub, 2001). Furthermore, rebuilding self-esteem had been found to be another positive reason given by disabled people as a motivator for being self-employed (Boylan and Burchardt, 2002). Nevertheless, these authors concluded that their representative survey data from disabled entrepreneurs suggested that those with lower educational qualifications tended to have fewer positive motivators for entering entrepreneurship in the first instance compared to non-disabled entrepreneurs:

> For those with professional qualifications, self-employment could be a matter of free choice (although they reported limitations in employment opportunities), but for those with low or no educational qualifications, while recognizing that it had positive aspects, self-employment was more often a last resort. (Boylan and Burchardt, 2002, p. 90)

While recognizing both the 'push' and 'pull' factors influencing disabled individuals to set up new business ventures, Cooney (2008) acknowledged the strong discriminatory 'push' forces linked to disadvantaged earning and employment opportunities. Without doubt, however, entrepreneurship also helps to accommodate the individual needs of disabled individuals, whether it be flexibility (for those requiring frequent medical attention) or accessible work space (ibid.).

DISABLED ENTREPRENEURS: CHALLENGES AND BARRIERS

Having established both similarities and differences between disabled and non-disabled entrepreneurs in terms of characteristics and motivators, it is important to review the potential challenges and barriers facing this group of entrepreneurs. Potential barriers faced by both disabled and non-disabled entrepreneurs starting their own businesses can include problems with finance, lack of support from professional advisers and clients and access problems (Fielden and Davidson, 2010). However, many of these problems appear to be even more acute for disabled individuals. In their in-depth study of 12 disabled UK entrepreneurs, Boylan and Burchardt (2002) for example, concluded that lack of start-up capital was even more of a problem for this group of entrepreneurs as they were more likely to have been on 'benefits' and have poor credit ratings. This was a particular problem highlighted by the long-term sick and disabled interviewees, who were more likely to have been unemployed for longer periods. Interestingly, in contrast to research findings on non-disabled female entrepreneurs compared to their male counterparts (e.g., Fielden and Davidson, 2010), the Swedish study by Larsson (2006) suggested that disabled female entrepreneurs did not report more problems than their male counterparts in obtaining business investment.

Nevertheless, similar to other entrepreneurial minority groups included in this book, Boylan and Burchardt (2002) reported that a number of their interviewees had faced discrimination and this was due to their disability when attempting to set up their business, particularly from banks and business advisers who often had stereotyped views of what a disabled person may not be able to do. Another main issue raised was fear about losing the security of regular benefit income and there was a common lack of awareness concerning the available benefits (e.g., Disabled Person's Tax Credit) available to them. The final major barriers cited by the disabled entrepreneurs centred on the lack of access to appropriate training and support. This included lack of transport and financial support enabling travel to advice centres, inaccessibility of training locations and training sessions not being designed for individual needs, poor advertising of available services and lack of alternative forms of information formats (e.g., Braille) (ibid.). These authors also made the relevant point of how crucial educational qualifications were in influencing the financial rewards and experience of all entrepreneurship. Disabled entrepreneurs, however, as mentioned previously, tend to be potentially disadvantaged in this respect compared to their non-disabled counterparts as they are more likely to have lower educational and professional qualifications and consequently are concentrated in lower-status jobs, generating lower pay (ibid.).

In his study of Swedish disabled entrepreneurs, Larsson (2006) followed up his sample after two years and found that over half (i.e., 60 per cent) were no longer active in business and of those still in business, only 31.2 per cent maintained they were 100 per cent involved in their enterprise. Hence a large proportion worked part-time, with 52.8 per cent working full-time. The main reason given for less involvement was usually related to health reasons, which had tended to get worse over time. This was in sharp contrast to Swedish non-disabled entrepreneurs, with 84 per cent continuing to work full-time in their businesses (Larsson, 2006). Nevertheless, Larsson (2006) concluded that the proportion of 'business failures' wasn't

particularly higher for the disabled group after the two years than comparative studies on non-disabled entrepreneurs. However, reasons for ending
their businesses did illicit both similarities and differences:

> [T]he main personal reason for disabled entrepreneurs to end their firm is illness
> (34.8%). This reason is stated by only 7% of entrepreneurs in Grefwe's study
> (1999). Other powerful reasons for closing a firm include a sense of threatened
> social security (20.6%) and the feeling that the workload had become too great
> (17.2%). (Larsson, 2006, p.164)

Like their non-disabled counterparts, the most common economic reason
cited for ending the business in Larsson's (2006) follow up, was too low a
turnover in relation to expenses (33.3 per cent). Another major economic
reason given by just over a quarter of the Swedish disabled entrepreneurs
was shortage of capital. Larsson (2006) makes the important distinction
that this is a substantially higher proportion than cited by non-disabled
entrepreneurs in other studies (e.g., only 11 per cent of entrepreneurs in the
study by Bengtsson and Gustafsson, 1998).

Finally, on a more positive note, Boylan and Burchardt (2002) identified
a number of factors from their UK disabled entrepreneurs that contributed
to success in establishing a business. These included family support (providing start-up finance, encouragement, transport and practical help) and
in-work benefits such as Disabled Person's Tax Credit and Disabled Living
Allowance (all of which helped to make the business financially viable). In
addition, for younger disabled entrepreneurs, help from The Prince's Trust
was also deemed highly beneficial, particularly the availability of ongoing
mentoring (ibid.).

DISABLED ENTREPRENEURS: STORIES OF SUCCESS

The following case studies describe the experiences of four highly successful
disabled British entrepreneurs – Hazel Carter-Showell, Albert Thompson,
Vanessa Heywood and Amar Latif. Hazel had already launched her new
company before she became ill with a brain tumour; Albert began his
business after losing his leg during action in the army; Vanessa launched
her company after developing multiple sclerosis and Amar, after losing his
sight. All of them have different disabilities and all of them illustrate great
determination in defying initial negatives and turning these into amazing
positives and subsequent business success.

BOX 8.1 HAZEL CARTER-SHOWELL – MD OF CARTER AND CORSON – BUSINESS PSYCHOLOGISTS

Hazel Carter-Showell started her business Carter and Corson Partnership Ltd in 1999 (at the age of 33) with her business partner (John) and Hazel is MD of the company, which is made up of six staff and specializes in senior assessment, coaching and development in both the public and the private sectors. Her business partner (a former accountant) is a director and they both previously worked together in the same executive recruitment company. Hazel and John wanted to create a company that united their interest in psychology and business – the first business venture for either of them.

Unfortunately, within three months of starting the business, Hazel was diagnosed with a brain tumour, which left John keeping the business ticking over for three months whilst she was in hospital and during her initial post-operative recovery period. However, even when she was in hospital paralysed down her left side, Hazel continued to work on the business from her hospital bed! She went on to defy bleak predictions, including clinicians who said she may never walk again, and despite her disabilities (which involve problems with balance, coordination, walking, nerve pain and occasional blackouts), quickly got rid of her wheelchair and went on to build a highly successful business.

During the business set-up stage, Hazel did not mention her disability to the banks and hence the biggest barriers Hazel faced were to do with sexism rather than disability discrimination. During early meetings with (male) bank managers, Hazel was often the one asked to pour the tea and they seemed to have problems with the notion of a woman being an MD and being able to develop business strategies! In the end, she used her networking skills to find a female bank manager who set them up with a small business loan. Hazel is delighted, since then, to have met more enlightened financiers.

Despite having a lot of successful previous business experience between them, other initial challenges involved a lack of understanding from the banks as to what exactly business psychologists did, that is, unlike many entrepreneurs they didn't have a specific product to sell or produce. Some government support was based on taking on individuals who were long-term unemployed – less useful for a small business where even their administrators had Masters degrees in Organizational Psychology. Also, they resisted the pressure to take on a chairperson when investors only wanted one to break any deadlocked decision, stating that human relations was their expertise area and they shouldn't need someone to sort out disagreements!

The business was built up steadily and Hazel said that she quickly learned that she had to find a different way of working with an acquired brain injury (a disability that is sometimes hidden until faced with less accessible buildings, heat, stress or tiredness). One of Hazel's important support systems was finding a mentor and role model who was a chairperson with an acquired brain injury. The best advice she received was to always remember three 'Ps' – 'Planning', 'Pacing' and 'Prioritizing'. For Hazel, learning how to pace one's work, knowing when to push hard and importantly, when to 'sit on a rock and rest', were invaluable lessons for both her own and the business's survival and growth. She maintained that her biggest lesson had been her final acceptance of her own limitations, despite working over 70 hours a week! It took many years to consider herself disabled – despite the evidence. However, after suffering post-traumatic stress, with the help of a clinical psychologist, she was able to accept the loss of 'Hazel A' (with near photographic memory, physically able and with perfect vision) on the operating table and accept and value the new 'Hazel B' who had none of those things but who had more empathy and tolerance.

Recently, when Hazel considered raising investment to grow the business, her health issues were raised by advisers. However, she challenged their concerns successfully by pointing out she had already proved herself over many years and that her health was much more closely monitored than the majority of business owners – where stress can become the silent killer.

Hazel maintained she puts her heart and soul into the business and for her, 'success' is not about 'the money' but about 'knowing they made a difference'. Their corporate mission is about 'changing the world, one person at a time' and they are proud of having 11 years of unbroken references from satisfied clients. Not being able to have children of her own, due to the tumour, for Hazel her business is 'her baby' and she wants it to matter.

Undoubtedly, Hazel's main challenges in building the business have revolved around her disability and often included practical barriers and misunderstandings about her specific needs. Generally, she doesn't inform clients about her disability unless the working facilities are unsuitable physically (e.g., training rooms on floors without lifts). In some cases clients have overreacted and tried to 'wrap her in cotton wool', that is, they 'assume' rather than 'ask' her about her specific needs. When needed, she simply presents with one of the team (while only charging for one person) who would understand and know how to react should she black out (something that incidentally has never happened in that particular situation).

The business outsources all its main support needs, from accountants to IT specialists, on a regular basis. The long-term aim is to develop the company so it can be sold off in the future. It is being progressed and built for exit, into a recognizable brand that has value. According to Hazel, this will mean she will have to eventually step away from her 'baby' and let it go. She envisages being a non-executive in the future, enabling her to continue to shape policies and bring about organizational change. Taking on interesting consultancy challenges and corporate mentoring may be another future career option. At this point in time, Hazel can't imagine retirement!

Hazel's advice to other potential disabled entrepreneurs is not to listen to others about their limitations but at the same time to know themselves in order to keep themselves safe. Finding a business mentor who understands your disability is extremely important. She also believes that she achieved a lot more once she had 'embraced' her disability and advocates not being afraid to ask for help (including counselling/therapy) if needed. More knowledge and access to resources available to disabled entrepreneurs would have been a great advantage for her and Hazel believes there isn't enough being done to advertise these support services. She has fairly recently gained 'Access to Work' support, which she didn't know existed previously. This helps with sourcing the right equipment for her condition such as voice-activated IT software and as she is unable to drive due to her disability, supporting her to employ a driver. This support has made a huge difference to her life and business.

Finally, Hazel concludes that despite the extra challenges, her disability has undoubtedly equipped her with additional drive and determination, which has benefitted her company. Having already been tested to the full in life, she feels the only thing she is fighting is the assumption that all disabilities are the same and that every disabled person has the same needs.[1]

BOX 8.2 ALBERT THOMPSON – MD OF ACTION CASUALTY SIMULATIONS (ACS)

Albert Thompson served 18 years in the British army as a Colour Sergeant and left after having been seriously injured by 'friendly fire' whilst serving in Iraq in 2003. This resulted in having to have his left leg amputated above the knee. While recovering in hospital, he used the time to plan his future life and began to formulate the idea of starting a company that utilized amputees in military training scenarios, to give the 'shock factor' to training rescue and medical personnel. In particular, he acknowledged that his survival was due to the medical expertise of the army doctors who arrived quickly on the scene after he was injured: 'I re-create scenes of devastation such as blasts using amputees as casualties to give a more realistic simulation and have trained in the use of pyrotechnics and the application of specialist effect make-up'.

Albert's main motivations for starting his new business venture Action Casualty Simulations (ACS) in 2005, was to turn what was initially a major negative in his life into a positive, as well as 'give something back' and show that amputees can have a vital role in helping to train medical and rescue services. According to Albert: 'As soon as I began running ACS I knew I'd made the best decision of my life. I knew then this was the reason I'd survived because I was meant to help other amputees … It's too easy to sit at home feeling sorry for yourself but getting one job now and again helps to give many amputees a much needed boost'.

In 2008, Albert was awarded the UK Disabled Entrepreneur of the Year at Radar's People of the Year Awards. In his acceptance speech Albert commented: 'Disabled people are probably better qualified to start and run their own business, having already overcome, or be able to deal with their disability within their normal day-to-day living. Starting a business may seem daunting but when you are doing something that you really enjoy, it couldn't be easier. You put in as much, or as little, time as you can manage, but will probably find a drive and determination you never knew you had. It is fulfilling and satisfying and I would recommend it'.

Today, ACS includes a large database of both men and women amputees aged 16–88 years of age (including ex-military personnel) and Albert has even been known to recruit people he happens to meet on the street! He has gone on to develop and extend the services offered both by himself and the other amputees who are on his books, to include being 'extras' in movies. To date, he has appeared in films starring well-known Hollywood actors such as Sir Antony Hopkins, Colin Firth, Jude Law and Robert Downey Jr. and recent film appearances include *The Wolfman* and *Dorian Gray*. Albert recently asserted: 'When I lost my leg at first I thought my life was over. But now I'm rubbing shoulders with some of the best actors in Hollywood and things couldn't get any better'.[2]

BOX 8.3 VANESSA HEYWOOD – CREATOR/ FOUNDER TINY MITES MUSIC

Vanessa Heywood graduated from The Arts Educational School and performed in plays and musicals ranging from *The Boyfriend*, *Christmas Carol* and *Twelfth Night* on stage in the West End of London and in theatres across the UK. She came from a musical family and her father (Chris Smith) was a well-known professional trombonist who toured with such stars as Frank Sinatra.

In 1995, Vanessa Heywood was diagnosed with multiple sclerosis (MS) and had to give up her career as a professional dancer, singer and actress. She described the early signs of her disease as first becoming noticeable whilst she was dancing. In a recent interview with *Guardian* journalist Graham Snowden she said: 'As a dancer I was incredibly fit, obviously, but I was doing double pirouettes and not quite landing on a sixpence. At first I thought I wasn't practising hard enough, that I must practise harder. But then I started to realize it wasn't that'.

After her diagnosis of MS was confirmed, she made efforts to carry on with her career but found that it became increasingly difficult. In addition, having had two children in quick succession, her marriage broke up and she found herself as a single mother with two toddlers and no income coming in. She then decided to launch her company 'Tiny Mites Music', which provides recorded and live interaction music sessions targeted at young children.

For Vanessa, this new venture enabled her to manage the symptoms of her disability whilst at the same time allowing her to utilize her musical talent. Describing where the inspiration for her business came from she recalled: 'I took my kids to a sing-along session where the mums were drinking coffee and singing "The

Wheels on the Bus" rather half-heartedly, and I just realized I could do better than this. I had to make it work. The ideas grew from songs and stories I made up and sang to my children. I wrote one song after another, they tumbled out in a creative flurry. At the same time I created four little characters, The Tiny Mites; they became an important part of the concept'.

Indeed, Vanessa's very first music session for children was held in a church field in her home town of Radlett in Hertfordshire, as she couldn't afford the cost of hiring a hall! She eventually took her business plan and ideas for her company to the Dancers Trust and in 2002, they financed her first recording, paying for the studio fees and the musicians. Today, Tiny Mites Music sessions have a portfolio of more than 100 children's songs that are performed regularly in nearly 100 venues nationwide. Tiny Mites also has contracts with a variety of schools, nursery chains and holiday parks. In addition to producing Tiny Mites CDs, Vanessa also offers Tiny Mites birthday parties for under-fives and is in the process of franchising her business throughout the UK.

In 2010, at the age of 41, Vanessa Heywood was announced the winner of the Stelios Award for Disabled Entrepreneurs in the UK at the Growing Business Awards Ceremony and was presented with a £50 000 cheque, along with specialist support through the Stelios Scholar Reach-out Programme. On presenting her the award, the sponsor and famous entrepreneur and MD of easyJet, Stelios praised her entrepreneurial passion, originality, performance and her business acumen. He continued by saying: 'I would like to congratulate Vanessa on running a successful business and displaying the drive, creativity and determination to reach the top and really fly. The £50 000 will ensure Tiny Mites Music has an important boost for growth. Today, she joins our community of entrepreneurs who are making a difference'.[3]

BOX 8.4 AMAR LATIF – MANAGING DIRECTOR AND FOUNDER 'TRAVELEYES'

Amar Latif is a blind British entrepreneur and is founder and director of the business 'Traveleyes', which is the world's first commercial international air tour company to specialize in catering for blind as well as sighted travellers. He is also a film and TV programme-maker and director, an actor and motivational speaker. Amar was born in Scotland in 1974 and by the time he was 20 years of age, he had lost 95 per cent of his sight due to the incurable eye condition retinitis pigmentosa.

Amar was awarded a BSc in Mathematics, Statistics and Finance at the University of Strathclyde in Scotland and also spent some of his studies at Queen's University, Kingston, Ontario in Canada. Having graduated from university, he then went on to train as an accountant and later at British Telecom (BT), became Head of Commercial Finance. Amar recalls these early days by saying: 'I set off on my professional career as a Management Accountant at British Telecom in Leeds, in the northern part of England. I still work for BT, managing a team of accountants. I advise on the subject of disability access, and BT is an exemplary employer in this respect'.

However, as Amar's eyesight worsened as he got older, he described how this inspired him to take on innumerable (sometimes dangerous) challenges: 'Though every year my eyesight has become more restricted ... every year the sky becomes higher and the horizon becomes wider and more tantalizing, packed with fantastic, hidden mysteries ... all waiting to be revealed. As life began to present challenges, I seized every opportunity I could, taking on probably more of them than was either wise or advisable. I borrowed funds to start a portfolio of professional rental houses. I was a mad judo enthusiast, I climbed mountains in Poland, I surfed in Hawaii. One day, while a friend and I were raising funds for charity, I began to wonder just how 'safe' and conventional I could really claim to be. Perhaps I should mention that I was at the time abseiling down the side of a large public building, dressed in a Batman costume!'

Indeed, it was Amar's other passion for travel that eventually inspired him to launch Traveleyes. His aim was to set up a travel company that would enable blind people to experience and enjoy world travel as independent travellers, without having to rely on family and friends. The company also offers holidays at a substantial discount to sighted people and in return, they travel with visually impaired or blind people and can act as guides and describe sights.

When trying to secure finance in order to set up Traveleyes, Amar maintained he experienced quite a bit of discrimination due to his disability and he was refused finance from some of the banks he initially approached: 'It was clear all they saw was a blind man and appeared to equate disability with risk, without properly assessing my plans'. Having eventually secured financial backing from one of the banks, Traveleyes grew into a highly successful Leeds-based business. Amar also believes that the success of his company is due to the total commitment of his team in sharing his passion in offering blind people quality travel and experiences and opportunities that have often been denied to them in the past: 'Rather than lament our visual disability, we prefer to jet-ski across sparkling blue bays, and to explore the tactile treasures of fascinating ancient worlds, and to savour fine local cuisine and aromatic wines on the dreaming hillsides of Tuscany'.

In 2005, Amar's entrepreneurial success was recognized by the Junior Chamber International when they awarded him the 'Outstanding Young Business Entrepreneur of the Year Award'. Two years later in 2007, Amar was awarded the very first 'Stelios Disabled Entrepreneur Award' (specifically aimed at disabled British entrepreneurs with businesses less than three years old) and £50 000 prize money to help further develop his business. On receiving his award, Amar proclaimed: 'At present, disabled entrepreneurs have to be twice as good as non-disabled business owners to succeed ... I believe that the positive approach is the way to overcome the fear, prejudice and misconceptions that often stand in the way of disabled people. Many disabled people may, like me, wish to become entrepreneurs, but no one should be forced into self-employment by a lack of employment opportunity in the job market.'[4]

DISABLED ENTREPRENEURS: SUMMARY

Clearly, it is evident from the limited material presented in this chapter that there is need for further research in this area, particularly investigating regional and country variations (especially in developing countries) in self-employment rates among the disabled, isolating the different types of disabilities and their specific barriers and needs, investigating explanations for the wage gaps between the disabled and non-disabled and presenting worldwide examples of good practice supporting disabled entrepreneurs (Boylan and Burchardt, 2002; Association of Disabled Professionals, 2010). It would appear that while many of the barriers to self-employment and subsequent success are similar for both disabled and non-disabled individuals, these barriers and problems are often more acute and magnified for the disabled. Disabled people are more likely to face discrimination from advisers, employment institutions and business advisers. Furthermore, they are also likely to face more difficulties in accessing start-up capital, interacting effectively with the benefit system and accessing appropriate advice and training.

Indeed, more and more countries are now introducing specifically designed entrepreneurial training initiatives and programmes for disabled individuals. In the US, for example, the National Technical Assistance Center (2003) proposed that step-by-step entrepreneurial training programmes need to be offered in parallel to current services. The types of training suggested for the disabled self-employed included business plan development, business training, specific skills training in obtaining financial resources, direct financial assistance as well as financial resources, and mentoring programmes and professional business coaching (ibid.).

In the UK, Boylan and Burchardt (2002) also emphasized the importance of mentoring and maintained that sufficient funding should be made available to train and finance business mentors for the disabled self-employed in local communities. Also, they suggested training should be inclusive and made available to both non-disabled and disabled entrepreneurs in order to allow free exchange of ideas. Moreover, they proposed that the UK support initiative 'Business Link' should provide more accessible information sites for the disabled such as in libraries and in high streets, as well as the provision of subsidized business incubation units during the early business start-up stage.

In South Africa, Lorenzo et al. (2007) reported on the 'Community Disability Entrepreneurial Project', which was initiated in order to develop the entrepreneurial skills of disabled individuals inhabiting informal settlements around Cape Town. In particular, they emphasized how the main aim of this programme was to facilitate the 'upliftment' and economic empowerment of disabled people in those communities (ibid.).

There are also entrepreneurial training schemes that have specifically catered for certain types of individuals with disabilities. For example, Bender (2003) described how persons in the US with serious mental illness had been offered a 15-session entrepreneurial training programme by the private, non-profit organization 'Brooklyn Economic Development Corporation'. More recently, Shaheen and Myhill (2009) have described a programme developed by Syracuse University's Whitman School of Management in the US entitled 'The Entrepreneurial Boot Camp for Veterans with Disabilities' (EBV). By 2008, it had been estimated that US casualties from wars in Iraq and Afghanistan exceeded 40 000, with the number of soldiers suffering from post-traumatic stress and other psychological disorders (including substance abuse) being well over 100 000. According to Shaheen and Myhill (ibid.), there were over 37 000 veteran-owned small businesses in the US and more than 9600 of these were owned by service-disabled veterans. Indeed, the US federal and state governments have made legal changes to facilitate entrepreneurship among veterans with disabilities. Shaheen and Myhill (ibid., p. 1) maintained: 'Entrepreneurship offers veterans with disabilities increased opportunities to customize their employment to accommodate their challenges, maximize their strengths and skills, and achieve their financial and career goals'.

These authors emphasize the dearth of programmes providing for the specific needs of this particular group and disabled entrepreneurs generally. Moreover, monitoring and evaluation of the first of the EBV programmes has revealed positive results, with 65 per cent of the 12 disabled veterans (from hundreds of applicants) still running a revenue-generating business 14 months later and 11 per cent taking additional education courses (Shaheen and Myhill, 2009). Since 2008, EBV has been expanded to include another three universities across the US and by 2009, around 100 disabled veterans had successfully completed the programmes (ibid.).

DISABLED ENTREPRENEURS: THE FUTURE

Undoubtedly, one of the greatest recent assets to both present and future disabled entrepreneurs around the globe has been the development of both new information technology as well as assistance technology (AT). Angelocci et al. (2008, p. 9) defined AT as including: 'rehabilitative, adaptive and assistive devices and the procedure used in selecting and using them. AT helps a person with a disability to perform an everyday task, e.g. jar opener, magnifying glass – and can improve the quality of life as well as perform business functions'.

Certainly, with ever-advancing technology, communication systems (essential for small business development) offer exciting new opportunities for disabled entrepreneurs. These include specialist computer software such as telecommunication devices for the deaf (including phone applications, video conferencing with sign language and mobile phone texting), mobile laptop offices with reading machine software (for those with impaired sight), voice-sensitive writing programmes (for those with manual dexterity impairment) and so on (Angelocci et al., 2008). The advent of solar power has also enabled isolated communities and disabled individuals (especially in remote rural areas in the developing countries) to have access to electricity, and mobile phones have improved communication links throughout the world. Interestingly, Larsson (2006) makes the point that access to social networking is even more important for disabled entrepreneurs compared to their non-disabled counterparts. Hence, business websites, Internet purchase and selling and the relatively new Internet social network sites such as Facebook, Business Link and Twitter, have all made substantial positive contributions to enhancing business development and marketing for disabled entrepreneurs. In the words of Angelocci et al. (2008, pp. 4–5): 'The widespread use of the Internet has made the world a smaller place and has allowed small business owners with disabilities to reach distant markets, despite transportation and mobility challenges'. Indeed, in today's economic climate, these rapid advances in communication and information technology will help make entrepreneurship an attractive and beneficial alternative for increasing numbers of disabled individuals throughout the world.

NOTES

1. Sources: personal interview with authors, February, 2011 and www.cartercorson.co.uk; accessed 16 August 2011.
2. Sources: adapted from the following: Sally Matheson, *The Sun*, 'Losing a limb gave me a leg up in Hollywood', 27 April 2009; Amputee Casualty Simulations Ltd, available at: www.actionamps.co.uk/about.php, accessed 21 March 2011; 'Albert Thompson wins Disabled Entrepreneur of the Year at Radar's People of the Year awards', http://www. disabilitymeansbusiness.com/latest-posts/albert-thomson-wins-disabled-entrepreneur-of-the-year-at-radar%E2%80%99s-people-of-the-year-awards/, accessed 16 August 2011.
3. Sources: adapted from the following: Tiny Mites Music website, http://www. tinymitesmusic.com/vanessa-heywood-creator; G. Snowden (2010), 'Why disability shouldn't stop you being an entrepreneur', http://www.guardian.co.uk/money/2010/dec/ 04/disability-entrepreneurs-self-employment; Real Business (2010) 'Stelios Award for Disabled Entrepreneurs: winner announced', http://realbusiness.co.uk/growing_ business_awards_2010/stelios_award_for_disabled_entrepreneurs_winner_announced; all accessed 16 August 2011.
4. Sources: adapted from the following: http://www.traveleyes-international.com; Amar Latif, http://www.amarlatif.com/; Leonard Cheshire Disability: press release: 'Amar Latif wins the first ever Stelios Disabled Entrepreneurs Award', http://www.lcdisability. org/?lid=6205; Amar Latif, Wikipedia, http://en.wikipedia.org/wiki/Amar_Latif; H. Loveless, *The Mail on Sunday*, http://www.amarlatif.com/index.php?option=com_ content&view=article&id=54:mail-on-sunday&catid=34:press-releases&Itemid=53; Amar Latif webpage Vienna, http://amarlatif.com/index.php?option=com_content andview=articleandid=51:vien; Amar Latif webpage biography, http://www.amar latif.com/index.php?option=com_contentandview=articleandid=48andIte; Amar Latif webpage Real Travel Article, http://www.amarlatif.com/index.php?option= com_contentandview=articleandid=47:real-travel-article; all 16 August 2011.

REFERENCES

Anderson, R., D. De Clercq, B. Honig and F. Schlosser (2009), USABE (ANA-HEIM 2009), 'Workshop on fostering entrepreneurship among people with special needs through entrepreneurial mentoring programs', Anaheim: USABE Proceedings, pp. 1423–31.

Angelocci, R.M., K.J. Lacho, K.D. Lacho and W.P. Galle (2008), 'Entrepreneurs with disabilities: the role of assistive technology, current status and future outlook', *Proceedings of the Academy of Entrepreneurship*, **14** (1).

Association of Disabled Professionals (2010), 'Being self-employed as a disabled person', The ADP Employment Series, available at: http://www.adp.org.uk/downloads/Being%20Self%20Employed.pdf; accessed 20 November 2010.

Bender, E. (2003), 'Mental illness doesn't deter future entrepreneurs', *Psychiatric News*, **38** (7), 7–8.

Bengtsson, E. and G. Gustafsson (1998), *Starta eget foretag med hjalp av starta eget-bidrag; En uppfoljning av starta eget-bidraget under perioden 1992-1996 i Af Halmstad, Af Laholm. Af Falkenberg, Af Hyltebruk, AMI Halmstad, AMI Varberg samt Af Kungsbacka*, Stockhom: AMS.

Blanck, P.D., L.A. Sandler, J.L. Schmeling and H.A. Schartz (2000), 'The emerging workforce of entrepreneurs with disabilities: preliminary study of entrepreneurship in Iowa', *Law Review*, **85** (5), 1583–668.

Boylan, A. and T. Burchardt (2002), *Barriers of Self-employment for Disabled People*, London: Report for the Small Business Service, October.

Cooney, T.M. (2008), 'Entrepreneurs with disabilities – profile of a forgotten minority', *Irish Business Journal*, **V** (1), 119–29.

De Klerk., T. (2008), 'Funding for self-employment of people with disabilities. Grants, loans, revolving funds or linkage with microfinance programmes', *Leprosy Review*, **79** (1), 92–109.

Disabled World (2010), available at: http://www.disabled-world.com; accessed 20 November 2010.

European Foundation for the Improvement of Living and Working Conditions (2006), *The Employment of People with Disabilities in Small and Medium-sized Enterprises*, Dublin.

Fielden, S.L. and M.J. Davidson (eds) (2010), *International Research Handbook on Successful Women Entrepreneurs*, Cheltenham, UK and Northampton, MA, USA: Edward Elgar.

Grefwe, J. (1999), *Företagsetablering Stenungsund-Tjörn-Orust. 1999 års uppföljning av starta-eget-bidrag 1993-1998*, Stenungsund: Företagsetablering Stenungsund-Tjörn-Orust.

Harper, M. and W. Momm (1989), *Self-employment for Disabled People: Experiences from Africa and Asia*, Geneva: International Labour Office.

Holub, T. (2001), 'Entrepreneurs among people with disabilities', Los Angeles: adjunct ERIC clearinghouse on entrepreneurship education, available at: http://www.eric.ed.gov/PDFS/ED464453.pdf; accessed 16 August 2011.

Jones, M.J. and P.L. Latrielle (2006), 'Disability and self-employment: evidence from the UK', WELMERC, School of Business and Economics, University of Wales, Swansea, Working Paper, June.

Labour Force Survey (2006), June, London: Office for National Statistics.

Labour Force Survey (2009), May, London: Office for National Statistics.

Larsson, S. (2006), 'Disability management and entrepreneurship: results from a nationwide study in Sweden', *The International Journal of Disability Management Research*, **1** (1), 159–68.

Lorenzo, T., L. Van Niekerk and P. Mdlokolo (2007), 'Economic empowerment and black disabled entrepreneurs: negotiating partnerships in Cape Town, South Africa', *Disability and Rehabilitation*, **29** (5), 429–36.

Mathis, C. (2003), 'Disability and entrepreneurship: a formula for success', available at: http://www.halftheplanet.org/departments/entrepreneurs/formula_forsuccess. html; accessed 20 November 2010.

National Technical Assistance Center (2003), 'Disability and self-employment: a formula for success', *Employment Brief*, **4** (2), available at: http://www. ntac.hawaii.edu/downloads/products/briefs/employment/pdf/EB-Vol4-Iss02-formula.pdf; accessed 18 August 2011.

RTC Rural (Research and Training Center on Disability in Rural Communities) (2003), *First National Study of People with Disabilities Who Are Self Employed*, RTC Rural, University of Montana Rural Disability and Rehabilitation Research Progress Report, No. 8.

Schur, L. (2003), 'Barriers or opportunities? The causes of contingent and part-time work among people with disabilities', *Industrial Relations*, **42** (4), 589–622.

Shaheen, G. and W.N. Myhill (2009), 'Entrepreneurship for veterans with disabilities: lessons learned from the field', *In Brief, The NTAR Leadership Centre*, 1 October, 1–8.

Shaw Trust (2006), *Disability and Employment Statistics*, Chippenham: Shaw Trust.

Smith, A. and B. Twomey (2002), 'Labour market experiences of people with disabilities', *Labour Market Trends*, August.

Social Development Canada (2005), available at: http://www.hrsdc.gc.ca/eng/cs/comm/gol/2005.shtml; accessed 18 August 2011.

Stein, M.A. and P.J.S. Stein (2007), 'Beyond disability civil rights', *Hastings Law Journal*, **58**, 1203–40.

US Census Bureau (2006), 'More than 50 million Americans report some level of disability', *U.S. Census Bureau News*, May, 1–3.

Weiss-Doyel, A. (2001), 'Self-employment as a career choice for people with disabilities', available at: http:ruralinstitute.umt.edu/publications/BHB_SelfEmployment.asp; accessed 20 November 2010.

Williams, B., I. Copestake, J. Eversley and B. Stafford (2008), *Disability Issues, Experiences and Expectations of Disabled People*, London: DWP.

9. Indigenous entrepreneurs

> Well it's the fact that we – my Aboriginal people – we're so smart. For thousands
> of years we found ways to live richly in deserts and hard places where other
> people might have just shrivelled and died. And despite all the mistreatment of
> the last two hundred years, we're still here; we're still trying. We're resilient
> you know.
>
> (Leonore Dembski, cited in Hindle and Lansdowne, 2007, p. 15)

INTRODUCTION

There has been an upsurge in research focused on entrepreneurial behaviour, mainly in Western countries, but also in industrialized emerging economies over the past 25 years (Peredo et al., 2004; Peredo and Anderson, 2006). This has added greatly to our collective knowledge, particularly in relation to motivations, strategies and contributions to the economic development in each country; however, little is known about the applicability of these generalizations to Indigenous populations (Peredo et al., 2004). It may be that findings related to mainstream entrepreneurship are not applicable to Indigenous entrepreneurs (Hindle and Moroz, 2009).

Research into Indigenous entrepreneurship is expanding. One of the key reasons for this is that many Indigenous peoples have a high dependency on welfare, hence governments worldwide see benefits in policies and practices that effectively reduce the ongoing welfare systems required to sustain a population where unemployment is endemic. In addition, many authors consider that successful entrepreneurial business ventures are central to the economic development of Indigenous people (e.g., Peredo et al., 2004). There appears to be wide consensus that 'passive welfare has failed and Indigenous disadvantage is massive' (Hindle and Moroz, 2009, p. 2). Therefore, successful business ventures run by Indigenous entrepreneurs have the capacity to offer an economic alternative to the deeply entrenched problems brought about by a reliance on welfare from the state (Lindsay, 2005; Furneaux and Brown, 2007), and hence enhancing an understanding of the factors that optimize entrepreneurial ventures amongst Indigenous peoples is of great importance.

As new ventures that are capable of generating wealth have the capacity to 'enhance both the autonomy and economic development of Indigenous people, at all levels (individual, group, community and nation)' (Hindle and Moroz, 2009, p. 8), this is a very attractive outcome for governments and Indigenous people alike (Hindle and Moroz, 2009). Therefore, the topic of Indigenous entrepreneurship is now 'on the agenda' for governments as well as the private sector (Cant, 2007), and research into Indigenous entrepreneurship has been predicted to become a highly important area within the wider field of entrepreneurship (Hindle and Lansdowne, 2007). In addition, entrepreneurial activities are seen as a significant vehicle for Indigenous people to 'reclaim some of their traditional strengths' (Schaper, 2007, p. 526), and the possibility of enhancing self-determination through entrepreneurial business ventures has been viewed very positively by some Indigenous groups (Frederick and Foley, 2006).

However, despite the growing interest in the area, research into Indigenous entrepreneurship is at present underdeveloped (Frederick and Foley, 2006; Frederick, 2008). What is emerging is that there are some distinguishing differences between non-Indigenous and Indigenous people who enter into a business venture, such as the importance of 'community', rather than a focus on the individual, as has been the case in much of the mainstream entrepreneurial literature. Indigenous entrepreneurs may have to operate within the context of considering other individuals within their community, as well as a wider consideration of the community as a whole. Such contextual issues may not impact on the non-Indigenous entrepreneur to the same extent (Hindle and Moroz, 2009). These issues are very important, and they are capable of having major ramifications on any entrepreneurial activity by self-employed Indigenous people. One example of this is found in the communally held property rights of some Indigenous groups, making collateral leverage almost impossible to assist with the start-up of an individual Indigenous business venture.

While it is widely held that Indigenous communities are communal in nature (e.g., Dana, 1996; Peredo and Chrisman, 2006), it is acknowledged that other authors disagree with this perspective (e.g., Galbraith et al., 2006). These latter authors believe that the 'collective' characteristic is a relatively recent phenomenon brought about through enforced reservation-style living, or through the embryonic institutional structures of developing countries. Obviously, such opposing perspectives will have important ramifications on policy development aimed at fostering and developing Indigenous business ventures (Peredo and Anderson, 2006).

Foley (2008) raises the interesting point that when considering the influences of a dominant societal culture on entrepreneurial propensity, an understanding of the culture in which the Indigenous person lives should also be considered, as this may have more influence than that of the national culture. He believes this has been overlooked previously, and it needs to be taken into account when considering the barriers and facilitators of embarking on an entrepreneurial venture. Furthering our understanding of the characteristics, aspirations and motivations of the Indigenous entrepreneur can provide a useful benchmark to assist in policy development that will provide optimal conditions in which the Indigenous entrepreneur can thrive. Because of the potential for entrepreneurial activities to offer a vehicle to assist in improving the chronically disadvantaged Indigenous populations in the world (Peredo and Anderson, 2006), research into the area of Indigenous entrepreneurs must aim to provide a deeper understanding of the barriers and facilitators to Indigenous business ventures.

Therefore, the aim of this chapter is to consider these issues through a focus on Indigenous peoples and their entrepreneurial ventures in various countries in the world. The majority of papers reviewed in this chapter adopt the perspective of entrepreneurship 'as the prime driver of any meaningful hope for the economic and social improvement of Indigenous individuals, communities and nations' (Hindle and Moroz, 2009, p. 18), and this perspective is seen as dominant in the emerging field of Indigenous entrepreneurship. An exploration into how Indigenous people start up businesses, maintain and sustain them, expand, employ others and so on despite the disadvantages many of them face, could be illuminating. It should be noted that particular emphasis will be given to Australian Indigenous entrepreneurial populations, as this group of Indigenous entrepreneurs has been the subject of a number of recent studies over the past decade.

It has been estimated that there were 370 million Indigenous people in the world in 2007 (UN News Centre, 2007), on all continents, ranging from hunter-gatherers, farmers, subsistence fishermen and women, to professional people who operate in industrialized societies (Peredo and Anderson, 2006). Colonization through European settlement has brought dramatic changes to traditional values and lifestyles of Indigenous people, which have resulted in widespread loss, particularly in economic, legal and political arenas. For many, this has meant becoming dependent on various welfare systems in order to survive (Schaper, 2007). According to Hindle and Moroz (2009), Indigenous peoples 'now reside as disadvantaged minority citizens in lands they once controlled' (p. 2). These circumstances have also impacted very negatively on the Australian Indigenous population, many of whom have become 'socially, economically and culturally disadvantaged' in their own country (Foley, 2003, p. 133). Despite many commonalities, what needs to be kept in mind is that there is often a high degree of heterogeneity amongst Indigenous people (Dana and Anderson, 2007). Indigenous people have their own 'distinctive identity', and have exhibited a high degree of adaptability to change, and even to prosper (Cant, 2007).

Indigenous people are defined as such by their Indigenous descent, and also by their identification with their community, and there are a number of countries throughout the world with Indigenous populations. For example, Indigenous people include the Inuit in Alaska, and the Canadian Indian in Canada, where there are formal definitions of three groups of Indigenous Indian people (Hindle and Moroz, 2009). In the United States, Indigenous descent is also adopted to determine the status of descendants of the 500 Indian nations, and in Australia, two types of Indigenous people are recognized: Aboriginals and Torres Strait Islanders (ibid.). In New Zealand, the Maori population is recognized as Indigenous (Lindsay, 2005). It is possible that many Indigenous people share the experience captured in the following quote: 'Indigenous people are a dispossessed and disadvantaged minority living under a hegemony, which has much dissimilarity to their own social, economic and cultural traditions' (Hindle and Moroz, 2009, p. 7). Such circumstances are not conducive to entrepreneurial ventures (Frederick and Foley, 2006).

However, entrepreneurship is not a new concept to many Indigenous people. As Galbraith et al. (2006) have argued, Indigenous people were often highly entrepreneurial prior to any colonizing of their country. For example, the Maori Indigenous people have a long history of pre-colonization commerce, and were seen as successful entrepreneurs as far back as the 1860s (Frederick and Foley, 2006). Such a history has obviously equipped Maori Indigenous people with a passion for entrepreneurial activities; 12 per cent of the Maori population are entrepreneurs, which is only 2 per cent lower than the population as a whole (Cant, 2007). It is possible, therefore, that a background that has honed skills of survival for countless generations (McGregor, 2004) may well provide the skills required for an entrepreneurial venture in contemporary society. The following section outlines the general characteristics of Indigenous entrepreneurs in various parts of the world.

INDIGENOUS ENTREPRENEURS: GENERAL CHARACTERISTICS

According to Dana and Anderson (2007), there is enormous variability in the characteristics of Indigenous people across nations – sometimes even within a given community. 'Governing myths, family and community organization, values concerning work, play, sexual roles and relations, are among the many matters where different Indigenous groups exhibit striking differences' (Peredo and Anderson, 2006, p. 6). However, some similarities are recognized. Researchers are in agreement that in general, Indigenous populations are poor and severely disadvantaged in economic and socio-political measures (e.g., Foley, 2003; Peredo and Anderson, 2006; Schaper, 2007; Hindle and Moroz, 2009). In addition, collective or communal ways of operating are frequently attributed to Indigenous communities, along with a propensity to organize social interactions along the lines of kinship, rather than being driven by the needs of the market (Dana and Anderson, 2007).

While a disadvantaged background may motivate many Indigenous people to consider a business venture as a way of breaking the cycle of poverty in which they may exist, variations occur in the proportion of Indigenous peoples who become involved in entrepreneurial activity. For example, early research reported that Indigenous Maoris in New Zealand were approximately twice as likely to be an employer, or self-employed, compared to Indigenous Australians, or Torres Strait Islanders (Hunter, 1999). To understand why this may be the case, a detailed exploration of the characteristics of the Australian Indigenous entrepreneur will now be made for the purposes of comparison.

In June 2006, the Australian Indigenous population was estimated to be approximately 517 200, and women made up just over a half of this number (50.3 per cent) (Foley and Pio, 2009). A little known fact is that the majority of Indigenous Australian society live in the suburbs of larger cities (72.6 per cent) (ABS, 1999, 2007; Foley, 2006; Frederick and Foley, 2006), with an estimated 420 000 living in urban locations (Hindle and Moroz, 2009). Half of this population live in two states, Queensland and New South Wales; however, it is in the Northern Territory where the highest proportion of regional concentration is found (27.7 per cent) (Hindle and Moroz, 2009). In 2006, the Australian Bureau of Statistics (ABS, 2006) population census confirmed that over three-quarters of the Indigenous population resided either in major cities (31 per cent), inner regional (22 per cent, e.g., Hobart) or outer regional Australia (23 per cent, e.g., Darwin), both capital cities in Tasmania and Northern Territory, respectively. In this census, only 24 per cent of the Indigenous population lived in either remote or very remote locations in Australia (ABS, 2007).

According to the 2006 Census data (ABS, 2009), 121 500 Indigenous Australians between 15 and 64 years of age (i.e., 45 per cent) classified themselves as 'employed'. A small minority (6600) of Indigenous Australians over 15 years of age classified themselves as 'self-employed' (ibid.).

Therefore, at this time, the Australian Indigenous population had a self-employment rate of 6 per cent, which was approximately one-third the rate for non-Indigenous Australians in the same age group, that is, 15 to 64 (16 per cent). In remote areas, self-employment rates of Indigenous people are lower (2 per cent), than in regional areas (6 per cent), and in major cities, 7 per cent are self-employed (ibid.). According to Foley (2006) the majority of Indigenous Australian entrepreneurs are 'owners and managers of stand-alone commercial enterprises in urban environments' (p. 1), and they are not based in community organizations.

Most self-employed Indigenous people are between 35 and 44 years of age (33 per cent), with just over one-quarter (27 per cent) coming from the 45–54 age group (ABS, 2009). This is in contrast with Indigenous people who classify themselves as employees; they are younger, with the majority aged between 15 and 24 (27 per cent) and a quarter being between 25 and 34 (ibid.). More males are self-employed (68 per cent) than females (32 per cent) in the Indigenous population, which is similar to the statistics for the non-Indigenous population (ibid.). The majority of Indigenous self-employment is in the construction industry (25.7 per cent), with transport, postal and warehousing coming a distant second (8.6 per cent). Only 6.1 per cent of this group are self-employed in the professional, scientific and technical services. It is of interest to note that a higher proportion of self-employed Indigenous people are managers (18 per cent) compared to those who classify themselves as 'employees' (5 per cent) (ibid.).

In 2006, more self-employed Indigenous Australians were engaged in full-time work than those who classified themselves as employees (68 per cent compared to 59 per cent). Indigenous self-employed males were more likely to work full-time than were 'employees', with half of the self-employed Indigenous females working full-time, and half part-time (ibid.). On average, self-employed Indigenous people worked 41 hours per week, compared to employees who worked 34 hours per week. These patterns were quite similar for non-Indigenous Australians. A small proportion worked more than these hours; one in three self-employed Indigenous people (34 per cent) and one in ten of those who classified themselves as employees (11 per cent) worked 49 hours or more per week (ibid.).

In terms of weekly income, full-time self-employed Australian Indigenous people earned $749, which was higher than the $704 income of full-time Indigenous employees (ibid.). Self-employed Indigenous males earned a median weekly income of $802, slightly higher than the income of Indigenous male employees ($715). In contrast, self-employed Indigenous females earned $582, which was considerably lower than the median income ($687) of Indigenous female employees. Moreover, median incomes for Australian Indigenous people were lower than those for non-Indigenous people working in a similar area, and with a similar education qualification (ibid.). Self-employed Indigenous people are more likely to own their own home than Indigenous people who were classified as employees (68 per cent compared to 40 per cent) and are also less likely to speak an Australian Indigenous language at home (3 per cent compared to 12 per cent of Indigenous people classified as employees); in all age groups, the self-employed were more likely to be married (73 per cent) compared to Indigenous employees (49 per cent) (ibid.).

In summary, compared to their non-Indigenous counterparts, self-employed Australian Indigenous people were more likely to be older, have attained a Certificate III or higher in a trade school, and be working in the construction industry, possibly as managers. Self-employed Indigenous males are more likely to work full-time with a higher median weekly income compared to Indigenous employees. Indigenous females who are self-employed are equally likely to work full-time although they will have a lower median weekly income compared to those who are employees (ABS, 2006).

It is reasonable to conclude that the very low proportion of the Australian Indigenous population engaged in entrepreneurial activities indicates the existence of severe barriers. Disadvantaged socioeconomic well-being, a mismatch in terms of cultural values (Dockery, 2010), and/or discrimination and prejudice by the wider Australian community (Foley, 2003) may be experienced. Such factors explain in large part the variability in the rates of entrepreneurship in the New Zealand Maori population when compared to the Australian Indigenous population. These factors will be explored more fully in the section on challenges and barriers.

INDIGENOUS ENTREPRENEURS: ASPIRATIONS AND MOTIVATIONS

Mazzarol (2007) believes that the triggers for *all* entrepreneurs (Indigenous and non-Indigenous) are the creativity to pursue a dream or find new ways to utilize talents, have sufficient money to have an income, or earn a living, and the ability to be autonomous, working in the way that suits the individual best. In the mainstream field of entrepreneurship, there appears to be consensus that innovation and commercialization is a primary motivation for entrepreneurs starting off a new business venture. However, in relation to the consideration of Indigenous entrepreneurship, the prime motivator appears to be for self-determination through preservation of heritage, customs and traditions (Hindle and Lansdowne, 2007). This underpinning desire by Indigenous people has been viewed as 'looking back', compared with the mainstream view, which is labelled as 'looking forward' (ibid.). Rather than seeing this as a dichotomy, a more positive and exciting perspective would be to 'understand the dynamic potential inherent in heritage' (ibid., p. 10), rather than seeing it as a problem blocking commercial development.

One of the key motivators for Indigenous people is the desire to rebuild their nations and their communities primarily by exerting control over traditional territories they once occupied and in so doing, to improve their socioeconomic circumstances (Peredo et al., 2004). In many nations, such as in Canada and Peru, the Indigenous people believe that business ventures are key to providing a strong economy that will be a foundation of rebuilding their nation (Anderson and Gilbertson, 2004). Heritage and culture are therefore of great significance to Indigenous entrepreneurs (Hindle and Lansdowne, 2007), and there is often a focus on setting up new business ventures to benefit their own people. In contrast, a non-Indigenous mainstream entrepreneur is more likely to focus on the 'commercialization of innovation' (Lindsay, 2005, p. 2).

An interesting question is posed in the literature relating to whether disadvantaged people may have a higher likelihood of becoming entrepreneurs due to no other available options. For example, some authors have suggested that groups of deprived or marginal people may be more likely to foster entrepreneurship through sheer necessity, or through a sense of psychological disequilibrium (e.g., Frederick and Foley, 2006). More recently, Frederick (2008) concluded that for some Indigenous people, such as the Maori in New Zealand, 'disadvantage' may bode well for the success of entrepreneurial ventures. However, in the case of Indigenous Australians, the disadvantages relating to social, economic, health and culture status are so extreme that perceptions of the possibility of an entrepreneurial venture are outside the range of probability for many Indigenous people (Frederick and Foley, 2006). However, this relationship is complex; for the Maori, despite their disadvantaged status, their history and attitudes toward their culture creates a favourable basis for their entrepreneurial ventures. For Indigenous Australians, however, their disadvantages are so entrenched and pervasive, Frederick and Foley (ibid.) believe that entrepreneurial activity will remain as the exception, rather than the norm, for some time to come.

However, some of the challenges to Indigenous people becoming entrepreneurs may actually become significant motivators. For example, having limited employment opportunities can act as a motivator to set up an entrepreneurial venture. Lee-Ross and Mitchell (2007) reported that the high proportion of entrepreneurial activity carried out by the Torres Strait

Islander people derived from the limited paid employment and harsh economic conditions, and this motivated inhabitants to look toward self-employment opportunities, that is, the 'push' factor (ibid.).

Another significant motivator for Indigenous people is the desire for self-determination and financial independence (Hindle and Moroz, 2009). Frederick and Foley (2006) believe that the majority of Maori entrepreneurs are motivated by a desire for independence, rather than viewing the 'pull' factor of acquiring wealth as their main reason to become an entrepreneur. This view is supported by other authors who are of the view that Indigenous people do not place a great emphasis on 'wealth generation' alone (e.g., Morris, 2004). Indigenous entrepreneurial activities are often embarked upon to achieve desired social outcomes, rather than just economic goals (Peredo, 2004). Anderson (2004) also notes that a motivator for Indigenous people in Canada is 'not economic development alone, but economic development as part of the larger agenda or rebuilding their communities and nations and reasserting their control over their traditional territories' (p. 2). When self-determination and financial independence are achieved, this has the benefit of greatly improving the quality of life (Noorderhaven et al., 2004; Lee-Ross and Mitchell, 2007).

Further motivators are proposed by Foley's (2003) study into 18 Indigenous businesses, which concluded that the Australian Indigenous entrepreneur was motivated by a desire to 'correct negative social perceptions and resultant social stratification based on race' (p. 146). In a subsequent study, he described the dominating motivator to be one of 'hatred of poverty' (Foley, 2006, p. 10). Among his participants in a research study into 50 successful entrepreneurial ventures owned and operated by Indigenous Australians, a commonly expressed view was: 'We cannot afford to fail, we will succeed' (ibid.), which he described as a positive attitude that was instrumental in allowing entrepreneurs to take control of their own lives. According to Foley (2003) the successful Australian Indigenous entrepreneur is able to challenge their position in society by becoming successful in business. Therefore, overcoming the discrimination of the mainstream society is a motivating force for the Indigenous entrepreneur (ibid.), along with the desire to achieve economic independence through a successful business venture.

A further dominant intrinsic motivator suggested by the above study is the desire to provide adequately for families, and in so doing, enhancing the quality of life for their families and children – to improve on what they may have experienced in their own childhoods (Foley, 2006; Foley and Pio, 2009). One motivator believed to be particularly important for female Indigenous entrepreneurs in Australia is to overcome poverty. Female entrepreneurs also appeared to be motivated by the lack of male role models in their immediate or extended family networks, often due to early deaths of Indigenous men, or the high incarceration rates of other male family members (Foley, 2006; Wood and Davidson, 2011). Therefore, these women were motivated by kinship obligations to take on the role of provider not only for their own nuclear families, but for extended family members as well (Foley, 2006). Once again, the influence of community is clearly seen.

INDIGENOUS ENTREPRENEURS: CHALLENGES AND BARRIERS

Worldwide, Indigenous populations suffer from 'chronic poverty, lower education levels, and poor health' (Peredo et al., 2004, p. 1) and hence experience economic and social deprivation (Frederick, 2008). According to the World Bank (2001) 'Indigenous peoples are commonly among the poorest and most vulnerable segments of society' (p. 1). Therefore, many Indigenous people face extreme disadvantage on every level, and the emergence of an enterprising spirit is for many highly unlikely, and even impossible (Frederick and Foley, 2006).

According to Schaper (2007), Indigenous Australians face particular barriers that stand in the way of greater numbers starting up successful business ventures. These include being sidelined from the cash economy, having fewer successful role models and mentors, and little human capital through limited access to education or the opportunity to acquire technical or managerial skills. In addition, there is the geographical remoteness in which a number of Indigenous people exist, and the cultural differences in values between Indigenous people and the mainstream society.

Culture has often been understood as a 'collective programming of the mind' (Lindsay, 2005, p. 2), which has the effect of distinguishing peoples of various categories. Culture is deeply embedded in Indigenous communities, and has a pervasive influence on attitudes, behaviour and values (Wood and Davidson, 2011). It follows that culture will impact on attitudes toward the possibility of a new entrepreneurial venture. Some authors have proposed that cultures may be influential in producing people who may have a stronger desire to participate in business ventures than others (e.g., Busenitz and Lau, 1996). According to Dana (2007), culture may also influence perceptions: 'differences between ethnocultural groups suggest that opportunity identification and/or response to opportunity is culture-bound' (p. 3). Indeed, this quote further substantiates that perceptions, and not opportunity alone, define the way an individual views entrepreneurial possibilities, and that the role of culture is paramount. According to

Lindsay (2005, p. 5): 'Indigenous culture will shape Indigenous entrepreneur attitudes'.

Culture appears to exert a significant influence on the aspiring Indigenous entrepreneur in many important ways. Barriers may be placed in the way of Indigenous entrepreneurs as their activities may be deemed inappropriate to a communal culture by members of their own communities (Foley, 2006). For example, when Indigenous Australian people undertake an entrepreneurial venture, they often report feeling 'culturally, spiritually and physically isolated' (Foley, 2008, p. 209) as they are operating from a base of having no role models to draw from. Therefore, an awareness of cultural factors provides insight into the added barriers that can impact on the Indigenous entrepreneur.

In particular, any introduction of change in the way of new ideas that appear to undermine cultural practices and values may not be accepted by the Indigenous community (Lindsay, 2005). To achieve acceptance of a new business venture by the community, an aspiring entrepreneur would have to place a priority on conforming to the cultural norms of their group. In addition, they would have to ensure there was a collective focus on the new venture creation, the goals would need to be consistent with the goal of self-determination, and the development of the business venture would need to preserve the heritage of the community (Lindsay, 2005). If these elements were not considered, pressure would be brought to bear on the individual, which would potentially undermine the success of the project.

This suggests that 'cultural influences will restrict innovation to developing and acting upon new and unique business activities that only conform to cultural norms' (ibid., p. 6). Any entrepreneurial ideas that fall outside these cultural norms will be difficult for Indigenous groups to conceptualize, enact, or sustain (Lindsay, 2005). Certainly, Indigenous entrepreneurs recognize the opportunities that may be available to them, however they may focus on a community end result; such an 'opportunity' may be overlooked by a non-Indigenous entrepreneur. 'Success', in Western non-Indigenous terms tends to be at odds with Indigenous cultural norms (Foley, 2003) and hence this is a particularly difficult fine line for the Indigenous entrepreneur to walk.

Some authors consider that traditional cultures and values can cause barriers to entrepreneurial progress (e.g., Peredo et al., 2004; Schaper, 2007) because of the social relationships of family and kinship and the community in which the Indigenous person belongs. One perspective is that: 'successful entrepreneurial responses require that Indigenous people leave behind, or at least adapt, those features of culture, which are incompatible' (Peredo and Anderson, 2006, p. 262). However, other authors consider that Indigenous people can use their cultural heritage to their advantage; 'they do not have to lose it when they set out in pursuit of venture success' (Hindle and Lansdowne, 2007, p. 18). Whatever the perspective, culture plays a significant role in decisions made by the aspiring Indigenous entrepreneur. An illustration of the influence culture can exert is seen in a study of Torres Strait Islander entrepreneurs, where only 8 per cent of the sample were involved in a business venture focusing on arts and crafts. The reason for this was the concern that such activity may be seen as exploitation of traditional art for purely monetary gain; such activity would have been seen as unacceptable among the Islander community as a whole (Lee-Ross and Mitchell, 2007).

Perceptions of opportunity may also be culturally influenced, as will attitudes toward, and ways of measuring 'success' (Dana, 2007). Success in an Indigenous entrepreneurial venture may require an acceptance of the capitalistic environment of the mainstream culture. It may even result in the Indigenous entrepreneur being cut off from their own families and traditional networks (Frederick and Foley, 2006). Therefore, it would seem that one of the very poignant challenges to the Australian Indigenous entrepreneur is that the more successful they become, the more at risk they are of losing links to their Indigenous community and their culture. Indigenous culture is about communal sharing, and when an individual sets up a business that is seen to be successful, with some of the trappings associated with success, the Indigenous entrepreneur is often seen as violating this norm. One Indigenous entrepreneur expressed this view: 'They see me as no longer Aboriginal as I wear a tie, a suit and drive a new vehicle. They don't understand' (Foley, 2003, p. 146).

In addition to the complexities that are brought to bear because of cultural considerations of the Indigenous community, other significant barriers and challenges in the wider community are experienced by many Indigenous entrepreneurs that may make mere survival difficult. In the Australian context, these include a reduced life expectancy (20 years less than that of a non-Indigenous Australian), high unemployment, or for those in work, earning a median weekly income that is 68 per cent of that of the non-Indigenous population, an increased likelihood of incarceration, living in crowded conditions, and a reduced likelihood that children will complete their final year at high school or go on to achieve further higher education qualifications. Often interpersonal violence is also experienced by Indigenous women and children (Hindle and Moroz, 2009). Therefore, barriers to the Australian Indigenous entrepreneur may include the most basic individual hardships from the need for secure shelter and food, through to difficulty in obtaining finance. In addition, due to the low levels of education and literacy, there is also a lack of business skills (Frederick, 2008). In fact, previous employment may not have been experienced by the aspiring Indigenous entrepreneur. According to Frederick (ibid.), the barriers are all-encompassing, creating disadvantage in social, cultural, economic, political and geographical areas.

In relation to Maori entrepreneurs, they also experience specific disadvantages in the wider community in the areas of 'health, housing, income, education and social services' (Frederick and Foley, 2006, p. 3). Issues of life expectancy, lower level of health, poverty, family breakdowns, domestic violence, drug and alcohol problems and suicide all point to serious disadvantage in Maori society (Frederick and Foley, 2006). Maori entrepreneurs may also have difficulties in starting up their business ventures through a lack of acceptance by the wider European New Zealand population and issues with acceptance by extended families (ibid.).

In addition to these wider socioeconomic factors, specific operational barriers are evident for the Indigenous entrepreneur. The ability to network with a wider non-Indigenous population is seen as very important for Indigenous Australian entrepreneurs (Foley, 2006). Networking 'provides role models, industry advice, the sharing of experiences and access to suppliers and customers' and hence is a key motivator for Indigenous entrepreneurs (ibid., p. 15). Such networking provides access to the dominant culture; it is seen as providing an opportunity to build credibility, and create a positive image in the wider community, as well as opening up possible customer bases (Foley, 2006). On the whole, networking is seen 'as a strategic and a purposeful activity by Indigenous entrepreneurs to gain entry into markets that are non-Indigenous' (Foley, 2008, p. 210), and hence efforts to set up and maintain appropriate networks will be pursued by the Indigenous entrepreneur.

However, networking for Australian Indigenous business operators often involves working with non-Indigenous business people, and this can cause additional difficulties. There has to be an accepting, mutual respect between the two parties for this type of networking to be successful (Foley, 2008). Racial discrimination is still a factor to be faced by many Australian Indigenous people, and this creates significant barriers to the Indigenous entrepreneur. One manifestation of racial discrimination may be that there is a limited number of potential 'mentors' who are prepared to work with the emerging Indigenous entrepreneur, or to become a meaningful member of a network for him or her. More insidiously, ongoing racial discrimination in the workplace continues to impact on the employment rates of Indigenous people in Australia. Hunter (2004) believes that more than two-thirds of the difference between employment rates of Indigenous and non-Indigenous Australians is the result of racial discrimination. Therefore, 'the dominating inhibitor to business growth and success would appear to be racism' (Foley, 2006, p. 19).

It is sobering to consider that such discrimination is not only found in the wider mainstream community. In Foley's (2006) study, 60 per cent of his sample had 'experienced discrimination from Indigenous communities themselves' (p. 20) as individuals begin to be seen as successful, or at least, different from the community of family networks from where they came. This is a further discrimination, and combined with that experienced from the dominant society, goes some way to explaining the very small numbers of Indigenous entrepreneurs in Australia.

In addition, other barriers have a particular impact on the setting up, maintaining and sustaining of an entrepreneurial business venture. These include impediments to obtaining finance and having a perceived lack of credibility. Challenges in relation to accessing finance stem from Indigenous Australians being excluded to a large extent from the cash economy, which has meant an inability to amass either the required capital, business acumen, or experience in managing others (Schaper, 2007). Conventional sources of capital may be cautious about taking a risk that an Indigenous business venture would succeed, or they may display discrimination because the client is Indigenous (Hunter, 1999). Both of these possibilities result in lack of finance being available to many potential Indigenous entrepreneurs. According to Foley (2000), obtaining a commercial loan for financial assistance in a business venture is 'almost impossible' for Australian Indigenous entrepreneurs, with up to 40 per cent of the participants in his study using credit cards to provide the necessary working capital for their business venture. However, where there are non-Indigenous spouses, access to finance becomes more possible. In one study, 19 out of 20 of the non-Indigenous spouses were able to obtain bank finance, in contrast to all 16 of the Indigenous couples who were unable to obtain bank finance, clearly suggesting that having a non-Indigenous spouse appears to facilitate the ability to access credit (Foley, 2006).

In addition, education is limited in many Indigenous populations (Schaper, 2007). Hunter (1999) agrees with this, believing that lower levels of education are one of the main constraints on Indigenous people being able to become self-employed. Furthermore, a proportion of Indigenous people are located in outback areas, making access to cities difficult (Daly, 1993). This isolation can impact on an inability to procure a local population who will want to avail themselves of the product or service being offered. In addition, in remote areas, there may be a lack of successful role models, which makes it difficult for Indigenous people to perceive that an entrepreneurial venture is possible. Nevertheless, despite the barriers that are experienced by the Indigenous entrepreneur, inspirational success stories abound.

INDIGENOUS ENTREPRENEURS: STORIES OF SUCCESS

The two Australian case studies that follow illustrate this very clearly, and exemplify that the entrepreneurial spirit is alive and well in these two young Australian Indigenous entrepreneurs. The first case outlines the success achieved by Michelle Earl through sheer hard work and a determination that failure will not be contemplated. The second case (Jack Manning Bancroft) illustrates a creative and innovative entrepreneurial venture that is helping Indigenous school children attain higher education, and in the process, positively changing community attitudes.

BOX 9.1 MICHELLE EARL, SOLE OWNER AND OPERATOR OF 'THE CRITTER SITTER'

Michelle is a 39-year-old Indigenous Australian and the sole owner of 'The Critter Sitter', a business that looks after other people's animals, and covers a geographic spread of approximately 3500 square kilometres in a regional city in New South Wales, Australia. The idea to start this business grew from periods of hospitalization, during which Michelle desperately sought to find a service that would take care of her animals. However, the idea sat on the 'back-burner' for some time, until she came across an advertisement for people who wished to start their own business to contact the Hunter Business Enterprise Centre and enrol in their New Enterprise Incentive Scheme (NEIS) Programme. She immersed herself fully in the course, completing the programme in eight weeks by attending classes three or four full days per week.

Her kernel of a business idea took off. The business started on 20 October 2005. Within three days, Michelle had people ringing her from other regional centres, and within a fortnight, she had two other people working for her. The business today has grown and diversified into other areas, such as offering grooming from home and 'babysitting' for pets in their own environment, whether it be their own home or other accommodation. According to Michelle: 'We don't have high profit, but we are not running in the red either. Any money that comes in, I put straight back into the business, and use it for promotional purposes to keep it all going. Almost five years after starting the business, I now employ 17 people'.

The early years were difficult; Michelle was a single mum with two boys, aged 11 and 13 years old, and therefore juggled family

commitments, household chores, working, completing assign-
ments and studying for a Tertiary and Further Education (TAFE)
course with the support of her ageing mother. She often completed
homework, studies or caught up on much-needed sleep while
sitting in the car at soccer practice. Her boys would ask: 'When do
we get our mum back?', and on occasions, she would wonder if
she should give it all up.

Michelle acknowledges that specific barriers were experienced
along the way. First, she found business itself difficult, because she
was not comfortable in saying 'No' to people, particularly if they
were having difficulties themselves because of economics or ill
health. Second, she found the paperwork side of the business was
stressful. Third, obtaining insurance policies was a major problem,
and this had to be achieved before Department of Employment
and Workplace Relations (DEWR) support payments could be
received. Fourth, she initially lacked some of the technological
skills necessary to run a successful business. She attacked this
problem with her usual total commitment and enthusiasm by
organizing to sit in on Year 6 (primary school) computer lessons to
learn the basics. 'Between that, asking my boys for help, and trial
and error, at home, I got by'. She has honed these skills to the point
where she now devises her own database without assistance.

However, she is quick to acknowledge the support she received.
Michelle believes that the NEIS Programme offered her invaluable
assistance. Once her business idea was judged to be likely to
succeed, then DEWR funding of $10 000 was accessible, spread
over fortnightly payments for 12 months. All expenditure had to be
on the business. This funding got 'The Critter Sitter' off to a great
start, and was used for business cards, brochures, letterheads,
printing off forms, filing cabinet, an advertisement in the Yellow
Pages telephone book, sign writing on the four-wheel-drive vehicle, and marketing help.

Additional support was gained from an Indigenous mentor, who
helped her access assistance through Indigenous Business Australia. 'This support funded MYOB training [MYOB, 'Mind Your Own
Business', is the name of an Australian multinational corporation
that provides accounting, payroll and retail software and web
hosting to small and medium businesses], the purchasing of the
MYOB package, paid the fees for a few stalls at expos and markets
and the purchase of a banner to display whilst there, and because I
was still having problems with marketing, I was able to engage an
expert to assist me in finding the best avenues for ads and who to

target.' In addition, business mentors were very supportive and helped reduce 'very expensive mistakes'. Professional support through accounting services is called on monthly.

Although ongoing support is received from Michelle's sons and they have helped her in running the business during periods where she has been unable to carry out the work herself, Michelle feels she does not get a lot of support from the rest of her extended family. There are times when demands are made on her from family members that seem to reflect a lack of awareness about the requirements of her business, and the need to stay focused and on budget.

She defines 'success' as having clients coming back repeatedly and word of mouth referrals. Within the next five years, Michelle wants to franchise her business, starting off in the lower Hunter Valley, then extending the franchising in Sydney and across New South Wales; in the next ten years and beyond, she plans to be fully franchised. Michelle also wants more people to recognize the name of her company and realizes further marketing needs to be done in this area. Her 'can do' perspective is summed up in this quote: 'I try to make ends meet, bring the money in, and want to renovate the house. I also want to give the boys a better lifestyle than what we had years ago. I am quite confident that I will be in this business in another five to ten years: failure is not in my vocabulary!'

Michelle has received numerous awards for her business 'The Critter Sitter' over the past five years, which testify to this philosophy.[1]

BOX 9.2 JACK MANNING BANCROFT, CEO, 'AUSTRALIAN INDIGENOUS MENTORING EXPERIENCE'

Jack Manning Bancroft is a young man with a vision. In 2005 when he was 19 years of age and a student at Sydney University he became aware that the lower rates of Indigenous students graduating at universities were directly linked to the poor social and economic indicators in later life. He started AIME (Australian Indigenous Mentoring Experience) which had three key objectives:

1. to increase Indigenous student retention to Year 10;
2. to increase Indigenous student retention to Year 12; and
3. to increase university admission enrolments of Indigenous students.

Initially, he ran a pilot project with a nearby Community School where a large number of Indigenous students were enrolled. This resulted in a 40 per cent increase in attendance, and the experience led to the refinement and development of a six-year programme for Indigenous students from Year 7 through to Year 12. As the need for the service expanded, AIME continued to grow.

In March 2008, AIME was incorporated as a company limited by guarantee through CATSIA – Corporations (Aboriginal and Torres Strait Islander) Act 2006 – which provides additional support if it is needed. At the age of 22, Jack took on the role of CEO. There is a board and a small membership base; Jack reports to the board and then back to members at the end of the financial year. He has an operational team of 34 staff under him, in addition to a huge suite of volunteers, estimated to reach over 1250 in 2011.

Initially, finance was obtained through Social Ventures Australia (SVA), an independent non-profit organization that caters for the needs of social entrepreneurs and philanthropists with a desire to make a real difference to some of Australia's most pressing community challenges. In addition, Jack also called on the services of appropriate professionals, and has done this since the very beginning. He particularly values being able to use experts to assist in setting up appropriate structures for governance, board directors, HR, financial planning and so on and to embed this into what AIME requires.

Some significant facilitators have operated in getting AIME established. One key enabler was that the programme had been running successfully for three years before incorporating, therefore the idea had been tested and there was significant momentum. In addition, there was great pro bono support, and Jack considers he was very lucky to work with staff members and mentors who worked very hard to get the programme up and running. The early results were encouraging, and this provided a base to go on from.

Jack believes that effective networking was crucial in establishing AIME, so he 'skilled up quickly' in this area. At only 22 years of age, it was difficult initially trying to broker a partnership, especially with a Vice Chancellor in a university. The task was to get a foot in the door in the corporate space, to learn who the best person was to deal with in the university, and to be able to be in the room with the decision-makers. In addition, Jack considered that he was very fortunate to be mentored by Dr Chris Sarra, a world-class educationalist, who has himself experienced first-hand the issues faced by Indigenous students throughout their schooling. For over a decade, Dr Sarra has implemented his 'Strong and Smart' philosophy into his role as Principal of Cherbourg State School in South East Queensland. Dramatic improvements in educational outcomes have been observed.

On a personal level, Jack sees it as a significant strength that he knows both worlds, having been an Aboriginal high school kid as well as having the perspective of a university student. Having a deep understanding of the experiences of the participants gave the programme a great start. Knowing what Aboriginal kids go through, he wanted the mentoring programme to be accountable, and to bring about real change. Jack believed the idea was a good one and that it would resonate with people.

Jack also considered that a commitment to excellence is one of the most important attributes for an entrepreneur, and he described himself as 'highly competitive'. If he puts his name to something, he wants it to be good. Having the right work ethic to make an idea work is also essential. Jack was also highly motivated through a strong sense of responsibility to do something worthwhile because of the opportunities he had been given, such as receiving a scholarship to go to university. His vision is to responsibly share as quickly as he can, and to 'give back' to others who have been less fortunate.

In terms of barriers, initially there was the challenge of any new idea; having to position the new idea in someone else's mind. 'We hit road blocks, which every organization does at the start.' At this time, people hadn't seen the programme, and the feedback received was that it hadn't been around for long enough, although some people were willing to take a calculated risk early. In this regard, Jack considers that timing is crucial. There is a real challenge when decisions span over five or six months; ideally, AIME works with people who believe in the idea and come on board straight away. In addition to these difficulties, another primary barrier experienced in setting up AIME was a knowledge gap in legal, compliance and financial areas.

Despite these barriers, the successes that have been achieved over a relatively short period of time have been impressive. The programme has grown from working with 25 mentees and 25 mentors in 2005 to the point where, in 2011, AIME is partnering 1250 mentees and 1250 mentors together at ten university campuses across the East Coast of Australia. In 2009, Year 10 students participating in the AIME programme had a completion rate of 76 per cent, compared to the NSW rate of 59 per cent; the Year 12 completion rates were 82 per cent and 60 per cent respectively.

Jack's perspective on the success of AIME is interesting. First, he measures success in the educational context as this is one of the controllable risk factors to overcome Indigenous disadvantage. Success is seeing educated Indigenous students standing in a modern world and 'playing ball' with anybody – defining their destiny and being proud of their identity and their culture. In addition, success is seen as educating the non-Indigenous populace, and using mentors from the non-Indigenous population.

His advice to others contemplating entering into a new business venture is to develop an idea that will stand out from other businesses, and be good enough to carry the business forward successfully. This core idea has to be believed in with a total commitment as it has the capacity to enable the organization to achieve its full potential.

The goal of AIME is to have 6000 mentors and 6000 mentees a year by 2020, and to have every Aboriginal student finishing school at the same rate as every Australian child. This is the long-term objective and goal that drives the company, and informs the structure of their operations. The vision is that the company will continue to go forward, and that the next five to ten years will provide an opportunity for AIME to enjoy the hard work that has already been done.

However, from a personal perspective, Jack feels he is reflecting and taking stock at the moment. He does not know if he will be personally involved in AIME in five to ten years' time although he is committed to growing the business and developing future Australian leaders. In terms of the big picture, Jack considers that if AIME can exist without him, then he has done a good job with the sustainability of the concept. The vision is beginning to have an impact on the culture of education. Year 12 kids are now mentoring Year 7 kids, reflecting a fundamental change in attitudes toward the value of education. However, he hopes to see a day when AIME doesn't need to be around and Aboriginal kids are finishing school by themselves. This is his dream for the future. Many non-Indigenous Australians would share this dream with Jack, and under his impressive stewardship, significant progress is being made in the right direction.[2]

INDIGENOUS ENTREPRENEURS: SUMMARY

In summary, the Indigenous entrepreneur is commonly characterized by a disadvantaged background that may include low levels of education, limited previous work experience, problems with access to finance and a communal style of living. They may view 'success' in a different way to the mainstream entrepreneur, as they focus on opportunities to better themselves, and their family situations, through reducing or eliminating discrimination and forging an acceptance in the mainstream community (Foley, 2003). Of interest is the fact that the discrimination and prejudice experienced by the Indigenous entrepreneur may not only be from the larger society in which they live; it may be generated from within their own community as they begin to be seen as outsiders (Foley, 2006).

A further difference in the Indigenous entrepreneur appears to be in the perception of 'risk'. Lee-Ross and Mitchell (2007) raise the interesting point that 'risk' may be interpreted differently by some Indigenous populations. When considering an entrepreneurial venture, the respondents in a study remarked that 'either you do it or you don't', but did not see 'risk' in terms of a potential business failure.

Cultural influences appear to be dominant in Indigenous populations. In particular, cultures tend to dictate whether an entrepreneurial venture will be accepted in the community. Acceptance may be based on whether the project is judged to be something that will benefit the community as a whole, and whether it will be something that is seen as showing respect for the heritage of the Indigenous group. Culture can also create a barrier to Indigenous entrepreneurs through successful individuals being seen as outsiders to their own group, and facing discrimination and prejudice because of this. Other barriers are created through social and economic disadvantage in the wider society, as well as specific barriers associated with difficulties accessing finance, potential mentors, or networks.

INDIGENOUS ENTREPRENEURS: THE FUTURE

This review of a selection of the Indigenous entrepreneurial literature has highlighted the clear differences that exist between mainstream and Indigenous entrepreneurship. It would seem that a deeper understanding of

Indigenous entrepreneurship must encompass knowledge of the role of culture. It is obvious that some cultural values are incompatible with some mainstream theories and practices (Dana, 2007). One of the key differences is the Indigenous entrepreneurship focus on communal outcomes that reflect a respect for heritage. This frequently raises the question of compatibility between cultural heritage of the Indigenous individual and the commonly held views of what is required to be a successful entrepreneur (Peredo and Anderson, 2006, p. 270).

These questions need to be addressed, as they have serious policy implications. For example, in order to ensure economic development, what balance between individual business ventures and collective business ventures should be pursued (Peredo et al., 2004)? Some Indigenous groups may function best through supporting individual business ventures (e.g., the Apache tribes of Arizona), whereas others will focus on more communal-based economic development (e.g., the Andean and Canadian tribes) (ibid.). There is an obvious need to recognize the validity and effectiveness of existing social and organizational structures – otherwise intervention strategies that encompass training and development may be doomed to fail. An understanding of cultural values and an appreciation of heritage and history are essential, as is an awareness that culture will also impact on the way an individual thinks about an entrepreneurial venture (Lindsay, 2005).

One illustration of this is that economic goals are not the dominant driver for Indigenous people in taking up an entrepreneurial venture, although they may be seen as a mediating variable in obtaining a better quality of life for the entrepreneur and their family. Attitudes toward entrepreneurial ventures will also impact on the range of cognitive processes that will influence views on the *possibility* that an entrepreneurial venture may be undertaken. These include the type of business that may be considered, through to motivations to start up a business after recognizing a potential opportunity, the degree of self-confidence and the motivation and desire to participate in networking opportunities (Peredo et al., 2004). Indigenous people appear to have different values; these will influence the decisions they make in relation to an entrepreneurial venture.

In terms of future directions, the need to 'find ways to reconcile and blend the best in mainstream and Indigenous cultures was and is the number one issue for Indigenous entrepreneurship' (Hindle and Lansdowne, 2007, p. 14). The benefits gained from successful Indigenous entrepreneurial ventures are seen at both a personal as well as a community level; they are able to show the wider population at large that they are worthy of respect, hence pushing back negative stereotypes and discriminatory attitudes they may experience from the population at large.

Despite the many profound disadvantages Indigenous peoples may face, there are great strengths in Indigenous societies. Many Indigenous people believe that the strength they draw from their traditional backgrounds and the 'spirit' of Indigenous people individually is sufficient to guide them toward economic self-determination (Wood and Davidson, 2011). One female Indigenous entrepreneur expressed this as follows:

> Well it's the fact that we – my Aboriginal people – we're so smart. For thousands of years we found ways to live richly in deserts and hard places where other people might have just shrivelled and died. And despite all the mistreatment of the last two hundred years, we're still here; we're still trying. We're resilient you know. (Leonore Dembski, cited in Hindle and Lansdowne, 2007, p. 15)

Further development of the field of research into Indigenous entrepreneurship will benefit from a mutually respectful partnership. Academics with a respect for Indigenous values, heritage and culture, working from a perspective of mainstream society should ideally work with Indigenous communities who know a different reality; their knowledge of being a member of a disadvantaged minority will ensure that both perspectives are recognized, understood and valued. In this way, research in this area of significant importance will develop and expand (Hindle and Moroz, 2009). It would seem that Indigenous peoples, communities and societies at large will benefit from the outcomes of such a partnership.

NOTES

1. Source: personal interview with authors, December 2010.
2. Source: personal interview with authors, November 2010.

REFERENCES

Anderson, R. (2004), 'Indigenous entrepreneurship: the 5 w's', Annual Meeting of the Academy of Management, New Orleans, LA, USA.

Anderson, R.B. and R. Gilbertson (2004), 'Aboriginal entrepreneurship and economic development in Canada: thoughts on current theory and practice', in C. Stiles and C. Galbraith (eds), *Ethnic Entrepreneurship: Structure and Process*, Amsterdam: Elsevier Science, pp. 141–70.

Australian Bureau of Statistics (ABS) (1999), 'Population. Special article – Aboriginal and Torres Strait Islander Australians: a statistical profile from the 1996 Census', *Year Book Australia, 1999*, Canberra: Australian Government Publishing Service.

Australian Bureau of Statistics (ABS) (2006), 'Experimental estimates of Aboriginal and Torres Strait Islander Australians', Catalogue No. 3238.0.55.01, Canberra: Australian Government Publishing Service.

Australian Bureau of Statistics (ABS) (2007), 'Population distribution, Aboriginal
and Torres Strait Islander Australians', Catalogue No. 4705.0, Canberra: Australian Government Publishing Service.

Australian Bureau of Statistics (2009), 'Self-employed Aboriginal and Torres Strait
Islander people', Catalogue No. 4722.0.55.009, Canberra: Australian Government Publishing Service.

Busenitz, L.W. and C.-M. Lau (1996), 'A cross-cultural cognitive model of new
venture creation', *Entrepreneurship Theory and Practice*, **20** (4), 25–39.

Cant, G. (2007), 'The South Pacific: Australia, New Zealand and the Pacific Islands
– insights into the theory and praxis of Indigenous entrepreneurship', in L.-P.
Dana and R.B. Anderson (eds), *International Handbook of Research on Indigenous Entrepreneurship*, Cheltenham, UK and Northampton, MA, USA:
Edward Elgar, pp. 459–69.

Daly, A.E. (1993), 'Self-employment among Aboriginal people', CAEPR Discussion Paper No. 39, Centre for Aboriginal Economic Policy Research, The
Australian National University, Canberra.

Dana, L.-P. (2007), 'Toward a multidisciplinary definition of Indigenous entrepre-
neurship', in L.-P. Dana and R.B. Anderson (eds), *International Handbook of
Research on Indigenous Entrepreneurship*, Cheltenham, UK and Northampton,
MA, USA: Edward Elgar pp. 3–7.

Dana, L.-P. and R.B. Anderson (2007), 'A multidisciplinary theory of entrepre-
neurship as a function of cultural perceptions of opportunity', in L.-P. Dana and
R.B. Anderson (eds), *International Handbook of Indigenous Entrepreneurship*,
Cheltenham, UK and Northampton, MA, USA: Edward Elgar, pp. 595–604.

Dana, P.J. (1996), 'Commercial enterprise ownership among Australian women:
economic control through entrepreneurship', unpublished PhD thesis, University of Southern California, California.

Dockery, A.M. (2010), 'Culture and well-being: the case of Indigenous Australians', *Social Indicators Research*, **99** (2), 315–32.

Foley, D. (2000), 'Successful Indigenous Australian entrepreneurs: a case study
analysis', Aboriginal and Torres Strait Islander Studies Unit Research Report
Series 4, ATSI Unit, University of Queensland, Brisbane.

Foley, D. (2003), 'An examination of Indigenous Australian entrepreneurs', *Journal
of Developmental Entrepreneurship*, **8** (2), 133–51.

Foley, D. (2006), 'Indigenous Australian entrepreneurs: not all community organisations, not all in the outback', Discussion Paper No. 279/2006, Centre for
Aboriginal Economic Policy Research.

Foley, D. (2008), 'Does culture and social capital impact on the networking
attributes of Indigenous entrepreneurs?', *Journal of Enterprising Communities:
People and Places in the Global Economy*, **2** (3), 204–24.

Foley, D. and E. Pio (2009), 'Inextricable identity and ideology: Indigenous women
entrepreneurs in Australia and Hawaii', 6th Annual Australian Graduate School
of Entrepreneurs (AGSE) Conference, Adelaide, South Australia.

Frederick, H.H. (2008), 'Introduction to special issue on Indigenous entrepreneurs', *Journal of Enterprising Communities: People and Places in the Global
Economy*, **2** (3), 185–91.

Frederick, H.H. and D. Foley (2006), 'Indigenous populations as disadvantaged entrepreneurs in Australia and New Zealand', *The International Indigenous Journal of Entrepreneurship, Advancement, Strategy and Education*, **11** (2).

Furneaux, C. and K. Brown (2007), 'Indigenous entrepreneurship: an analysis of capital constraints', Australian Graduate School of Entrepreneurship Conference, 4th AGSE International Entrepreneurship Research Exchange, QUT, Brisbane, 2007.

Galbraith, C., C. Rodriguez and C. Stiles (2006), 'False myths and Indigenous entrepreneurial strategies', *Journal of Small Business and Entrepreneurship*, **8** (2), 1–20.

Hindle, K. and M. Lansdowne (2007), 'Brave spirits on new paths: toward a globally relevant paradigm of Indigenous entrepreneurship research', *Journal of Small Business and Entrepreneurship*, **18** (2), 131–41.

Hindle, K. and P. Moroz (2009), 'Indigenous entrepreneurship as a research field: developing a definitional framework from the emerging canon', *International Entrepreneurial Management Journal*, DOI 10.1007/s11365-009-0111-x, published online 11 August 2009.

Hunter, B.H. (1999), 'Indigenous self-employment: miracle cure or risky business?', Discussion Paper No. 176, Centre for Aboriginal Economic Policy Research, The Australian National University, Canberra.

Hunter, B.H. (2004), 'Indigenous Australians in the contemporary labour market', Australian Bureau of Statistics, Catalogue No. 2052.0, Canberra: Australian Government Publishing Service.

Lee-Ross, D. and B. Mitchell (2007), 'Doing business in the Torres Straits: a study of the relationship between culture and the nature of Indigenous entrepreneurs', *Journal of Developmental Entrepreneurship*, **12** (2), 199–216.

Lindsay, N.J. (2005), 'Toward a cultural model of Indigenous entrepreneurial attitude', *Academy of Marketing Science Review*, **5**, 12–15, available at: http://www.amsreview.org/articles/lindsay05-2005.pdf; accessed 13 July 2010.

Mazzarol, T. (2007), 'Different strokes for different folks: stimulating entrepreneurship in regional communities', in L.-P. Dana and R.B. Anderson (eds), *International Handbook of Research on Indigenous Entrepreneurship*, Cheltenham, UK and Northampton, MA, USA, pp. 494–507.

McGregor, D. (2004), 'Coming full circle: Indigenous knowledge, environment, and our future', *American Indian Quarterly*, **28** (3 and 4), 385–410.

Morris, M.H. (2004), 'Is entrepreneurship universal: a values perspective', Annual Meeting of the Academy of Management, New Orleans, LA, USA.

Noorderhaven, N., R. Thurik, S. Wennekers and A. van Stel (2004), 'The role of dissatisfaction and per capita income in explaining self-employment across 15 European countries', *Entrepreneurship Theory and Practice*, **28** (5), 447–66.

Peredo, A.M. (2004), 'Entrepreneurship and diversity', Annual Meeting of the Academy of Management, New Orleans, LA, USA.

Peredo, A.M. and R.W. Anderson (2006), 'Indigenous entrepreneurship research: themes and variations', in C.S. Galbraith and C.H. Stiles (eds), *Developmental Entrepreneurship: Adversity, Risk, and Isolation*, Oxford: Elsevier, pp. 253–73.

Peredo, A.M. and J. Chrisman (2006), 'Toward a theory of community-based enterprise', *Academy of Management Review*, **31** (2), 309–28.

Peredo, A.M., R.B. Anderson, C.S. Galbraith, B. Honig and L.-P. Dana (2004), 'Towards a theory of Indigenous entrepreneurship', *International Journal of Entrepreneurship and Small Business*, **1** (1/2), 1–20.

Schaper, M. (2007), 'Aboriginal and Torres Strait Islander entrepreneurship in Australia: looking forward, looking back', in L.-P. Dana, and R.B. Anderson (eds), *International Handbook of Research on Indigenous Entrepreneurship*, Cheltenham, UK and Northampton, MA, USA: Edward Elgar, pp. 526–35.

United Nations News Centre (2007), 'United Nations adopts Declaration on Rights of Indigenous Peoples', 13 September 2007, available at: http://www.un.org/apps/news/story.asp?NewsID=23794; accessed 28 July 2011.

Wood, G.J. and M.D. Davidson (2011), 'A review of male and female Australian Indigenous entrepreneurs: disadvantaged past – promising future?', *Gender in Management*, **26** (4), 311–26.

World Bank (2001), 'Draft operational policies (op 4.10), Indigenous peoples', available at: http://www.sari-energy.org/training/eia/course_files/WBOP410 policies.pdf; accessed 17 August 2011).

10. Conclusion: minorities in entrepreneurship – an international review

> Entrepreneurs have the dynamism to get something started. They view the world differently from other people. They create opportunity that others don't necessarily see and have the guts to give it a go.
>
> (Sir Richard Branson, Chairman of Virgin Group, 2009, p. 259)

INTRODUCTION

This book has aimed to further contribute to the limited literature on the experiences of non-mainstream entrepreneurs by presenting chapters reviewing literature pertaining to eight categories of minority business owners: younger entrepreneurs, older entrepreneurs, women entrepreneurs, ethnic minority entrepreneurs, immigrant entrepreneurs, LGB entrepreneurs, disabled entrepreneurs and Indigenous entrepreneurs. As mentioned in Chapter 1, we acknowledge that the selection of these specific entrepreneurial minority groups was not comprehensive of all business owner minorities, but their inclusion was determined by the availability (which in some cases was limited) of published research and literature.

In this final chapter, we pull together the main themes that have evolved from the various entrepreneurial minority groups in relation to their characteristics and aspirations/motivations for starting up a business, as well as the potential challenges and barriers faced during business venture development. We also summarize the challenges and barriers experienced by the various minority groups, and go on to present predictions for the future development of entrepreneurial minorities worldwide. Here, we emphasize the need for future research initiatives and also propose recommendations in terms of future government support for entrepreneurial education, training, business support and development.

MINORITIES IN ENTREPRENEURSHIP: GENERAL CHARACTERISTICS

Entrepreneurship is a global phenomenon and has taken numerous forms in communities and groups across the world. Our book clearly indicates that cultural attitudes towards entrepreneurship vary. According to the World Economic Forum (2009) only a relatively few countries embrace and support entrepreneurial behaviour and leading examples include the UK, the US, Australia, Poland, Norway, South Korea, China, the Baltic Republics (and former Eastern Bloc countries), Nigeria, Ghana and other parts of West Africa. It is therefore not surprising that the majority of research studies on minority business owners included in this book were restricted to a small number of countries and were predominantly North American, Australasian, British and European. Furthermore, globally, information about the characteristics of minority business owners (including statistical demographics) is often sparse and in many cases, simply does not exist. Hence, we have only been able to provide a limited 'snapshot' of the characteristics and experiences of minority entrepreneurs in a limited number of countries and communities.

When analysing the overall demographic profiles and characteristics of the eight groups of minority entrepreneurs, certain distinguishing factors stood out. For example, compared to all the other minority business owners, disabled entrepreneurs were the most likely to be home-based (allowing them more freedom to cope with their specific disability especially if they had mobility restrictions and/or health problems), were more likely to work part-time and were twice as likely to be self-employed compared to non-disabled individuals (Holub, 2001; Cooney, 2008). LGB entrepreneurs on the other hand, were an entrepreneurial group who were most likely to be single and childless and also have the highest disposable incomes (Galloway, 2007; GLBT Market Demographics, 2010).

Not surprisingly, as with mainstream entrepreneurs, in every minority group the male population greatly outnumbered that of the female, and women entrepreneurs tended to earn less. Furthermore, in all the entrepreneurial categories reviewed in the book the women business owners had the least available demographic statistical monitoring and research data compared to their male counterparts.

It is also important to acknowledge that even within these different entrepreneurial minorities, each group was diverse and did not have homogeneous characteristics. Despite this, similarities and differences were noted in each of the entrepreneurial categories. Individual business owners' experiences within the minority groups can be influenced by a whole array of factors such as gender, education, socioeconomic class, previous business experience and training, economic status, age, marital status, family dynamics, health, disability, sexual orientation, appearance, nationality, place of birth, country of residence (developed versus developing countries), religion, culture and so on. All of these multiple factors can in different and various combinations impact on the types of business ventures members of various minority groups enter into, their starting capital, and the subsequent growth, development and sustainability of the business. In ethnic minority entrepreneurs for example, religion is an important variable in the Muslim and Sikh communities in relation to their positive attitudes towards business ownership, as both have prominent figures in these religions who themselves were successful entrepreneurs (Rafiq, 1992). What is evident is that despite some explanations (such as religious entrepreneurial role models), there are still unanswered questions as to why certain ethnic groups such as Asians in the US are more prominent and successful compared to African Americans, who have the lowest rate of business ownership (Bogan and Darity, 2008). Conversely, in the UK, with the exception of women from black African, Indian and Pakistani backgrounds, women entrepreneurs from other ethnic minority groups outnumber those of their non-ethnic minority counterparts. It is also very apparent throughout each of the chapters that to date, there is still a dearth of literature on many specific types of entrepreneurial minorities within the different groups, for example, ethnic minority LGBs, disabled immigrants and so on. Much of the research has failed to include and acknowledge these complexities and the non-homogeneous factors within these different entrepreneurial groups.

A consistent finding throughout the book is that compared to their mainstream counterparts, many of the minority business owners were disadvantaged in terms of gaining finance during business start-up stage. Individuals within the immigrant, disabled and Indigenous entrepreneurial groups who came from poorer socioeconomic backgrounds and had lower educational attainments, were the most vulnerable in this respect (Boylan and Burchardt, 2002; Foley, 2003, 2006; Frederick and Foley, 2006; Shinnar and Young, 2008). Indeed, with studies consistently showing a positive relationship between business ownership and economic well-being, business venture development is an important vehicle for escaping the 'poverty trap'. This was endorsed by Lowrey (2007, p. 176) who asserted: 'continuously fostering minority business ownership should be considered as one of the most effective economic policies'. Interestingly, the most financially secure entrepreneurial groups as a whole were older entrepreneurs (in developed countries) who often had the advantage of accumulated financial backing, combined with previous business experience (Weber and

Schaper, 2004), and gay men who were also the most highly educated with the largest financial business turnovers (once established) of any of the entrepreneurial groups (including mainstream heterosexual male business owners) (GLBT Market Demographics, 2010).

A final demographic characteristic that appeared to be featured in a number of the entrepreneurial minorities (e.g., LGBs, disabled, immigrants and ethnic minorities) and stood out as being quite different from mainstream entrepreneurs, was the tendency to cater for specific niche markets in their own minority communities. This was particularly the case during early business venture development when affinity with their respective community needs, knowledge of market demographics, availability of same-minority employees and increased marketing opportunities all provided important self-protection (particularly from discrimination and prejudice) and safer environments for their businesses to thrive (Lowrey, 2007; Kidney and Cooney, 2009). Certainly, these particular minority business owners were much more likely to experience social exclusion from their mainstream communities; this is particularly noticeable in some Indigenous communities (e.g., Foley, 2006). In addition, with the exception of disabled entrepreneurs, they were also much more inclined to be located in geographical areas of 'same-community enclaves'. This provided them with important access to networks and family, legal and financial support, as well as availability of same-minority employees (Fadahunsi et al., 2000; Sequeira and Rasheed, 2004; Schaper, 2007; Kidney and Cooney, 2009).

MINORITIES IN ENTREPRENEURSHIP: ASPIRATIONS AND MOTIVATIONS

When reviewing the aspirations and motivations of the entrepreneurial minorities featured in this book, an appraisal of varying attitudes towards definitions of 'business success' certainly adds a useful dimension. In the mainstream field of entrepreneurship, the general consensus in the literature had been that financial incentives, commercialization and innovation have been the primary motivators for starting up a new business venture (Scarborough and Zimmerer, 2000). However, a repeated theme that emerged from the different minority entrepreneurial groups, was that many had very different attitudes and views towards what constituted 'success' compared to their mainstream counterparts. Young entrepreneurs, for example, have been reported as stating freedom to be in charge of their lives and the ability to be independent were major elements in their attitudes toward being successful in their business venture (Cull, 2006). Women entrepreneurs, on the other hand, have been found to equate success with self-worth and reward for hard work with financial profits and respect in the workforce being secondary motivations (Newton et al., 2001; Fielden and Davidson, 2010). A further insight into 'success' is seen in research focusing on Australian Indigenous entrepreneurs (e.g., Foley, 2003). It appears that this group of entrepreneurs see 'success' in a different way from the mainstream entrepreneur, as their primary focus is on opportunities to better themselves, and their family situations, through diminishing discrimination and forging an acceptance in the mainstream community (ibid.), rather than on achieving commercial gain alone.

For those entrepreneurial minority groups facing higher degrees of social exclusion from mainstream society (sometimes also combined with poverty), motivations towards business success were often linked with complex combinations of providing same-community support and sustaining cultures, as well as improving socioeconomic circumstances for their family (including extended family). Indigenous entrepreneurs, for instance, tend to be poor and are often driven more by kinship and self-determination through preservation of customs, traditions and heritage, rather than market needs (Hindle and Lansdowne, 2007). Like other entrepreneurial minorities who often experience social exclusion from their respective mainstream communities, for Indigenous business owners, business success was often deemed a vehicle to act as important role models for both members of their own and the mainstream communities. Furthermore, these particular entrepreneurs often felt their success and subsequent enhanced visibility helped correct negative social perceptions from society to their particular group and helped break down stereotyped prejudices and discrimination (Wood and Davidson, 2011). Ironically, however, unlike mainstream entrepreneurs, economic and high business success in some entrepreneurial minorities (e.g., Indigenous and ethnic minority entrepreneurs) may also result in alienation and isolation from their own communities for 'having sold out' to the mainstream (white) community (Davidson, 1997; Foley, 2003; Wood and Davidson, 2011).

Another interesting thread running throughout the book in relation to business start-up motivations, is the recognition that at least half of the minority groups reviewed appeared to have been predominantly 'pushed' as opposed to 'pulled' into entrepreneurial activity (the latter being much more common in mainstream business owners). According to the Global Entrepreneurship Monitor (Bosma et al., 2008), where there is 'opportunity recognition', people may be 'pulled' into a business venture as their main motivator. This seemed to be much more the case for young, older, female and LGB entrepreneurs. In the case of older entrepreneurs in the

UK for example, almost a third of retirees go on to take up paid employment again and are 'pulled' by the advantages of acquired capital, combined with years of business experience (Singh, 1998). Surprisingly, 'push'
factors related to homophobia appeared not to be the main motivator for
LGB business owners who were much more likely to be influenced by 'pull'
factors such as freedom and financial independence (Schindehutte et al.,
2005; Willsdon, 2005). Nevertheless, similar to much of the research
included throughout the book, the LGB entrepreneurial research was
confined to predominantly North American and UK studies on gay men.
Future research in other countries, where LGBs face greater degrees of
social exclusion and ostracization, may possibly reveal a dominance of
'push' versus 'pull' factors.

According to Bosma et al. (2008), individuals who feel that they may be
unemployed in the near future, or who believe that they are unable to earn a
living in any other way, may be 'pushed' into taking up an entrepreneurial
venture. This group of entrepreneurs have been labelled 'necessity-
motivated', and it was evident that ethnic minority, immigrants, disabled
and Indigenous individuals who entered entrepreneurial ventures were
more likely to be categorized in this way (ibid.). Indeed, 'necessity motivators' in these particular minority groups often included different combinations of reported 'glass ceiling' career development issues, discrimination
and prejudice, job dissatisfaction and high unemployment (Cooney, 2008;
Shinnar and Young, 2008). While these 'push' factors were often common
for both men and women in these particular minority groups, some
research did highlight occasional gender differences. For example,
Raghuram and Strange (2001) in their investigation of UK ethnic minority
entrepreneurs reported that lack of career progression (due to glass ceiling
and prejudicial factors) was an important 'push' motivator for both genders especially those from Indian and South Asian backgrounds, but for
black men lack of employment was the greatest 'push' motivator. Conversely, in relation to British disabled entrepreneurs, women were most
likely to cite 'push' factors associated with family commitments, compared
to disabled men who tended to quote 'push' factors linked to lack of local
jobs or redundancy (Boylan and Burchardt, 2002).

A final theme that emerged from all the entrepreneurial minority groups,
when reviewing motivational issues linked to business venture development, was the highly important role of educational attainment in potential
business owners. Without exception, within every entrepreneurial category
group, lower educational qualifications were linked to business motivational 'push' rather than 'pull' factors (Schur, 2003). Perhaps this explains
why LGBs, who were one of the most highly educated and professional
group of entrepreneurs, were much more likely to quote 'pull' factors

despite being a vulnerable group in terms of social exclusion and discrimination (GLBT Market Demographics, 2010).

MINORITIES IN ENTREPRENEURSHIP: CHALLENGES AND BARRIERS

When assessing the challenges and barriers facing minority business owners, the degree to which these barriers were experienced was very much contingent on cultural, ethnic, religious and societal norms and they were often country-specific. Nevertheless, compared to mainstream entrepreneurs, every entrepreneurial minority group experienced greater degrees of discrimination and prejudice, which had varying impacts on their business venture development.

Without doubt, the biggest challenges faced by the majority of the minorities (with the possible exception of LGBs), were poor access to finance and business training in the business start-up stages and this was most prevalent in the poorer, less-educated individuals. Prejudicial and discriminatory attitudes from banks, in respect to business loans, were reported by both older and younger entrepreneurs (citing ageism issues) (Burchardt et al., 2002; Singh and DeNoble, 2003), as well as by women entrepreneurs (citing sexism) (Fielden and Davidson, 2010). Financial barriers were particularly acute and magnified for disabled entrepreneurs compared to the non-disabled and they commonly reported discriminatory experiences from banks, advisers and employment institutions (Boylan and Burchardt, 2002).

Similar negative experiences were also revealed in ethnic minority entrepreneurs compared to their non-ethnic minority counterparts. In his recent testimony to the US Senate, the economist Professor Robert Fairlie stated that discrimination was the main reason why US ethnic minority business owners are rejected at twice the rate of their non-ethnic counterparts when applying for business loans and those who do obtain loans pay one-and-a-half percentage points higher interest than white-owned firms (*The Wall Street Journal*, 2011). Furthermore, indications are that ethnic minority women business owners are facing greater social, cultural and personal barriers – the double negative of both gender and racial discrimination (Omar et al., 2007). Immigrant and Indigenous entrepreneurs also had major problems gaining business bank loans and this was often enhanced by language barriers and lack of knowledge regarding business practices and legislation (Shinnar and Young, 2008).

Alienation and isolation from the main culture and cultural differences in values, combined with exclusion from business networks and lack of role models and mentors were all major barriers faced by entrepreneurial groups most vulnerable to social exclusion (i.e., ethnic minorities, immigrant, Indigenous and disabled entrepreneurs). Indeed, the importance and positive impact of access to business mentors was a common factor mentioned by many of the case studies featured throughout the book.

For many of these minority groups, problems were identified when developing their business markets into the wider mainstream community away from their same-group niche markets (Rowley, 2004). It should also be noted that poor health problems could also be a particular challenge facing certain vulnerable groups such as the older, disabled and Indigenous entrepreneurs (Boylan and Burchardt, 2002; Frederick and Foley, 2006). For example, in relation to Indigenous Australians, Frederick and Foley (2006) consider that the severe disadvantages relating to social, economic, health and culture status, produce perceptions that an entrepreneurial venture may be a possibility outside the realm of probability for many Indigenous people in these circumstances. When disadvantages are entrenched and pervasive, it has been suggested that entrepreneurial activity will continue to remain as the exception, rather than the norm (ibid.). However, this is not the case for all Indigenous peoples; although New Zealand Maori people were classified as having 'disadvantaged status', their favourable perception of entrepreneurial opportunities creates the possibility of an optimistic future for their involvement in business ventures (ibid.).

Interestingly, one of the themes that threads throughout the book is that of 'invisibility'. Whole subsections and nationalities of minority group business owners are missing from the global entrepreneurial demographics and published entrepreneurial literature and hence we are still unaware of the multitude of challenges and barriers facing these groups. For example, millions of LGB business owners throughout the world still 'stay in the closet' and continue to hide their sexual orientation, due to fears of discrimination, prejudice and even legal proceedings (or worse) if they reveal their sexuality (IDAHO-UK, 2009; Resources for Gay and Lesbian Entrepreneurs, 2010). Millions of women acting as 'non-registered' business partners in family businesses continue to remain hidden from the entrepreneurial statistics (Fielden and Davidson, 2010).

Moreover, there are still many unanswered questions related to numerous discriminatory barriers facing various categories of individuals within these different minority entrepreneurial 'invisible' groups. For instance, we still need to ascertain why certain ethnic groups, such as black African Americans, are the least likely of US ethnic minorities to establish small business ventures. Certainly, the evidence continues to suggest that potential challenges and barriers facing these individuals are complex and involve entrenched discrimination and negative stereotyping towards certain particular ethnic groups by the mainstream population (Bogan and Darity, 2008). In conclusion, it is evident that the material included in this book is only able to 'scratch the surface' in relation to isolating the numerous challenges and barriers facing entrepreneurial minorities throughout the world.

MINORITIES IN ENTREPRENEURSHIP: SUMMARY

Clearly, for many of the entrepreneurial minorities, compared to their mainstream counterparts, they often continue to struggle with the challenges of social inclusion in mainstream society and interventions to overcome barriers to business progress. Many similarities were noted in reviewing the eight minority groups of entrepreneurs in this book. It is clear that for many of these groups, initial disadvantage, or in fact, severe prolonged disadvantage, can create a powerful impetus to start up a business venture in order to survive (as illustrated by many of our case studies included throughout the book). Many minority groups appear to experience difficulties of acceptance in the mainstream societies in which they live. This marginalization can lead to difficulties in obtaining finance to develop an innovative idea into an entrepreneurial venture. In addition, not belonging to the mainstream society can mean that access to networks – so important in establishing, maintaining and sustaining business ventures – is denied to minority groups, or at least entry into such networks is made more difficult.

However, there is enormous variability in other features of minority entrepreneurs. One striking difference is noted in attitudes towards success. Other aspects of motivation are also worthy of consideration. Throughout the chapters in this book, there are numerous examples of various minority groups being both 'pushed' and 'pulled' into their entrepreneurial ventures. Therefore, it is not possible to say that all minority groups reviewed in this book are driven by similar motivators. Such levels of variability make it impossible to pull together the various motivating factors for all minority groups in order to be able to make a clear, coherent statement that would provide a framework for understanding what would be meaningful for 'all minority groups'.

MINORITIES IN ENTREPRENEURSHIP: THE FUTURE

Despite all the potential challenges and barriers, on an optimistic note, the future overall is looking positive for the majority of entrepreneurial minorities reviewed in this book, especially in the developed countries. What was repeatedly apparent throughout was the important (but often unrecognized and undervalued) economic and social contribution these minority business owners make to their respective economies and communities as a whole. In the UK for instance, in 2010, while immigrants constituted only 8 per cent of the population, they contributed 10 per cent to the GDP (Migration Watch UK, 2010). Moreover, Desiderio and Salt (2011, p. 1) proposed from an economic perspective that the immigrant entrepreneur had the capacity to 'contribute to expanding trade between the host country and their countries of origin'.

In addition, indications are that the number and sizes of minority-owned businesses are often growing at phenomenal rates. In the US for example, LGB business owners account for over 10 per cent of all US businesses and the percentages are growing annually (Hamar, 2010). Furthermore, aspirations to become an entrepreneur appear to be on the increase, especially in the young (UK Women's Enterprise Task Force, 2007).

Changing population demographics will also have an influence on entrepreneurial growth for both younger and older entrepreneurs in the not too distant future. The new Generation Y young people (born between 1977 and 1995) make up almost a quarter of the populations in countries such as the US and Australia and are forecast to constitute a third of the population in the US by 2015 (Pelton and True, 2004). Similar trends are evident in India, China, Latin America and throughout the Arab World (World Economic Forum, 2009); the exception is Europe. These young people entering the workforce will undoubtedly add substantially to the growing numbers of young business owners in all minority groups, and bring with them highly sophisticated technical and IT skills not possessed by former entrepreneurial generations. The World Economic Forum (2009) maintained that these younger more 'digitally savvy' entrepreneurs (unlike their predecessors), will have the capacity to break down some of the former geographical barriers to entrepreneurial success. This forum also emphasized the need for the right environments and structures for future global entrepreneurial development: 'For entrepreneurship to thrive it must operate in a well-functioning business and regulatory environment. Without the proper framework conditions, even potential entrepreneurs wanting to start companies will not do so' (ibid., p. 18). Furthermore, with the exception of some groups, such as Indigenous populations, increasing life expectancy in developed countries means that increasing numbers of retirees are also projected to join the world of entrepreneurship.

In relation to older entrepreneurs, there has been a dramatic increase in the proportions of early retirees who are taking up an entrepreneurial self-employment option. In the past, it had been estimated that approximately a third of early retirees would take up an entrepreneurial venture, or some other form of paid employment (Singh, 1998). We are now aware that this prediction underrated the numbers of older entrepreneurs who are becoming self-employed after they have completed their 'formal' working lives, and retiring in their 50s and 60s. The rapid increase in this phenomenon is highlighted by the Merrill Lynch Retirement Survey (Harris Interactive, 2005), which reported that three-quarters of their large sample planned to continue earning a living throughout their retirement, possibly in a new career. The start-up success rate of entrepreneurs over 55 years of age in the US (Vaughn, 2011) will no doubt act as an incentive for many people in this age category to view an entrepreneurial venture as a highly positive possibility.

It is also interesting to note that in Western countries there have been continual increases in the number of young educated women from corporate backgrounds starting their own businesses rather than face glass ceilings and career development prejudices in the mainstream workforce. Unlike former female entrepreneurial generations who tended to be mothers turning to business ownership (often home-based) in order to balance home/work conflicts and childcare duties, these new younger female entrepreneurs are often single, delay motherhood, are highly educated and have much higher levels of both social and human capital at their disposal (Fielden and Davidson, 2010).

One of the biggest entrepreneurial growth areas in the US and the UK has been in ethnic minority business ownership, which has grown faster than any other entrepreneurial minority group and is forecast to continue to rise over the next 25 years (Bates, 2007). Even though ethnic minority businesses have been particularly hit by the global economic downturn and in the US have 40 per cent less revenue than non-ethnic businesses, they continue to grow and according to the US Senator Mary Landrieu, who chaired the Senate Committee on Small Business and Entrepreneurship: 'Minority-owned business enterprises accounted for more than 50% of the 2 million businesses over the last 10 years' (Trading Markets, 2011). Not only are the number and sizes of ethnic minority-owned businesses in many countries on the increase, but they are diversifying much more and targeting mainstream markets rather than just supplying niche products catering predominantly for their own ethnic communities (Sequeira and Rasheed,

2004; Trading Markets, 2011). Similar trends are forecast for future immigrant business owners and long-range planners have predicted that immigrants will continue to play a key role in the economic growth of the future, including entrepreneurial activities (Desiderio and Salt, 2011).

Clearly, the continued development of advancing technology and IT communications around the globe is essential for small business development and offers tremendous opportunities for present and future entrepreneurial minorities. Solar power (especially in remote rural areas in the developing countries) enables minority entrepreneurs to have access to mobile phones, electricity, computers, Skype and so on, and improved communication links throughout the world (Angelocci et al., 2008). The World Economic Forum (2009) emphasized how these new advances in IT and telecommunication industries (including the media), were creating dramatic changes in relation to social inclusion and new opportunities for minority groups in the world of entrepreneurship:

> The growth of the Internet and use of computers and mobile phones have also made a huge impact, particularly with small business and education. The role of the media is also important for raising awareness and creating role models. Radio and television have grown across the world, especially after satellite television. (World Economic Forum, 2009, p. 17)

Throughout the different chapters on the various groups of entrepreneurs, consistent barriers to entrepreneurial opportunities, development and growth (particularly for lower socioeconomic status individuals), was linked to lack of education and training opportunities. In his foreword to the recent World Economic Forum report entitled *Educating the Next Wave of Entrepreneurs* (2009), the Founder and Executive Chairman Klaus Schwab emphasized the global need for stronger educational systems and effective leaders in order to prepare the present and future generations of entrepreneurs. Schwab believes that:

> Entrepreneurship is the engine fuelling innovation, employment generation and economic growth. Only by creating an environment where entrepreneurship can prosper and where entrepreneurs can try new ideas and empower others, can we ensure that many of the world's issues will not go unaddressed. (World Economic Forum, 2009, p. 6)

This global educational initiative facilitated by the World Economic Forum (2009) continues to raise awareness of the importance of entrepreneurship education and to provide recommendations to numerous bodies including the private and public sector, academia and governments, on the delivery and development of effective entrepreneurship education programmes. In addition, the forum intends to encourage the development of innovative approaches and new tools aimed at consolidating existing good practices, knowledge and case studies in entrepreneurial education (ibid.). Interestingly, the world-renowned, iconic entrepreneur, Sir Richard Branson (Chairman of the Virgin Group), also suggested we should look for inspiration from successful case studies and quoted the example of the Grameen Bank in Bangladesh (Branson, 2009). This was set up by one of the Elder Group, Professor Muhammad Yunus, offering small (affordable) loans to mainly poor women who wanted to consider an entrepreneurial venture, and in so doing, successfully elevated whole communities out of poverty. Like many of the case studies included throughout this book, Richard Branson is a classic example of a highly successful entrepreneur who started out his early business life as a minority (very) young entrepreneur, with a number of adversities, which ultimately led him to make different and important entrepreneurial choices:

> If I hadn't badly damaged my knee as a teenager, I would likely have been a sportsman. If I hadn't been dyslexic I wouldn't have left school at sixteen and created a magazine, which means I wouldn't have ended up running *Student*, which means Virgin Records would never have been born, which means … There are different paths that you can take in this life, and choosing the correct path is supremely important. (Branson, 2009, p. 331)

Obviously, it is vital globally, that government policies in particular need to be much more geared toward minority business development initiatives that are *inclusive* of all minority groups within their respective countries. There is also an urgent need for more in-depth, cross-cultural academic research into the multidimensional complexities of minority business owners, ensuring practical, constructive recommendations for future business development as an integral part of the applied research process.

In the final analysis, despite the additional challenges and barriers facing minority entrepreneurs compared to their mainstream counterparts, the future of minority-owned businesses looks generally bright, despite the world economic downturn. Interestingly, Richard Branson maintained that in retrospect, he would have only ever invested in business during recessions when costs are often 50–90 per cent less than their worth during economic upturns (Branson, 2009).

More and more successful entrepreneurs originate from a minority group, and they provide powerful role models to other aspiring entrepreneurs who see themselves as outside the mainstream of society. In addition, an increasing number of governments, institutions, private and public bodies and organizations are providing an expanding variety of support services (including mentoring programmes), possibly fuelled by a recognition of the economic benefits to society at large. Indeed, entrepreneur

Richard Branson (ibid.) believes that future entrepreneurial businesses should be those that are based initially on simple, small and lean business ideas that can be taken forward and made to happen. His advice to all future entrepreneurs is: 'Think big, but build small. Create something you're proud of, but don't let it swallow you financially. You don't need to slather money over a good idea. A good idea will grow by itself' (ibid., p. xvii). It would appear that this advice could be particularly relevant to entrepreneurial minority groups as they take their first step into business ventures, in their desire to improve their social and economic circumstances, and in so doing, make a significant contribution to their own communities and the wider society as a whole.

REFERENCES

Angelocci, R.M., K.J. Lacho, K.D. Lacho and W.P. Galle (2008),'Entrepreneurs with disabilities: the role of assistant technology, current status and future outlook', *Proceedings of the Academy of Entrepreneurship*, **14** (1), 1–5.

Bates, T. (2007), 'The urban development potential of black-owned businesses', *Journal of the American Planning Association*, **72** (2), 272–91.

Bogan, V. and W. Darity (2008), 'Culture and entrepreneurship? African American and immigrant self-employment in the United States', *The Journal of Socio-Ethnic Economics*, **37** (5), 1999–2019.

Bosma, N., Z. Acs, E. Autio, A. Coduras and J. Levie (2008), *Global Entrepreneurship Monitor, 2008 Executive Report*, Universidad del Desarrollo, Santiago, Chile, Babson College, MA, USA and London Business School, UK.

Boylan, A. and T. Burchardt (2002), *Barriers of Self-employment for Disabled People*, London: Report for the Small Business Service, October.

Branson, R. (2009), *Business Stripped Bare*, London: Virgin Books.

Burchardt, T., J. Le Grand and D. Piachaud (2002), 'Degrees of exclusion: developing a dynamic multidimensional measure', in J. Hills, J. Le Grand and D. Piachaud (eds), *Understanding Social Exclusion*, Oxford: Oxford University Press.

Cooney, T.M. (2008), 'Entrepreneurs with disabilities – profile of a forgotten minority', *Irish Business Journal*, **5** (1), 119–29.

Cull, J. (2006), 'Mentoring young entrepreneurs: what leads to success?', *International Journal of Evidence Based Coaching and Mentoring*, **4** (2), 8–18.

Davidson, M.J. (1997), *The Black and Ethnic Minority Woman Manager: Cracking the Concrete Ceiling*, London: Paul Chapman.

Desiderio, M.V. and J. Salt (2011), *Main Findings of the Conference on Entrepreneurship and Employment Creation of Immigrants in OECD Countries*, 9–10 June, Paris: OECD.

Fadahunsi, A., D. Smallbone and S. Supri (2000), 'Networking and ethnic minority enterprise development: insights from a North London study', *Journal of Small Business and Enterprise Development*, **7** (3), 28–40.

Fielden, S.L. and M.J. Davidson (eds) (2010), *International Research Handbook on Successful Women Entrepreneurs*, Cheltenham, UK and Northampton, MA, USA: Edward Elgar.

Foley, D. (2003), 'An examination of Indigenous Australian entrepreneurs', *Journal of Developmental Entrepreneurship*, **8** (2), 133–51.

Foley, D. (2006), 'Indigenous Australian entrepreneurs: not all community organizations, not all in the outback', Discussion Paper No. 279/2006, Canberra: Centre for Aboriginal Economic Policy Research.

Frederick, H.H. and D. Foley (2006), 'Indigenous populations as disadvantaged entrepreneurs in Australia and New Zealand', *The International Journal of Entrepreneurship, Advancement, Strategy and Education*, **11** (2).

Galloway, L. (2007), 'Entrepreneurship and the gay minority. Why the silence?', *Entrepreneurship and Innovation*, **8** (4), 271–80.

GLBT Market Demographics (2010), available at: http://www.gaydays.com/Advertising/gay-and-lesbian-market-demographics.html; accessed 16 November 2010.

Hamar, M. (2010), 'Bilerico project: building a network of gay entrepreneurs', available at: http://www.bilerico.com/2010/06/building_a_network_of_gay_entrepreneurs.php; accessed 16 November 2010.

Harris Interactive (2005), *The New Retirement Survey*, Merrill Lynch, available at: http://www.retirement-jobs-online.com/retirement-survey.html; accessed 10 May 2010.

Hindle, K. and M. Lansdowne (2007), 'Brave spirits on new paths: towards a globally relevant paradigm of Indigenous entrepreneurship research', *Journal of Small Business and Entrepreneurship*, **18** (2), 131–41.

Holub, T. (2001), 'Entrepreneurs among people with disabilities', Los Angeles: adjunct ERIC clearinghouse on entrepreneurship education, available at: http://www.eric.ed.gov/PDFS/ED464453.pdf; accessed 16 August 2011.

IDAHO-UK (2009), 'International day against homophobia and transphobia', available at: http://www.idahomophobia.net/spip.php?rubrique=47; accessed 16 November 2010.

Kidney, E. and T.M. Cooney (2009), 'How do gay entrepreneurs differ?', *Irish Academy of Management Conference Proceedings*, Galway, Ireland, 2–9 September.

Lowrey, Y. (2007), 'Minority entrepreneurship in the USA', *International Journal of Business Globalisation*, **1** (2), 176–220.

Migration Watch UK (2010), 'Economic contribution of A8 migrants', available at: http://www.migrationwatchuk.org/Briefingpaper/document/14; accessed 7 December 2010.

Newton, J., L. Gottschalk and G. Wood (2001), *A Model for Success: Women's Entrepreneurial and Small Business Activity in Regional Areas*, report prepared for the Department of State and Regional Development, Ballarat: School of Business, University of Ballarat.

Omar, A., M.J. Davidson and S.L. Fielden (2007), *Black and Minority Ethnic (BME) Small Business Owners: A Comparative Study Investigating the Problems, Experiences and Barriers Faced by BME Female and Male Entrepreneurs in North West England*, Report Centre for Equality and Diversity at Work, available at: http://www.train2000.org.uk/research-reports/pdfs/BME-report.pdf; accessed 10 August 2011.

Pelton, L.E. and S.L. True (2004), 'Teaching business ethics: why Generation Y?', *Marketing Education Review*, **14** (3), 63–70.

Rafiq, M. (1992), 'Ethnicity and enterprise: a comparison of Muslim and non-Muslim-owned Asian businesses in Britain', *New Community*, **19** (1), 43–60.

Raghuram, P. and A. Strange (2001), 'Studying economic institutions, placing cultural politics: methodological musings from a study of ethnic minority enterprise', *Geoforum*, **32** (3), 377–88.

Resources for Gay and Lesbian Entrepreneurs (2010), available at: http:www.gaebler.com/help-for-gay-entrepreneurs.htm; accessed 16 November 2010.

Rowley, T. (2004), 'Entrepreneurship means adaption', available at: http://www.matr.net/print-12097.html; accessed 4 August 2010.

Scarborough, N.M. and T.W. Zimmerer (2000), *Effective Small Business Management: An Entrepreneurial Approach*, Upper Saddle River, NJ: Prentice-Hall.

Schaper, M. (2007), 'Aboriginal and Torres Strait Islander entrepreneurship in Australia: looking forward, looking back', in L.-P. Dana and R.B. Anderson (eds), *International Handbook of Research on Indigenous Entrepreneurship*, Cheltenham, UK and Northampton, MA, USA: Edward Elgar.

Schindehutte, M., M. Morris and J. Allen (2005), 'Homosexuality and entrepreneurship – implications of gay identity for the venture-creation experience', *Entrepreneurship and Innovation*, **6** (1), 27–40.

Schur, L. (2003), 'Barriers or opportunities? The causes of contingent and part-time work among people with disabilities', *Industrial Relations*, **42** (4), 589–622.

Sequeira, J.M. and A.A. Rasheed (2004), 'The role of social and human capital in start-up and growth of immigrant businesses', *Ethnic Entrepreneurship Structure and Process – International Research in the Business Disciplines*, **4**, 77–94.

Shinnar, R.S. and C.A. Young (2008), 'Hispanic immigrant entrepreneurs in the Las Vegas Metropolitan Area: motivations for entry into and outcomes of self-employment', *Journal of Small Business Management*, **46** (2), 242–62.

Singh, G. (1998), 'Work after early retirement', unpublished PhD dissertation, School of Graduate Studies, University of Toronto, Canada.

Singh, G. and A. DeNoble (2003), 'Early retirees as the next generation of entrepreneurs', *Entrepreneurship Theory and Practice*, **27** (3), 207–26.

The Wall Street Journal (2011), 'Minority entrepreneurs still face bias, Prof says', available at: http://blogs.wsj.com/in-charge/2011/03/10/minority-entrepreneurs-still-face-bias-prof/; accessed 7 May 2011.

Trading Markets (2011), 'Landrieu: closing the wealth gap for minority entrepreneurs should be a top priority', available at: http://www.tradingmarkets.com/adv.php?ref=%2Fnews%2Fstock-alert%2Fsbcod_landrieu-closing-the-wealth-gap-for-minority-entrepreneurs-should-be-a-top-priority-1534686.html; accessed 17 August 2011.

UK Women's Enterprise Task Force (2007), *Increasing the Quantity and Quality of Women's Enterprise. Statistics and Trends*, UK: SBS Analytical Unit.

Vaughn, C. (2011), 'The Zuckerberg fallacy: older entrepreneurs as the drivers of innovation', Founder's Toolbox Blog, available at: http://www.goodwinfoundersworkbench.com/posts/zuckerberg-fallacy-older-entrepreneurs-drivers-innovation/; accessed 8 August 2011.

Weber, P. and M. Schaper (2004), 'Understanding the grey entrepreneur', *Journal of Enterprising Culture*, **12** (2), 147–64.

Willsdon, J. (2005), 'Homosexual entrepreneurs: different but the same', *Irish Journal of Management*, **26** (1), 107–21.

Wood, G.J. and M.J. Davidson (2011), 'A review of male and female Australian Indigenous entrepreneurs: disadvantaged past – promising future?', *Gender in Management – An International Journal*, **25** (4), 311–26.

World Economic Forum (2009), *Educating the Next Wave of Entrepreneurs – Unlocking Entrepreneurial Capabilities to Meet the Global Challenges of the 21st Century*, Report of the Global Education Initiative, Switzerland: World Economic Forum.

Index